MW01592976

Praise for
"I Did Not Burn the Church Down...I Only Started the Fire!"

"Don Farrior shares much pastoral wisdom in this book. Along the way we are treated to an inside glimpse of a faithful and effective life and ministry in the making. It is a glimpse that overflows with the joy and pain, hilarity and grief of which life and wisdom are made. He is searingly and poignantly honest about the church, the ministry, and himself. This book will make you laugh, cry, and hope! I have known Don Farrior as a friend and colleague in ministry for 34 years, beginning with the days in which he served as my field education supervisor. Having learned much from Don and having seen his ministry bear excellent fruit through the years in diverse settings, I am proud to call him and Janet dear friends."—Dr. Richard L. Hamm, former General Minister and President of the Christian Church (Disciples of Christ) in the U.S. and Canada.

"As a preacher, and now as a writer, Don Farrior has an amazing ability to communicate in a way that is immediate and personally engaging. Even when people disagree with something he says, they still have the feeling that he has delivered a positive, confident word and that he has spoken directly to them."—Dr. Keith Watkins, Professor of Worship (ret.), Christian Theological Seminary.

"Don Farrior is an extraordinary man. I have known him as pastor, advisor, confidant, golfing companion and, above all, a very close personal friend. He is personable, kind, compassionate and…yes…humorous. He has a genuine love for people…and a true zest for life. He is a reflection of what Christ means when he taught us to 'love your neighbor as you love yourself.'"—Clarence E. "Jack" Jordan, Brigadier General, U.S. National Guard (Ret).

"I generally go to church in a bad or gloomy mood and fall asleep soon after the choir quits singing. But if Dr. Farrior is preaching it takes but a few minutes until I am wide awake smiling or giggling over his spiritual and humorous comments.—Sam Ingram, Captain, U.S. Navy (Ret).

"This is an amazing collection of humorous stories told from the heart and woven around an inspirational life. This is a 'must-read' for anyone who has faced a tragedy, hit bumps in the road or who wants a positive life! It has been my privilege to know Don Farrior as a spiritual mentor and a friend who knows the real value of humor."—Janice A. Ferguson, Ph.D., former Dean of Students and VP for Student Affairs, Adrian College and Pennsylvania College of Podiatric Medicine, CEO, Concepts in Creative Communication.

"Dr. Farrior has created an enlightening, entertaining, thoughtful, and joyful piece of art that depicts how a person such as myself can relate to the suffering of others who lose a loved one. What a wonderful tribute to his son."—Yolanda B. Payne, Clinical Laboratory Department Secretary, Del E. Webb Memorial Hospital, Sun City West, Arizona.

"I DID NOT BURN THE CHURCH DOWN...I ONLY STARTED THE FIRE!"

"I DID NOT BURN THE CHURCH DOWN...I ONLY STARTED THE FIRE!"

by Dr. Donald G. Farrior

with Dr. Diane Holloway

iUniverse, Inc.

New York Lincoln Shanghai

"I DID NOT BURN THE CHURCH DOWN...I ONLY STARTED THE FIRE!"

iUniverse books may be ordered through booksellers or by contacting:

iUniverse
2021 Pine Lake Road, Suite 100
Lincoln, NE 68512
www.iuniverse.com
1-800-Authors (1-800-288-4677)

ISBN-13: 978-0-595-37359-8 (pbk)
ISBN-13: 978-0-595-81756-6 (ebk)
ISBN-10: 0-595-37359-3 (pbk)
ISBN-10: 0-595-81756-4 (ebk)

Printed in the United States of America

Contents

Dedication and Acknowledgments

This book is dedicated to our much-loved son Christopher Farrior whose struggle with a bi-polar disorder led him to end his life long before his time.

This book is also dedicated to my devoted wife, Janet Farrior, and to our daughter, Melissa Gish, and our two granddaughters Brittney and Halsey.

A very special thank you to the members and friends of all the congregations I have served including:

First Christian Church, my home church, in Richlands, North Carolina, the Sugar Grove Community Church, the Lizton, Pfafftown, Crestview, Parkway, Sun City Christian Churches and First Christian Church in Independence, Missouri.

I owe an unpayable debt of gratitude to Dr. Joe Wick who was the first to teach me that it is okay to laugh—even in church.

Special acknowledgments to my two supervisors at Sun Health Corporation who gave me a much needed leave of absence—Jane Harker and Dr. Ron Hamilton, and a most hearty "thank you" to Dr. Diane Holloway, my editor, consultant and advisor, and to Bob Cheney for invaluable counsel and help in proofreading the text.

Finally, I want to thank Sam Ingram for his beautiful and clever painting for my book cover. Sam, a retired captain in the U.S. Navy, has been recognized as one of America's leading artists over the past 50 years. He painted and designed the presidential inaugural booklets for both of Dwight D. Eisenhower's terms. The Oklahoma Christian University in Oklahoma City will house his enormous collection of world-famous artifacts and paintings in 2006.

Preface

Who am I writing this book for? Well, certainly it is for all members in all churches where I have served as pastor. It is also for all staff persons and volunteers related to Sun Health, and especially those in Boswell and Del Webb Hospitals.

This book is also for a wider audience of anyone and everyone who has dealt with "dark clouds" and especially suicide in their family, and the trauma of bipolar behavior.

However, it is especially for America's retirees. This may be the best audience of all, some 35,000,000 of them, to show that "We ain't down yet!"

It is for this audience that I decided to make the type size a little larger so older people could read it easily.

1

"I Did Not Burn the Church Down...I Only Started the Fire!"

It stuck like a burr in cotton. It's now been over 40 years since Bill spoke that memorable phrase: "I did not burn the church down...I only started the fire!"

Whatever could it mean? Rev. Bill, a senior in our graduate seminary, was having a most successful pastorate at his little country church in central Indiana. He had "gotten religion" and was abundantly enthusiastic about the reception by his congregation and the town folk.

Attendance at worship had doubled in only two years—and the offerings more than tripled. The youth group came to life with young people from all the other churches attending his exciting youth meetings. Yes, there was some jealousy on the part of the other pastors who felt they might be losing their youth to Rev. Bill and his church. But nothing serious surfaced.

What did surface shocked us—no, stunned us is more accurate. Bill had told with great pride how his church had grown and how the offering plates were full to over-flowing. In addition, we were all jealous of his obvious success. If only we could do it as Rev. Bill was doing it.

Then the jolt came from out of the blue. Bill announced to his closest friends at the seminary that he had suddenly and inexplicably been fired.

What? Why? What on earth happened?

Bill explained that the Board of Directors was made up of the older members who had been "running the church" for many years.

Now suddenly that had all changed. There was new leadership by all these young people who were coming here from "God knows where." They showed no respect to their seniors.

When confronted by the Board's decision, they added, "Our church is on fire and it's your fault."

Rev. Bill responded, "Yes, our church is alive with the fire of the Holy Spirit. But you need to know, 'I did not burn the church down...I only started the fire!'"

It was memorable. It made me think of the place of humor in the church and pulpit—and the first time I tried to tell something funny.

In the early days of my ministry, there was little humor in the church. Back in the early 1950s and even in the 1960s, religion was heavy, serious, and at times even morbid. I often wonder now why people ever bothered to go to church—except that in my case I got to see a cute blonde who liked me. However, something was missing, really missing, and I began to find out what it was as I served my very own pastorate in North Carolina.

I knew as a young person that I loved to laugh. However, the rather stern admonition that I got from my school, my home and from my community was that "laughter is frivolous."

I recall my own saintly mother telling us that she was suspicious of people who laughed a little too much!

Yes, we did laugh at family reunions and at church homecomings—but again, Mother would remind us, "It's okay to laugh as long as it doesn't go on too long."

Laughing in church? Never! It just was not done. I think it never really occurred to me to do or say anything that would result in what some call a "belly laugh."

Yet, the great French writer Francois Voltaire had said, "God was a comedian playing for an audience afraid to laugh!" I heard that many years ago and it took me some time to truly appreciate it. Nevertheless, I did and do.

The first time I remember laughing vigorously and heartily in church was when we celebrated our 100th anniversary at the Pfafftown church in Winston-Salem in 1965.

It was to be a grand occasion. We had invited Dr. Fred Helsabeck, president of Culver-Stockton College, to be our featured speaker. We flew him all the way from St. Louis to Winston-Salem. His trip plus the gratuity which we gave him totaled over $200. Wow! "That's a lot of money," we reasoned. He had better be good.

And people came. Dozens, hundreds, close to 250 people crowded into the packed little country church to hear Dr. Helsabeck at 3 p.m. on Sunday afternoon.

Ray, the chairman of the 100th anniversary celebration, was obviously shaken by the enormity of the event. He stood before the waiting audience—hesitated, started again and then intended to say, "We welcome you to this historical occasion." What he said in fact was, "We welcome you to this *hysterical* occasion."

My wife, sitting in the second row directly in front of the pulpit, burst out laughing—and then embarrassed, took out her handkerchief and began to feign a cough.

Incredibly, just as she was about to get over her first outburst of laughter, the chairman Ray again welcomed everyone to this "hysterical" occasion.

Five times he used the wrong word—and not once did he seem to catch on to the fact that "hysterical" is funny and "historical" is serious.

Presently the entire congregation came to life. Everyone laughed at poor Ray. We never did determine if he used the wrong word on purpose or not. Only Ray knows for sure.

One thing surfaced: people enjoyed laughing in church. It has been now more than thirty-five years—but I remember it like yesterday.

It taught me something I was to use over the next thirty-five plus years. Perhaps there is, after all, a place appropriate for humor—even in church on Sunday morning.

2

When Dark Clouds Come

I wanted this book to be fun. I wanted people to laugh and have a good time. However, something happened to change all that.

I remember it with anguished pain. We had been cruising for several years on what seemed like a smooth sea. No storm clouds on the horizon—a beautiful home, friends, and enough money to buy things that were important to our family.

Life was good, exciting, and deeply satisfying. It never ever occurred to us that all that was about to change—in a moment—with one phone call.

Like other families, we were blessed with children—two of them—a son and a daughter. Yes, there were problems but somehow they seemed manageable. We stepped in to help when it seemed appropriate, but those times were few. Their sense of pride kept them from burdening us with their problems or asking for favors.

Mainly there were good times, happy times, fun times—so much so that I never really saw the dark cloud that was settling in over his life.

I recall the visits—being with him at our home in Ft. Lauderdale and in Phoenix. We both loved to kid and tease—and laugh.

I recall the hundred times or so my son would say, "Dad, the problem with you is you never listen"…and my response, "I'm sorry, son, what did you say?" In addition, the laughter and smiles and the question, "I wonder how many times we have told that to Dad." Again the retort, "I'm sorry, son, did you say something?"

I was going to write a book about that—and tell all the funny things we had done and said over his forty-one years.

I wanted to write a book about humor and the funny incidents that had happened as a pastor over these thirty-five years. I wanted to write about the struggles and rewards, the joys and, yes, the sorrows that I had known as a father, a husband, a pastor, and more recently as a staff chaplain. In addition, I knew the positive effect of laughter on one's health.

Bob Hope, perhaps America's most popular entertainer, echoed my deepest thoughts and feelings when he said, "I have seen what a laugh can do. It can transform almost unbearable tears into something bearable, even hopeful."

Little did I know as I heard Bob Hope speak those words years ago, just how soon that dark cloud would move in to test everything I thought and believed. I would move without warning from laughter to tears.

Dr. Joe Wick, one of our country's most popular after-dinner speakers, said to me, "There's a fine line separating humor from tears—the two are so close as to almost be cut from the same piece of fabric." Dr. Wick went on to say, "We move from laughter to tears and from tears to laughter."

He then added the words that were to help us walk through the approaching darkness: "When your tears begin to be mixed with humor, you will know that the healing process has begun."

Strange that of all the words Dr. Wick spoke when he came to be our guest speaker a few years ago, these are the ones that would cling to us and remind us that the light does shine even in the face of darkness and despair. Moreover, the moment we begin to smile and laugh through our tears is the time when our recovery starts.

"Manageable problems." That is what we called them…but looking back there were times that seemed unmanageable, out of bounds—especially with our son.

Truth be known, I never knew a wilder child. It was maddening at times to be around him. He was hyperactive, restless, impulsive, a disaster waiting to happen. He was blessed or cursed with a quick mind, able to spell adult words by the time he was five. I recall his first day of school—waiting for the bus. He began to cry and I asked what was wrong.

"Daddy," he asked, "What if they ask me to spell 'abdominous'?"

"Oh, son," I replied, "that's a college word and they won't ask you that for at least twelve years."

I had to look the word up, myself. It means pot-bellied, but where did he learn about it.

The first day at school was trouble, and the second and the third and the fourth. And always it was the same problem. "Your son Christopher can't sit still or listen or pay attention...he wants to get up and walk around...we don't know what to do with him."

Fact was, he could not sit still or listen to a teacher or any speaker for more than four or five minutes.

"Hyperactive" they said of him at the office of the psychologist when he was only eight. "ADD—Attention Deficit Disorder" they declared when he was ten. Then came the most painful sting of all—worse, I think, than the bite of a cobra—"bipolar."

I knew that the word was a euphemism, a more pleasant way of saying what we used to call it: Manic depressive disorder.

Yes, I had heard of a medication called lithium and knew of people in the parish where I served who used it with great success. However, it did not work for him.

Now he was forty-one—far too young to die. Nevertheless, the news came from his wife early Tuesday morning at 7:22 a.m., September 21: "Christopher is dead...He took his own life..."

The anguish of telling you this is almost more painful than I can bear. I thought telling it would be easy—but now as I write, it feels as painful as that phone call with the news a year ago.

I was paralyzed—stunned. In a state of shock and total disbelief.

I can hardly speak of it. My God...My God. I so identified with the words spoken from a cross 2,000 years ago. "My God, why have you forsaken me?"

How can I tell you? I had been a pastor for forty years. I knew death, had seen it, had touched it, but always it was a safe distance away—because it was not my family and therefore not my problem.

I had conducted over three hundred memorial services and had, on occasion, shed tears of sadness and sorrow for some of the very special people I knew and loved. But that was different.

I was there when my ninety-one-year old mother died but there was no deep grief, no heavy sadness. Actually, there was a feeling of quiet celebration—that a life had been lived fully, completely, and there were no regrets. In addition, if there were tears, they were tears of gratitude and thanksgiving and relief.

Perhaps this will be hard for some people to understand. However, the death of one's elderly mother who had lived a full and complete life is very different from losing your son—long before his time.

When I thought of the violence with which Christopher had ended his life, I sank into the very depths of despair. For whatever reason the word that came to me was from the Bible where the writer spoke of the anguish of God upon watching his own son die. It said "There is no sorrow like unto God's sorrow." Now I knew. I really felt the anguish of God.

Perhaps you have lost someone you loved more than life, and you, too, know something of the anguish of God.

The phone call at 7:22 a.m. That is where I was.

I was paralyzed, frozen, powerless, and confused. And for the first time that I could recall, I reached the depths of despair.

Where now was the joyful confidence I had preached about for forty years? Where now were the laughter and the positivism and the certainty and the all-conquering faith I had proclaimed all these years?

It seemed like the end of everything. It felt like the end of everything. It seemed like the end of the world. Where was the promise of heaven now? In fact, where was God? Where was the faith I had preached to others over all those years?

The reality of our son's death hit hard, and I began to weep—softly at first, then frantically, and I recall shouting, "No, no, my God, no!" It is hard to be objective about that first hour. I was hurt, angry, and sad beyond my ability to describe to you. But if you ever lost a child, you will surely understand.

I knew I had to gain my composure long enough to call Janet, my wife of forty-five years, who was out taking her morning walk with our friend Nancy. Her cell phone rang. We had agreed that if I heard anything I would call her.

We had been expecting something but we did not know what. Our daughter-in-law, Pam, had called Monday night to say that Christopher had not returned home from his job. He could not be found. So the police in Wisconsin Rapids were asked to help find his car—a maroon-colored Cadillac—and the search began.

It seems now that he had been "down" for many months—and seemed unable to pull himself out of a deep, dark depression. He had spoken on occasion of not wanting to live and it frightened us. I had learned enough in working with families in the parish that people who talk about not wanting to live must be taken seriously—and help for them must be found.

I recall that Christopher was taking a number of antidepressants but the pills seemed ineffective and the darkness seemed to deepen.

Soon family and friends from across the country heard the news and each of them tried desperately to offer us comfort and hope.

I have been astounded by the large number of people who have faced a nearly identical family crisis. For whatever reason, it helps to talk to them for they seem to understand the full range of your emotions.

It is strange that the least helpful responses from well-intentioned friends were those that told us that our son was in a "better place" or "in heaven"—or "with the Lord."

I did not want to hear it. I wanted him back. I did not like some of the spiritual platitudes that we were receiving. I wanted another chance to intervene, to stop him, to talk him out of taking his own life. If only I could have five minutes with him. I would ask him to come to Phoenix to be with us. We would go together to see a physician and get his medication adjusted.

One thing did help: tears. I was shocked by the flow of tears. Yes, I had said to others, "It's good to cry"—but they were things I had heard others say. Suddenly the tears came—and the memories—and more tears—and it all took on a new meaning.

I learned that tears—and almost tears alone—were therapeutic. I don't know how it works, or why it works but each intense session of tears helped me to face the reality of what had happened.

I knew that we were not alone at the depth of our loss—and wondered if anything good could ever come from it. I thought of our despair and for whatever reasons recalled the devastating flood that hit Portsmouth, Ohio, back in the 1920s. The story shook me, but comforted me as well.

George L. Willetts described it. He said that the flood waters rushed down the center of the streets of the city. Many people's lives were in danger. There were heroic rescues attempted with people in boats pulling residents from roof tops and two-story dwellings. Dozens of residents drowned.

In one of the higher places, the water had reached the top of the front door. Two rescuers shined their flashlights in the flood waters and saw two small children bobbing up and down in the water. As they reached into the water to rescue the last child, they felt the hand and arm of some adult who was suddenly swept away by the rushing waters.

The picture that came to them was that of a mother holding each child with upstretched arms while she herself was submerged. The moment of rescue for the children became the moment of ultimate sacrifice for the mother. She died so that they could live.

Yes, I knew in my heart that we were not alone in facing this dark night of the soul. Someone said to me, "The most painful loss of all is yours." Think of the tears we shed for those we know and love. You can read of misfortune, loss, and even tragedies of one thousand other people—but when it comes home to where you live, your response to it is not the same.

Today we heard that the number of deaths from the tsunami tidal wave in December of 2004 is expected to pass 400,000 people. We have responded as generously as we were able. It may turn out to be the most devastating natural disaster in world history—much more human loss than Hurricane Katrina in New Orleans and the Gulf Coast.

However, it occurs to me that while we did not know any of them by name, their families' grief, and sorrow and the depth of their loss is greater than our own. How those who lived through it can go on with their lives is a mystery. Perhaps they believe as we do that the light shines in the darkness, faint and flickering though it be, and the darkness has not overcome it.

It seems so strange that their tragic loss makes ours a little easier to bear. I recall a brilliant message by Dr. James Armstrong forty years ago at the Broadway Methodist Church in Indianapolis titled, "Into Each Life Some Rain Must Fall." The memory of it helped for I knew it was true.

3

When Attitude Is Your Only Friend

Strange that something so totally shocking and negative would have moved me so forcefully into the world of a positive attitude and joyful praise.

I had known about it, had read about it, and had tried to practice the tenets of Christian positivism for 30 years. I had already come to believe that attitude is pivotal in recovery. Now it became real to me.

Looking back, I realize now that it was Dr. Robert Schuller whose bold positive thoughts, words, and writings helped us get through this dark night of the soul. Anyone who has ever heard Dr. Schuller's inspiring messages at the Crystal Cathedral or on the telecast, "Hour of Power," will discover what my wife and I discovered: that setbacks, hurts, and even tragic loss are not the final word.

Two of Dr. Schuller's books, *Power Thoughts* and *Life's Not Fair—But God Is Good,* contain numerous inspirational real-life stories that brought us through the darkness which we had encountered.

More than any other person we know, Dr. Schuller's emphasis on the biblical themes of positive attitudes and possibility thinking have helped us see the good that can and does come out of the bad. Suddenly this world of infinite possibilities began to make sense.

Attitude Is Everything

Dr. Schuller and Dr. Chopra have told us what we already know—and yet, don't really know. Bad things do happen to good people—but that is not the end.

God did not single you out for punishment or sorrow or loss, or pain or tragedy. The rain falls on the just and the unjust alike. Bad things happen to all of us—and for the most part, they are things that cannot be helped.

The simple fact is that people grow old, slow down, have accidents, and lose their eyesight, their hearing, their ability to walk and a dozen other misfortunes. In addition, we experience death—even at a very early age.

I still recall the anguish of almost losing my beloved pet dog. I was six and Buster was four. I came home from school and Mother said, "Buster has been hit by a car...and I think he's going to die."

I began to cry and ran to the shed where his little helpless body lay. His pleading eyes looked up at me and with all his power and might, he managed to lick my hand as if to say, "I love you."

I recall asking God to spare Buster's life. A day or two later, Buster drank some water and on the third day, stood and ate food. By week's end, he was back on his feet—not running or jumping—but walking. That was 60 years ago. It still seems like it was yesterday. It was both a great victory and a very close encounter with death. It would help to prepare me for what lay ahead.

I've heard it said that you don't appreciate what you have until you lose it. I knew it was true but I didn't really know it was true. Perhaps I took our son for granted. It never occurred to me that he would leave us.

Suddenly his leaving brought back a flood of memories—so many of them funny—almost hilarious, like the week he went to camp. His mother carefully packed his suitcase with a change of clothes for every day. She went over the "to do" list most carefully—feeling proud that he would follow her instructions to the last detail. Secretly no mother ever believes her children are going to do exactly as instructed. But we were not prepared for the day our son came back from camp.

We opened his suitcase—and, alas, all the clean clothes were untouched—exactly as they had been placed there a week earlier.

Think of it—one full week wearing the same shorts, T-shirt, pants, socks, and shirt. In addition, his tooth brush and toothpaste had not been touched all week.

However, what do parents know? He smiled and said, "I had a really good time…they didn't make me take a single bath."

Maybe it's a good thing that parents don't know what really goes on at camp.

Recently I came across a letter from a Boy Scout at camp to his parents:

Letter from Camp (or Why Parents Turn Gray)

Dear Mom and Dad,

Our Scoutmaster told us to write to our parents in case you saw the flood on TV and were worried. We are OK. Only one of our tents and two sleeping bags got washed away. Luckily, none of us got drowned because we were all up on the mountain looking for Chad when it happened.

Oh, yes, please call Chad's mother and tell her he is OK. He can't write because of the cast. I got to ride in one of the search and rescue jeeps. It was neat. We never would have found him in the dark if it wasn't for the lightning. Scoutmaster Walt got mad at Chad for going on a hike alone without telling anyone. Chad said he did tell him, but it was during the fire so he probably didn't hear him.

Did you know that if you put gas on a fire, the gas can will blow up? The wet wood didn't burn, but one of the tents did. Also some of our clothes. John is going to look weird until his hair grows back.

We will be home on Saturday if Scoutmaster Walt gets the car fixed. It wasn't his fault about the wreck. The brakes worked OK when we left. Scoutmaster Walt said that with a car that old you have to expect something to break down; that's probably why he can't get insurance. We think it's a neat car. He doesn't care if we get it dirty, and if it's hot, sometimes he lets us ride on the fenders. It gets pretty hot with ten people in a car. He let us take turns riding in the trailer until the highway patrolman stopped and talked to us.

Scoutmaster Walt is a neat guy. Don't worry, he is a good driver. In fact, he is teaching Terry how to drive on the mountain roads where there isn't any traffic. All we ever see up here is logging trucks.

This morning, all of the guys were diving off the rocks and swimming out in the lake. Scoutmaster Walt wouldn't let me because I can't swim, and Chad was afraid he would sink because of his cast, so he let us take the canoe across the lake. It was great. You can still see some of the trees under the water from the flood.

Scoutmaster Walt isn't crabby like some scoutmasters. He didn't even get mad about the lifejackets. He has to spend a lot of time working on the car so we are trying not to cause him any trouble.

Guess what? We have all passed our first-aid merit badges. When Dave dove in the lake and cut his arm, we got to see how a tourniquet works. Wade and I threw up, but Scoutmaster Walt said it probably was just food poisoning from the leftover chicken. He said they got sick that way with food they ate when he was in prison.

I'm so glad he got out and became our scoutmaster. He said he sure figured out how to get things done better while he was doing his time.

By the way, Mom, what is a pedophile?

I have to go now. We are going to town to mail our letters and buy bullets. Don't worry about anything. We are fine and having a lot of fun.

Love, Jordie

We can laugh at this because it's a joke. And I need to laugh and shed the black cloud if only for a moment because nothing, no, nothing in this life is more devastating than hearing the news that one of your children is dead. Nothing!

You may think all the positive thoughts you want. You may make yourself smile and pretend that in this vast darkness, the sun is shining.

You may even be comforted by the thought of heaven and the world to come—or even of how much God loves you—but ultimately nothing works quite like tears and the passage of time.

Recovery is like walking through a fiery furnace. It does no good to pretend that the fire is not hot or that "you'll get over this."

Time and tears—and only then do we speak of the power of a positive attitude.

For me, and I think for my wife, simple little one-step assertions began to help. I began to say the things I believe: "God is so good...He's so good to me." There were other helpful affirmations sprinkled in with all the tears. I made myself say them:

Life is good.
I believe in God the Father, Almighty Maker of heaven and earth.
Thank you for my son Christopher.
Thank you for our forty-one years together.
I believe in the sunshine even when it rains.
I can do all things through Christ.

How many times I sang (to myself, of course) the comforting words of many old gospel hymns:

Blessed assurance, Jesus is mine…
To God be the glory; great things he hath done…
O Lord, my God, when I in awesome wonder…
Consider all the worlds thy hand has made…
Then sings my soul, my Savior, God to thee…
How great thou art…

I don't know why. I don't know how, but these old hymns began, slowly, to replace the anger, the bitterness, the sadness and the sorrow that had flooded my soul for so many months.

There came to me a deep peace—a knowing—that, "It is well with my soul…" and it was well with my son Christopher.

You can't control what happens but you can always control your attitude and your response.

Abraham Lincoln was attacked, criticized, and vilified by many of his peers. Even in the courtroom, Lincoln was attacked by the opposition attorney who once told the jury that Lincoln was two-faced and could not be believed.

It hurt. He knew that he was not handsome or attractive but Lincoln knew how to turn a negative into a positive. He stood slowly, carefully, to his full stature, (someone said he was so tall it took him five minutes to stand). He placed his hand upon his face and said, "Does anyone in this court believe that if I had a face other than this one, that I would choose to wear this one all the time?"

The members of the jury roared with laughter and Lincoln won the case for his client.

Lincoln once commented: "It is my observation that most people are about as happy as what they make up their minds to be."

Ironic perhaps that one with such humble origins could have achieved such a level of greatness. Lincoln never quit. Discouraged? Yes. Despondent and even severely depressed at times? Yes. However, always he kept on keeping on.

I recall reading a long list of negatives—failures that seemed to engulf his life. Lesser men would have given up or drowned in despair. Attitude was everything. Of bitterness—none. Of hatred—none. Of harbored resentment and revenge—none.

Repeatedly in this world, we see evidence that God plants majesty in the world's mangers. The Eternal lures the highest and noblest qualities from the humblest quarters.

Lincoln's biography is an incarnation of this contention. He is now recognized as perhaps the man of greatest moral stature in the 19th century. Yet his greatness is garbed in such humility that most of his contemporaries missed it.

As late as June, 1864, less than a year before his assassination, *The New York World* published this paragraph:

> The age of statesmen is gone. The age of rail-splitters and tailors, of buffoons, boors, and fanatics has succeeded. In a crisis of almost appalling magnitude, the country is asked to consider the claims of two ignorant, boorish, third-rate, backwoods lawyers for the highest station in government. God save the Republic. (The second person referred to is newly-elected Vice-President Andrew Johnson.)

God did exactly that. He saved the Republic with the help of one of those backwoods lawyers.

Attitude. Mind set. Positive reactions. Call it what you will—but wherever it is found there is also found solutions and answers to the most divisive problems.

Historians are still talking about the negativity of Edwin Stanton toward President Lincoln. His words were vicious—his attack cruel and unrelenting.

Yet when the President wanted to fill the post of Secretary of War, he selected this same Edwin Stanton. "Why," asked the reporters, "would you select someone who doesn't even like you?"

"It isn't important that he like me. What matters is that I like him and besides he's the best man for the job…"

"With malice toward none…and justice for all."

Historians will remember that after the assassination, Edwin Stanton stood over the lifeless body of Mr. Lincoln—and wiping tears from his eyes said, "Here lies the greatest ruler of men this world ever knew. Now he belongs to the ages."

Let us harbor no hatred toward anyone. Let us give others the benefit of the doubt. Let us assert life in the face of death, light in the presence of darkness, and hope in the face of despair.

Moreover, let us turn doubts and fears and all forms of negativity into something useful, helpful, and positive.

Does it work? Let me tell you about Suzanne Kunkel and her remarkable study done at the University of Miami Gerontology Center.

There she worked with some six hundred persons—along with another three hundred at Yale University. The respondents were asked one simple question related to their attitude: Do you see yourself as being essentially a positive person or a negative person?

She carefully monitored the group over a period of more than ten years. At the end of the study, she and her colleagues at Yale University unearthed some amazing data.

Persons who professed a positive attitude were healthier, happier, sick less often, had more friends and—incredibly—lived an average of seven and one-half years longer than those with a professed negative attitude.

Attitude is everything—and it has nothing to do with one's age.

Our friend Roy Jones told of a man who moved to Sun City, Arizona, a senior retirement community, at sixty-five. He went to see the doctor for his physical. The doctor said, "You're in good condition for a man who is sixty-five. May I ask how old your father was when he died?"

The man responded, "Did I say my father was dead? My father is eighty-five and lives right here in Sun City."

"Amazing," said the doctor. "Well, how old was your grandfather when he died?"

"Did I say my grandfather was dead?" asked the patient. "No, my grandfather is very much alive. He's one-hundred and five; lives right here in Arizona, and, in fact, just got married last month."

The doctor, astonished, asked, "Why on earth would a man one-hundred and five want to get married?"

"Did I say my grandfather *wanted* to get married?"

Some readers have perhaps heard or read about the Martha Berry School in Rome, Georgia. Martha was quite a lady—and one who knew how to turn insults into compliments and negatives into positives.

She was a friend of Henry Ford. Once in Mr. Ford's presence she told him about the new school in Rome, Georgia, and asked if he would consider a contribution. Mr. Ford reached into his pocket and gave her a dime.

Instead of being discouraged at the size of the gift, Miss Berry determined to use it for the school's good.

She happened upon an idea. She bought a package of "seed" peanuts, planted them, harvested, and sold the small crop she produced.

Again, she appeared with Mr. Ford. "Here's the dime you gave me last year," she said, handing him the coin. Then she told him of the return she had realized from his meager investment.

Mr. Ford was so impressed with her perseverance that, in the years that followed, he contributed millions of dollars to her school.

I confess to you that I have wasted many hours pouting over things I don't possess—money, talent, material things—and then I read about someone like Martha Berry and I realize that

It's Not What Happens to Us but How We React To It.

Anyone who can allow himself to turn a negative into a positive is already walking on the road to success, health, and happiness.

Many readers are acquainted with the *Tufts University Newsletter*. In one copy from a couple of years ago, the writer reported on studies done with persons whose outlook was positive and optimistic.

This same conclusion was reached years ago by Dr. Norman Vincent Peale. Peale, who could be called the father of positivism and optimistic thinking, was right in his assertions: optimism actually improves your health—even into the retirement years.

The *Tufts Newsletter* study found that optimists and people with a positive attitude recover faster from surgery, have less heart disease, less pain, better blood pressure, and fewer physical and emotional problems. Not surprisingly, the study found that optimists and positive-attitude people live longer and, in essence, become masters of their own fate.

Some doubtless accuse positive people with being simplistic, naïve, and "burying their heads in the sand." The truth is, say the researchers, positive attitude people pay attention to negative events and learn how to maneuver around them.

We have known for years that prolonged stressful situations trigger an automatic negative response in the human body. Chemicals including cortisol and adrenaline are released into the blood stream affecting breathing, blood pressure, heart rate, and muscle tension. The fact of being "uptight" or "tied up in knots" is often the result of these long periods of stress. Left unattended, these chemicals will in time weaken your immune system, making you more susceptible to disease.

Fortunately, psychologists are telling us that optimism can be learned. Dr. Herbert Benson at the Harvard Medical School helps patients learn a relaxation exercise that dramatically reduces the tense muscles and the "tied up in knots" feeling.

He asks patients to sit quietly, close their eyes, breathe slowly, repeat a certain word—like peace, calm, easy, love, gentle—and give your muscles permission to relax and to be "at ease."

The results of this and other types of mind-body exercises show a dramatic and positive effect upon the levels of stress and tension. The overwhelming majority of people who do these exercises declare "It really works!"

I came early to know that we are not alone in our grief—that there were hundreds of others who had received the same kind of phone call with unbelievable news. Caroline V. Clarke writes about the trauma of a phone call that came to Terri James in the winter of 1997.

The unbearable news said that Terri's mother had died—and that she had chosen to end her own life. Terri said of the call and the dark days that followed: "I had no idea how I was going to get through it...It's hard to imagine a darker time."

Somehow, someway, she did get through it. Two weeks after returning to her work with a financial services firm, Terri realized that she had become overwhelmed by the trauma of her mother's death. She asked for and received a leave of absence to try to recover. She sought grief counseling and traditional therapy and began as well to try to find the foster family she lost when she was adopted at age four. She found them and enjoyed a wonderful reunion. It was a blessing but it also opened emotional doors that had been closed for years.

Then one day came a joyful serendipity. A close friend came to see her and asked for her help in the preparation of a speech. Terri's counsel was that the speech was too heavy and needed to be lightened up a little. The friend suggested to Terri that with her inclination toward humor that she should do stand-up comedy writing.

Terri thought, in light of the darkness that had encroached itself in her life, "No way!" She said that it is easy to laugh when you feel good...but when you're angry or hurting, laughter is not part of your lexicon. However, wallowing in misery may cause more damage than we realize.

So Terri moved, hesitantly, into the field of humor and comedy. She went to her first class of comedy workshops and found it, and all the others that followed, to be extremely helpful.

"Crying can be therapeutic," she said, "but laughing feels so much better."

Terri returned to her old job, but now with tools that would help her face even the dark side of life when it comes. (Clarke)

The American Association for Therapeutic Humor says one of the things too often missing from our day is a good laugh. A 1966 study of hundreds of adults found happiness to be directly related to humor—and they agreed that humor can help to turn our mental and spiritual struggles around—even if we are walking through life's deepest darkness.

Gratitude Works

I was taught that gratitude and thanksgiving must become a way of life for anyone who considers himself civilized. I knew that my mother was right when she gently, yet firmly said to me and my eight brothers and sisters, "Always say thank you when someone does something nice for you."

More recently I have come across numerous studies that go well beyond the social courtesy necessity—which prove that a thankful spirit and manner actually makes you feel better and improves your health.

Yet in our daily experience, repeatedly we hear and see evidence of people who either forget or were not taught to say thank you.

I was intrigued by a story that appeared in Dale Carnegie's book, *How to Stop Worrying and Start Living.*

Carnegie asks, "If you saved a man's life, would you expect him to be grateful?" Yes, you would expect that—but Samuel Leibowitz, who was a well-known criminal lawyer before he became a judge, saved seventy-eight men from going to the electric chair. How many of those men do you suppose stopped to thank Samuel Leibowitz, or even took the trouble to send him a letter or even a card? How many? Guess…That's right—not one!

I confess that health and happiness may not come as a direct result of learning to say "thank you" but it is surely a first step in the process of recovery.

Some will say that being grateful and positive is a mark of rich and privileged people. I think not. What I have discovered is that gratitude is often very slow in coming from those who have everything given to them. I saw this demonstrated at Christmas when a grandchild was overwhelmed with eight or ten gifts. The child expressed hearty thanks for the first gift and the second and to some degree, the third. By the time, he opened his last gift he was heard to say, "Oh, no, not another Christmas present!"

I still recall how as a small lad growing up in a family that had so little, we often had nothing at all to open on Christmas day. When I was eight, we celebrated the best Christmas I ever knew. Somehow, my father was able to purchase an entire box of red Delicious apples as a gift to the children. I can still recall the deep joy I felt when mother gave me not one or two but three big red Delicious apples. We had nothing else—and that was somehow okay. I was for a day or two flooded by joy and gratitude.

Attitude, mind-set, thankfulness, and a bold positive assertion that the very best is possible are traits we can add to our character. Somehow, I have come to see the truth of the Biblical passage that says "The Kingdom of God is inside you."

Some of the most compelling samples of gratitude have come from people who seemed to have the least. A grateful, positive countenance is a beautiful thing to see.

The German mystic Johannes Tauler tells of meeting such a man way back in 14th century Germany. In his travels, Tauler met a very poor man, a beggar, on the street. Tauler said, "May God give you a good day, my friend."

The beggar answered, "I thank God I never have a bad day."

Tauler said, "May God give you a happy life, my friend."

The beggar answered, "I thank God I am never unhappy."

Tauler said to him in amazement, "What do you mean?"

"Well," said the beggar, "when it is fine I thank God. When it rains, I thank God. When I have plenty, I thank God. When I am hungry, I thank God. And since God's will is my will, whatever pleases him pleases me. Why should I say I am unhappy when I am not?"

Tauler was astonished and asked, "Who are you?"

"I am a King," came the reply.

"And where is your kingdom," asked Tauler.

The beggar pointed to his heart and said, "Here inside of me."

It may be called by different names: gratitude, thanksgiving, a positive spirit. One thing seems clear: the Kingdom of God really is inside of each of us.

I would not want readers to misunderstand what I am about to say. However, during my prayers at night, I began to tell Christopher how I felt. I told him, aloud, that I loved him more than life, and that I had been angry at what he chose to do. If a psychiatrist had been listening to my "prayers," he might have thought me totally crazy.

This process of talking aloud to our son seemed to me to be a step toward my healing. I have no idea why it worked or how it worked—and I would not presume to recommend that any other person do this. All I know is that it worked for me.

As improbable as it might seem, that idea came from a book written by a medical doctor. This man normally writes about medicine and the human body, but not about the world of the spirit. The book was *Vibrational Medicine* by Dr. Richard Gerber.

I found myself disagreeing with some of the points made in this stimulating book, but it did make a deep and lasting point that assured me that life and consciousness do not end at death. When I first read this, I was quite literally ecstatic, and immediately began telling Christopher how I felt and what I thought.

All this is a roundabout way of saying that my own recovery from our son's tragic, self-inflicted death also progressed as I started to express thanks to God for the life that he had lived, and not for the thirty or forty years unlived.

Yes, it was done at times through heavy tears and an anguished heart—mingled, I suspect, with feelings of anger—but the gratitude began to come out. Often alone, I found myself saying aloud, "Thank you for my wonderful son, Christopher." I found myself repeating this repeatedly. I would add things like, "I had forty-one years with him. Thank you, Eternal Spirit, for this great gift."

When I mixed this vocal expression of thankfulness with all the tears, with a positive confession about his life, and about our own future—the healing I so desperately needed and wanted began to come. Humor? Yes, it was, in a strange and weird sort of way, mingled in among all the other emotions. Together they helped me to believe, really believe that our son was somehow alive—even if it were a non-visible, spiritual existence.

Humor Wears Many Dresses

I was to learn that humor comes in many shapes and sizes. It has a diverse and multi-faceted persona—but the essence of humor is doing or saying the unexpected. Humor's personality may include preposterous thoughts, outlandish conclusions, illogical statements, surprise endings, or dramatic turns. It is all wonderfully therapeutic.

A quick example is the mountain school district that raised the "no drinking" age to thirty-five to allow everyone enough time to graduate from high school.

Another surprise form of humor was the story that appeared in our local paper about an older lady who went to get in her car in a shopping center lot. She owned a white Cadillac and knew exactly where she left it. When she got to the car, she noticed four young men getting into her car. She pulled a gun out of her purse and threatened to shoot the "thugs" if they didn't get out immediately. The men ran for their lives. The lady got in, put her key in the ignition, but the key didn't work. After several minutes, she got to looking around and saw another white Cadillac. Her key worked perfectly in her own car. She eventually went to the police to tell her side of the story and the folly of what she had done.

"Madam," the officer said, pointing to the four men who also came to the police station, "your version of the story is nothing compared to the one they told about a little old lady who pulled a gun on them and tried to steal their car."

Saying the totally unexpected often produces humor.

An E-mail page told about a middle-aged man who applied for a government job. The interview went something like this:

Q: Do you come late to work?

A: Not more than two or three days a week.

Q: Have you ever told lies to your boss?

A: Well, only on occasion.

Q: Have you ever been arrested?

A: Well, yes, but not often.

Q: Do you keep secrets and confidences?

A: On most things, yes.

Q: Have you ever spent time in jail or prison?

A: Well, once, but only for five years.

The interviewer sat back in his chair. He smiled broadly and stood as he extended his hand and exclaimed, "You're hired. You're perfect for this job." Well, no one actually believes this story. But it shows how humor comes when you stretch a story to extremes and arrive at a preposterous conclusion.

It is like the totally absurd things which you hope you will never hear during a surgical procedure like:

Oops. Dropped the knife. Oh, well, the floor is clean, isn't it?

Why, yes, I used these same scissors yesterday. It's one way we have of saving money.

Well, if that is the appendix, what on earth is this?

Whoops! There go my glasses. Well, I'll try it without them.

What do you mean, I pulled the wrong tooth?

God Goes Where You Can't

Some readers will remember the writings of the late Joseph Bayly, and the story he told about his own rebellious son. At an early age, the son declared his independence from his family, cut all his ties with them and hitch-hiked across America to live his own life on the west coast.

With his son so far away, Joseph became very depressed. But his wife, Mary Lou, said, "We must pray all the more. We're not in San Diego with our son, but God is."

I thought of the prayer poem called *Mother's Covers:*

When you were small
And just a touch away,
I covered you with blankets

Against the cool night air.
But now that you are tall
And out of reach,
I fold my hands
And cover you with prayer.

Among the hardest things we ever have to do is to stop trying to control and manage and manipulate our adult children. Somehow, someway we must release them, let them go, give them up, and give them over to the care of the Eternal God even if that could mean that they choose not to live.

He Walked In My Shoes

I do not know what it is about sharing your grief with others that seems to lift your own spirits. Admittedly, we are grateful for anyone who will listen and who seems to understand. Nevertheless, the people we prize the most, the ones who really seem to help us, are those who have themselves walked through some dark and tragic loss.

For whatever reason, the name that kept coming to my mind in those early days was that of Jacob DeShazer. He was a bombardier on one of our American B-25 bombers flying over Japan. He was assigned to Jimmy Doolittle's unit.

In April 1942, he was captured by the Japanese and held as a prisoner of war for over three years. When he described the harsh and brutal treatment in the Japanese prison, I could hardly bear to read it. Desperate for food and clean drinking water, he lost half his body weight. He was beaten, tortured, slapped, blind-folded and filled with seventy-five boils and sores on his body.

He asked for a Bible and after many requests was given one. While reading the Bible, he came upon a verse in Romans 10:9. "...if you confess with your lips that Jesus is Lord and believe in your heart...you will be saved." He somehow knew that he would live, and that changed everything.

He was aware of the deep hatred, bitterness, and anger that consumed his every waking moment. Suddenly that little passage gave him hope. He would give his Japanese captors the benefit of the doubt. He would be kind to them regardless of how they treated him.

Days later, DeShazer was a little too slow returning to his prison cell. The Japanese guard pushed him, and with his foot caught in the door, slammed the large steel door, crushing his foot. Hatred, intense and deep, welled up in his heart. Suddenly there came to him the picture of Jesus on the cross. In his anguish and pain, he prayed to his Father, "Forgive them for they know not what they do."

DeShazer's hatred lifted and he said, in his own mind, "I forgive you."

The next day, the guard came to the cell. Jacob stood on his one foot, raised his hand in a salute, and with cheerful Japanese words said to his captor, "Good morning, sir."

The guard was stunned and began immediately to show him respect in return. A day later, that same guard slipped Jacob a large sweet potato and smiled, but motioned him to tell no one.

He said in that instant he knew that the victory was won.

Incredibly DeShazer lived. He returned to the United States and decided to become a Christian missionary—to the very people who held him captive.

Following the war, he held tent meetings and many Japanese citizens heard him speak about God's love, forgiveness and his living presence in life's darkest hours.

Then the most amazing thing happened. One night a small Japanese man came to Jacob's home and stated that he had attended many of the tent meetings and wanted to be baptized as a follower of Christ. He then told Jacob, "My name is Mitsuo Fuchido. I am the man who led the raid on Pearl Harbor."

I thought of the dark night through which DeShazer had walked. If God could come to him, comfort him, and bring something good, something redemptive out of all that suffering, then the same God could bring comfort to me in my hour of loss.

Peggy Rynk wrote about the power of a positive attitude. She told of a study done at the University of Chicago with two hundred telecommunication executives who were observed as their companies downsized. The health of the executives who saw the downsizing as an opportunity for growth fared much better than those who saw it as a threat. (Rynk, 2003)

Less than one third of the executives with the positive, hopeful attitude contracted a serious illness during or soon after the downsizing. However, the executives who saw downsizing as a personal threat suffered more than a ninety percent likelihood of becoming seriously ill. Our body responds to what our mind is doing!

In another study related to attitude and health, researchers wondered what, if any, effect on cancer patients might be made by attending a support group. A study at Stanford University showed that cancer patients in support groups stayed in remission longer and lived longer. Again, Rynk concluded that when a person is anxious, angry, or depressed, it is helpful to talk to someone who listens, understands, and cares.

Rynk thinks that attitude, talking and humor all have a significant impact on one's health. Taken as a whole or individually, those factors reduce stress, boost immunoglobulin A (which helps to fight upper respiratory disease), and tend to increase killer T-cells (which fight infection). Humor tends to displace destructive emotions like anger. Some have gone so far as to say, "Laugh and live."

A physician with a great sense of humor told about a middle-aged woman named Helen. She had a critical heart attack and was taken to the hospital. While on the operating table, she had a near-death experience. She saw God and asked if this was the end for her. God looked at her and then at his chart and said, "No, you still have another forty years to live."

Upon her recovery, she decided to stay in the hospital, have a face lift, a liposuction, tummy tuck and a change in the color of her hair. She left the hospital a beautiful, trim, young woman. Out in the street she was run over by a speeding ambulance and once again arrived before God. She yelled at him and said, "You told me I had another forty years."

God said, "Is that you, Helen? For Heaven's sake, I didn't recognize you."

Oh, it feels good to laugh.

4

Was It God Who Called,
Or a Blue-Eyed Blonde?

The "call" was clear and unmistakable—I was to prepare to be a pastor. To be perfectly honest, I was excited about the prospects—only four years of college and three years of graduate school at the seminary.

No big deal, I thought. As I recall, I had a singleness of purpose and mind: I was going to be an ordained pastor—fully prepared, blessed, licensed, sanctified, holified, authorized but hopefully not scandalized. It was fun, those days.

I began to play the part at church, at college, on Sundays when I met with my brothers and sisters to play euchre—a card game played a lot in Central Indiana. I told everyone with an air of excitement: "I am going to be a minister."

Even the employees at Bob's Marathon where I worked heard about it. One said "Oh, God, what's next?" I just laughed and went on working.

I wasn't interested in much else. The idea of going to college and formally preparing for the ministry consumed most of my thoughts, my time, and my feelings.

The Blue-Eyed Blonde Appears

Then it happened. I went to church that first Sunday in September, 1956. My eye fell upon a beautiful teenage lady dressed in a royal blue velvet suit. And the rest is history—well, not quite. She had an air of royalty. She was dignified, refined, polished, and, I thought, very sophisticated.

It occurred to me that she stood in sharp contrast to the person that I was—an old country boy, unpolished, tall, skinny, awkward, anxious, nervous, and very impulsive. I recall hiding my hands so she wouldn't notice the accumulation of grease in my fingernails from my work at the service station. Then she said, "Hello" or something like that, and I responded, but not in English.

Being from the deep South was no advantage. I spoke no English—only "southernese" which is like gibberish to educated Yankees. I think she asked me three, four or five times what it was I had said.

But something happened—something big and wonderful that has now lasted forty-six years—and counting.

She went home that day after church and unbeknownst to me announced to her parents, "I have met the man I am going to marry."

To set the record straight, she really did not have blue eyes but hazel, and she really wasn't blonde, but a brunette. But suddenly that didn't matter. She was indescribably beautiful—and refined and poised and dignified. And I went to work pursuing her. It took the better part of three years before we tied the knot—time to remember my first passion, preparing to be a pastor.

Now I had two passions: Janet, who quickly became the center of my life, and slightly less important, the Christian ministry.

Early on I recall how devastated I was when her mother mentioned that her daughter was determined never to marry a minister. Fortunately, that news didn't surface until we were both madly in love with each other. She concluded: being married to the minister of a church might not be too bad.

I had so little to offer and she, so much. I had come from a background of near poverty, and she, a family of means. I felt supremely blessed, lucky—as if it were all a dream.

I was like the old fellow who won the Irish Sweepstakes—all 2.6 million dollars. Problem was he had a serious heart condition and they figured any sudden shock could be fatal. How to tell him the good news without causing his death became the overriding concern. "Let's ask Father O'Connor.

Perhaps he can think of a soft way to tell him…" It was agreed and Father O'Connor began.

"Mr. O'Reilley, God is good. He's always coming up with big and sometimes shocking surprises. Suppose for a moment, Mr. O'Reilley, that you had won the Irish Sweepstakes—all $2.6 million," intoned the Reverend.

"Father O'Connor, as God is my witness—and all these people standing here, if I won that much money, I'd give every dime of it to my church."

And the priest had a heart attack.

I didn't have a heart attack over my good fortune, so we were married on Flag Day, June 14, 1959, nearly three years after I first saw her there at University Park Christian Church. I felt for many months that she was blinded by her fantasy of a "southern gentleman" but I was ecstatic and determined to live up to the gentleman she believed me to be.

Over the years, both of us came to believe that marriage was somehow sacred—that our vows were binding and for life. I knew that marriage was not intended to be a "trial and error" or a short-term arrangement or an experiment to see if we like it.

Perhaps I am wrong but I see all too many people who imply that they will try it for a few months and if it works, fine, and if it doesn't work, that too is fine. For better or for worse should mean exactly that.

With all of my own father's weaknesses, he remained devoted and loyal to my mother for all of their sixty plus years together. When I was fourteen, he stopped using and abusing alcohol. The effect on our family for good was immediate and overwhelmingly positive. Mother and Daddy became a team in every sense of the word. No, he never accompanied her to church, but they became in every other way a team.

This is not an attempt to be harsh or judgmental toward people who have had many marriage partners. Doubtless there are always a dozen or so factors that go into one's decision to be divorced. But marriage is not the answer to a lot of the problems people face. Very often marriage adds to the problems people face. But they must learn it for themselves and often the hard way.

It was the dead of winter at Earlham College, where I was a senior student, and our town was in the middle of a winter blizzard. My appointment at the Yale Divinity School to enroll as a graduate student, however, prompted us to leave immediately.

We were poor as church mice and had no business starting out with so little money and on so bitterly cold a night. Through wind and blowing snow we headed out driving all night long on our way to New Haven. What did it matter to us if it was ten below zero? We were young, adventuresome, madly in love and about to take the trip of a lifetime. They say "love is blind." May I hasten to add that at times, it is also downright stupid!

After what seemed like a month's driving, just as we approached Harrisburg, Pennsylvania, we developed a loud clanking noise underneath the car and were forced into a service station to get it checked.

I had recently finished three years working as a mechanic at a service station and felt that I knew everything about cars. I had even given thought to writing my own book on "How to repair your own car." Big mistake! The mechanic indicated that he thought my problem was a broken universal joint. But headstrong me, I told him rather arrogantly to install a new pressure plate in the clutch and all would be well. He shook his head and did as I directed.

Now $150 poorer, we pulled onto the interstate highway, got up to speed and about fifty miles east of Harrisburg, the old clanking noise reappeared. Yes, it was a universal joint and I left the second service station greatly humbled, dramatically poorer and terribly late.

We wired my wife's parents for money and got it just in time to be one full day late for our appointment at Yale. When we appeared at the office of the registrar a day and seven hours late, and two days before Christmas, the staff members were not too excited about seeing us. I knew there had to be some reason she kept calling me John and then Ron, but never Don…

"Well, Ron, could you come back after Christmas?" Could she just give me the forms and have me send them back? Staring at the clock on the wall over the secretary's chair, I noticed it was 4:55 pm and quitting time was 5:00 pm, even at a seminary. The Rons and Johns became even more noticeable. I think she was trying to tell me something.

I thanked her politely for listening and apologized for my being late for my appointment by nearly two days and told her about my car problem, turned and walked out. That was the last time I ever saw the hallowed halls of Yale.

Strange, isn't it? My whole life might have been so dramatically different if only I had listened to that mechanic in Harrisburg and installed a universal joint instead of a pressure plate.

My new young bride never gave me a hard time about my pigheadedness, but we've enjoyed some good laughs about the incident. In fact, laughs are part of the glue that binds us together.

I Want a Guy Just Like the Guy That Married Dear Old Mom

My wife had such high expectations for her new husband. That was especially true when it came to house repairs, and for that matter, any work that required a "man's touch." She had received from her very own father this model of what all husbands are expected to do. Her dad was an engineer, practical minded, who could and did fix anything. She assumed that her new husband would be able and willing to step in and do all repairs around the house—just as good ole' Dad had done.

However, let's face it. Some men were just not cut out to do practical things—especially projects that might be accurately classified as "work." It got so bad around our house that when I finally did find time to do a few repairs, my wife regretted profoundly having bothered me with such mundane projects. The results of my work were usually disastrous.

I do recall trying to install a lid on a stool. Anyone can do that, I thought—anyone but I. As I recall, the screws would not come loose. I worked what seemed to be the better part of two days but the screws refused to break free. I happened upon an idea that seemed just short of genius. I would use a sharp screwdriver and a hammer and cut the plastic screws loose.

It really was a brilliant idea and it would have worked except that once, and only once, as I was pounding the screwdriver, the hammer slipped and I hit instead the side panel of the stool.

I did not know that those things would break, let alone shatter. Instantly the entire bathroom floor was flooded and the stool broke in 1,000 pieces.

A plumber was summoned. A new stool was purchased and installed to the tune of $300. If there was any redeeming feature about this event, it was that I was never again asked to repair anything in or around our house or anyone else's house. I cannot begin to tell you what a comfort that has been. I told Janet that God has a way of taking care of his own…but somehow, she never saw the humor in it.

"He Can't Even Change a Light Bulb…"

Early on, it became a joke when I showed up at the church for a "work day." They never assigned me to do anything important. I was permitted to change light bulbs until I managed to break two of them during one ordeal.

Once they allowed me to do some painting at the old scout hut, but when I finished painting the east wall, they distracted me long enough to have someone come and repaint the wall. It seems I had used the wrong color from the wrong can. When I found out what I had done, they laughed and joked and said now they could better understand what my poor wife had to deal with at our house.

Elder Bill added, "Don't worry, preacher…you are a good preacher and nobody's good at two things."

Well, I went home vindicated. I told my wife, "We had a really good time…, and they seemed to like my preaching." I supposed that she would never find out about my painting goof. It was a deep dark secret for almost a full day until Sunday morning when the Elders gathered to discuss my painting exploits. Moreover, yes, each of them individually told my wife every detail and said I should just stick to preaching.

Our friend Jake once told me that my lack of manual skills reminded him of a story. It seems a young fellow went to the home of a wealthy man and asked for a job. The owner said yes, he would like to get his porch painted and it was located out back. The brush and dark green paint were there ready to be used. A couple of hours later, the young buck said that he was finished and then added, "But, Sir, that ain't no Porsche, it's a Mercedes Benz." Yikes!

Mixed Signals from the Pastor's Wife

It hadn't started out as a problem. It was intended to solve a problem. The problem was simple: I talked so fast during my sermons that no one could understand me. What my new bride Janet did not realize at that time was that I probably secretly did not want anyone to hear me, let alone to understand me. I was in a dreadful hurry, racy, nervous, rapid-fire staccato that was so fast-paced that my sermon was over almost before it began.

"Honey, you've got to slow down...Can't you try to slow down in your delivery?" she said to me in her soft, sweet tones. The problem seemed fixable to her. But not to me.

"Dear, I can't tell when I'm speaking too fast or too slow. I just can't tell..." I said to her in my own defense. "What can I do?" I asked.

The problem continued. My sermons seemed to get shorter and shorter. But there was one advantage: Somebody said, "Well, at least we beat the Baptists to the restaurants!"

Another said, "I think you had a good sermon but you spoke so fast I'm not sure exactly what you said."

Then Janet happened upon an idea that would end all ideas. It was brilliant, insightful, timely and workable. "Let's do it this Sunday," I said enthusiastically. Unfortunately, that is what I did, or I should say, that is what we did. We put her plan into action. When I was talking too, too fast, she would place her right hand on her right cheek and that meant slow down.

I cannot tell you how beautifully this plan worked. I moved from ninety miles per hour to about thirty miles per hour. Now simple math will tell us that if you triple a ten minutes sermon, you've got thirty minutes.

What that meant was that we would no longer beat the Baptists to the restaurants. (I say Baptists because there were more of them than all the other denominations put together.) Well, the long and short of that brilliant idea was that I slowed down to a dreary, dull drawl, and half the congregation went to sleep.

Something had to be done, but what? What we needed was another plan that would tell me when I was speaking too slowly. Again, it was so simple, clear and sure, that nothing could go wrong with this plan. Right? Wrong!

She said to me, "Honey, when I put my left hand up on the left side of my face that means you're talking way too slowly."

Well, it worked fabulously for about four weeks. I discovered the exciting world of timing and pacing and articulation. I even learned such things as dramatic pause, vocal highs and lows and clear, precise enunciation (at least as clear as it ever gets for a Southerner). I was proud, and the congregation responded by asking me if I would consider becoming their "full time pastor."

How else can I say it? Her two hand signals worked really well. And then came the hay fever season in east central Indiana. I did not know it would be a problem. Ask anyone. "Will a wife's hay fever have any adverse effect upon her husband's preaching?" and the answer will always be no, no, no.

Well, don't believe it. I was preaching at what I thought was a good pace with good timing, rhythm, eye contact and I knew I had them in the "palm of my hand." I felt good because I had learned something interesting and helpful from my new bride.

Then her right hand rose to cover the right side of her face. I slowed down to what I thought was a snail's pace. She then tapped her face two or three times more as if to say to me in a far more dramatic vein, SLOW DOWN!

Well, I slowed down and the congregation looked puzzled, confused, and bewildered. The sermon lasted about two hours.

Then the unbelievable happened. She placed her left hand on the left side of her face but, at the same time, her right hand covered the right face.

I looked at her through disbelieving eyes. What, I wanted to say, are you trying to tell me? I'm too fast; too slow; what?

I knew it was a problem when the people said after the service, "What was wrong with you today, pastor? You seemed to be a snail and a race horse at the same time."

In the car going home I impatiently wanted to know what on earth she meant by her strong hand signals. Was it that we hadn't used our signals in a while, I inquired.

I still recall her reply. "Oh, honey, I forgot. I was so miserable with hay fever that I forgot all about our hand signals."

Well, that put an end to our "perfect" solution. I don't recommend that any pastor just starting out use it.

I sometimes had other problems in speaking. For example, as I concluded a sermon, I gave the congregation a challenge: "The choice is clear for each of you: either you can reject Christ—or you can deny him!" Of course, I meant to say, "...either you can accept Christ—or you can deny him," but it just didn't come out that way. One old farmer shook my hand as he was leaving the church and said, "Preacher, that ain't much of a choice you gave us this mornin'." Janet told me later what I'd said.

The Devil Made Me Do It

I regret having told it in church. I still can't believe I said it. But there it was on the tape—my voice—telling the entire congregation the story about my wife's new Easter dress.

It was Holy week and my wife, wanting very much to look her best for Easter Sunday went shopping. The dress was just two degrees short of spectacular. On Sunday I stood before the congregation and told them how nice they all looked and especially how lovely were the ladies' dresses. I then proceeded to tell them the following, and I still can't believe I said it.

My wife, like yours, is decked out in her new Easter dress. When she came home from the department store yesterday, I was struck by its beauty and asked how much she had to pay for it. When she told me, I protested vigorously saying that it was more than we could afford. She said she liked it and just couldn't resist the temptation. I told her we should resist these temptations and just tell the devil to "get thee behind me."

She smiled sheepishly and said, "I told the devil to get behind me." He did and said, "Why, Mrs. Farrior, it even looks good on you from back here."

"Please, Don't Sing"

If I happened to be a little deficient in manual skills, I was more so in vocal skills. I loved to sing—really loved it—and I thought I was quite good. At my very first church, I soon realized that my strong loud voice was carried all over the building by our speaker system.

The nursery attendants and babyland attendants were inflicted with the sound of the pastor's disharmonious cacophonies over the public address system. One of the babyland attendants told me that my singing always made the babies cry and there was no way to disconnect their speakers.

Well, it hurt my feelings, of course. But I knew that there were some people who simply could not appreciate quality when they heard it.

I suddenly recalled my encounter with the voice teacher, Mrs. Nordsieck at Earlham College only a few years earlier. My beloved mother-in-law felt that every pastor should have a good singing voice, and that even you could learn if I could get some lessons. I loved how she worded it, "Even I could learn to sing if only..."

Well, Mrs. Nordsieck had me start out doing the vocal scale, do re mi fa so la ti do, up and down, up and down. Try it again and now again. She stopped me, shook her head in total disbelief, and said, "Reverend, don't sing; stick to preaching." Well, it hurt my feelings again, and obviously she was wrong. Nobody who liked music as much as I did could sing that badly. When I told Janet about it at home, she smiled knowingly—because she had heard me sing.

Well, not to be discouraged by a few so-called "professionals," I charted my own course. At the little weekend church at Greensfork, Indiana, where I served as student pastor, the organist informed me that the congregation expected their pastor to do all the solos in church. Well, this was my moment in the sun and I readily agreed to sing regularly. That was, of course, before they actually heard me sing.

We practiced on Saturday, once, twice, three times, and I knew I was ready. I do not remember now what I sang, but my wife said that it was "promising." That was the least offensive thing she could think to say.

When church was over, the elders asked for a meeting with me. At that short meeting, they stated that they had been wanting to organize a church choir and that was exactly what they would do. I still recall the way they worded it, "Rev, you just stick to preaching and we'll take care of all the singing." Well, survival is the name of the game, so I brushed off their comments with the comforting thought that I must really be a great preacher.

I never did another solo in church, and even my loving wife has seemed comforted by that fact.

The Preacher's Wife

Janet says that being a minister's wife has been, for the most part, a happy and fulfilling life for her. When I began the ministry, the preacher's wife was expected to be able to do everything: teach Sunday School, teach Vacation Bible School, chair committees, do all sorts of jobs in Women's Fellowship, make pastoral calls, play the piano, sing solos, and just generally do any job that no one else wanted to do. She even had to preach for her husband on occasion if he was ill on a Sunday morning and did not have an Associate Minister.

This happened once shortly after our daughter, Melissa, was born. I developed laryngitis and could not speak above a whisper one Sunday morning. Janet had to go to church and preach for me. She's done all those things that wives do—except sing a solo!

The minister's wife was also supposed to be the perfect wife and perfect mother and perfect housekeeper. And she was not supposed to work in paid employment outside the home.

As the years have gone by, expectations have diminished. The minister's wife is allowed to be her own person far more now than she was in 1960. People are more willing to let her do the things that suit her temperament and her talents. Today most ministers' wives are employed outside the home because of economic necessity.

Janet always thought the most important thing a minister's wife could do for a church was to provide him with a peaceful and happy home to which he could come at day's end. That was far more important than any jobs that she might do at the church. I am truly blessed.

The Open Door Policy

Living in a parsonage next door to a church can be a problem—privacy. Our church did not have a telephone in the building, so whenever anyone was at the church and needed to use a telephone, they would just run over to the parsonage and often walk right in and start using the telephone.

One Sunday morning, Janet was in the midst of dressing to go to church. She walked out of the bathroom in just her slip and there was some man in the house, looking for the telephone! She was quite embarrassed and so was he.

Another thing about being so close to the church was that when we did laundry and hung the clothes outside to dry (this was in the days before we had a dryer), anyone coming by the church could look at our laundry. One day some woman said to my wife, "Your husband has more socks than any preacher we ever had. Ha ha!"

She waited for a reply. My wife, in stunned disbelief, said, "How in the world would you know that?"

"Oh, I stopped the car long enough to count them yesterday as they were hanging on the line in the back yard."

We thanked her for telling us and added something innocuous like, "Well, we're glad you care."

Many of our members were farmers who got up very, very early in the morning. They expected us to be up just as early as they were. Sometimes some of them would call us at 5:30 or 6:00 in the morning just like it was noontime. Or someone would call and say, "Why I drove past your house at 6:00 this morning and you didn't have a single light on. Were you still in bed that late?"

My Promotion

My wife, Janet, tells this story about being married to a pastor. One of the occupational hazards of the ministry, if the pastor is a nice-looking man, is that there are women who are lonely or unhappy and who become infatuated with him, seeing him as being a man who is kind, caring and understanding—the sort of man the infatuated woman has always wanted. This is especially true if the woman goes through some crisis in her life and turns to her pastor for counseling during this difficult time. It can become dangerous if the woman is mentally unstable.

There was one such woman in our church whom I'll call Hattie. This lady was very emotionally disturbed. I was aware of her instability right away and used extreme caution in dealing with her. However, that didn't stop her from thinking she was in love with me.

One day Hattie went to a beauty shop to get her hair done. It was a large busy shop with many customers and many hairdressers. Hattie stood up and clapped her hands to get everyone's attention.

"I just want to invite you all to come to my wedding this evening at 7 p.m. at the First Christian Church. Don Farrior and I are getting married," she said.

One of the customers knew her and said, "Hattie, I thought you were already married."

"Oh, you mean Frank! He and I are separated now. No, I'm marrying Don Farrior."

Another customer spoke up. "I thought Dr. Farrior was already married."

Hattie gave a dismissive wave of her hand and said, "Oh, her? She doesn't count!"

Some time later, Hattie called our house in the middle of the night. I answered the phone and in a saccharine sweet voice, Hattie said, "I just figured out who you are!"

"Is that you, Hattie?" I asked. "It's two o'clock in the morning! Why are you calling me at this hour?"

"You're the apostle Paul, aren't you?" Hattie said.

"Hattie, go back to bed and go to sleep. And let me do the same."

About fifteen minutes later, the telephone rang again. This time when I answered, Hattie's demeanor had totally changed. Now she was extremely hostile.

In a low, evil-sounding voice, Hattie said, "I know who you really are. You are the devil!"

Hattie continued to harass us over a two-year period, and once I even had to have an off-duty policeman to watch her in church when she had made some threatening comments. Eventually she was committed to a mental health facility. I think Janet was very happy when we moved away from that town with all members of our family alive and well.

Janet thought it was particularly amusing how quickly I was promoted to the apostle Paul, and then demoted to the Devil within a few minutes time.

Two Years to Live

I've heard it said that a man's "crown of glory" is his wife. To have someone with you, near you, who cares profoundly about you may be the most comforting thing that we ever experience in this life. When that vital relationship is threatened, when something happens to shake the foundations of that devotion, love, and loyalty, it is traumatic.

Little did we know after only thirteen years of marriage that there would come news that would shake us to the foundations. We both knew something was wrong with my health—dreadfully wrong, but we had no idea what it could be. I began to lose weight, become tired, exhausted, and lifeless. We went together to numerous doctors to find out what was wrong. No one had a clue.

When the news finally came, we were not prepared to hear it. Dr. Boyce said, "There is no way to make this easy...but you have a terminal blood disease...about two years to live..."

It is at moments like that when you realize how very precious the gift of life is. We had, for all these thirteen years, taken the gift of life for granted. We had been healthy, vigorous, strong, and deeply devoted to each other and to our two beautiful children.

I was thirty-four at the time. The thought of not living had never really occurred to me. I felt a sense of indestructibility. I was young, strong, and full of life.

Now, suddenly, harshly, cruelly to be struck down by this "fatal flaw" was unbearable. I recall the flow of tears, the near-panic feelings, the anxiety, the threat, the fear that dominated our thoughts and feelings. We hugged repeatedly. We embraced and wept and embraced some more.

Our son, age nine, wanted to know what was wrong and we tried desperately to spare him the worst of the news—that very soon he would not have a father. We skirted the issue by telling him that Daddy is sick and will have to see the doctor a lot. That seemed to satisfy him and off he would go to play.

The days that followed were the most unsettling, devastating, and shattering that we had ever known. The world that once seemed resplendent with beauty, excitement and joy now seemed to have been invaded by some dark and sinister force. It was the closest thing to despair that I had ever known. There appeared to be no place to turn, nothing to do—except to sit back and face the inevitable.

Strangely, I began a long and anguished period of adjusting to the news. In the weeks that followed, I came to realize the depth of my support system from friends, colleagues, and family. Janet was my Rock of Gibraltar, quietly determined to make these weeks and months the best that they could be. Yes, we cried often, in private, and shared with our children in as positive and hopeful tones as we could find. I remember that Janet's devoted parents, my own parents, and my brothers and sisters gave me such strong support.

Surprisingly the congregation where I had served as senior pastor sent a large check and a wonderfully-worded letter about the value they placed on my life and my seven-year ministry among them. I felt as if I had accomplished something at my first full-time church. It really felt good.

I recall the process that evolved. I found myself beginning to be at peace about my life. One day I awakened and found that the anger and bitterness were gone. Where did they go? Why did they go?

I recall feeling a deep sense of tranquility that had about it almost an air of soft optimism. I determined to live the last part of my life without regrets—without second guessing and playing the destructive game of "what if." Whatever fear there was, disappeared.

I believed profoundly in the future, in a living, loving God and in a new world coming. Perhaps I run the risk of being misunderstood when I tell you that there were moments in the day when I actually embraced my future with an almost joyful countenance. I still recall feeling a little guilt about leaving a beloved wife and two small children, but I was preparing myself for the end. I suspect others have done the same.

In the meantime, Dr. Boyce called to say that there was one other thing we could try. "It comes with no guarantees but it's worth a try." He called it a "therapeutic phlebotomy," a process of having 500 cc of blood drawn each week in the hopes that the excess iron in my body might be depleted. He called the disease "hemochromatosis" and yes, he had known one or two whose life expectancy had been extended by this intensive therapeutic procedure.

I recall attending a mid-week healing service in Indianapolis at a large Presbyterian church. I remember the elders who gathered around me and prayed for my complete and total healing.

As they prayed, I felt a warm glow, a kind of internal knowing—I knew I would live. And if I did not, that was okay, too. I would like to say that prayer brought about the complete miracle of healing. What it did give to me was the certainty that I was going to live, and that the new therapeutic procedure would prove to be the key. I left the church and that prayer group with the most alive feeling that I had ever known.

In the next few weeks, the laboratory at the blood center began the process of drawing 500 cc's of blood every seven days. During the first two years alone, I gave 100 pints of blood. Incredibly, I began to feel better after only four weeks. Instead of leaving me depleted and exhausted, the blood drawings left me feeling energized, excited, and hopeful and my "old self" again.

The wonderfully supportive people in our church were convinced that God had given me a full blown miracle. The miracle, as it turned out, was finding a doctor who knew just what to do. Was he sent by God? Yes, just as we are all sent by God to bring life and love and hope to all we meet. Wherever he is, I know that Dr. Boyce was God's gift to me.

Well, you guessed it. I lived! That has now been 33 years ago. In those intervening years, I found that I had given over 500 pints of blood which has left my body with normal levels of iron. Yes, there are "pot marks," scars on both my arms. If I were ever arrested, I would certainly be held as a "drugger" but those needle marks are beautiful to behold. Because of them, I got a new lease on life.

That long, dark night's journey into day would prove to be a key ingredient in coping during the coming years—especially as we tried to deal with the death of our only son.

Flag Day

It was June 14, Flag Day, and not coincidentally our wedding anniversary. It was late in the day, not long before bedtime. For whatever reason, Janet seemed sullen, quiet, withdrawn, and late in the day, was teary-eyed. I recall the event painfully, but oh so clearly.

I asked her if everything was okay. She had hardly said a word all afternoon. Instantly she started to cry. I was shocked, rattled, shaken. What was wrong? What could possibly be wrong, I asked. Then this revelation.

Haltingly through tears she said, "I can't believe that after only six years of marriage you have forgotten our anniversary." I was shattered to think that I really had forgotten. But what to do? All the stores were closed. We had no cards in the house. I was desperate for something to do, to say. I happened upon this:

"Honey, of course it's our anniversary. You thought I forgot. Well, our wedding date is June 14th, right? And it's still June 14th until midnight. I still have two full hours. Honey, please give me a break...I could never forget our anniversary. Now just cheer up. The day isn't over yet..."

I was desperate. I began searching for anything I could find to make a handmade card. No luck. None at all. Suddenly my eyes fell upon an old brown paper bag that had been used to bring in groceries. It was folded neatly and stacked in the cabinet. I grabbed it, disappeared to the office where I found four colored magic markers. I began to make designs on the bag, complete with two or three large hearts and arrows flying through them. I wrote a poem and used the words "I love you" repeatedly. I added, "It's not over till it's over" and "Bet you thought I forgot."

I softly, almost casually presented it to her just as she was about to go to bed. Well, the tall and the short of it was that there was great rejoicing at the Farrior house. Secondly, I never, ever forgot our anniversary again. Husbands of America, remember this: anything will work when you are desperate enough. Thank God for brown bags.

Tornadoes Are Not a Priority

Our daughter Melissa was sixteen at the time—incredibly beautiful if I may be permitted to tell you what I think, and she was getting ready for a date. It was Saturday and it was spring—and just the worst time of the year in that part of the country for storms. To be perfectly honest, we never once thought about a tornado—not where we lived, not near our house. Tornadoes happen to other people—people who live in far away places like Illinois and Indiana, but definitely not in the Kansas City area—and certainly not in Independence. She was in her room getting dressed for the date, and had settled finally on getting her hair "done."

Yes, we had on occasion heard the early warning siren sound go off alerting us to the possibility of tornadoes. However, the idea of a real tornado seemed absurd, unreal. However, we looked out the rear door window and noticed that the clouds were dark and gray and churning. It felt nervous. Was it possible that this could be the real thing?

Suddenly the alarms sounded. We looked out and saw the dark funnel clouds churning, twisting, and coming toward our house. Janet ran to Melissa's bedroom, knocked on the door and shouted "Come quickly, a tornado is coming." I could imagine the look on her face: a look of irritation and disgust. She finally stood, comb in hand, and continuing to "do" her hair, exclaimed with impatience, "I have a date. I don't have time to worry about tornadoes."

She literally sauntered to the steps, and casually made her way to the basement. The tornado hit with a sense of fury and rage, ripping off roofs and tearing down small buildings. It lifted our little red bridge off its foundation and hurled it like a small pebble into our neighbor's yard. But we were spared the full force of its fury. Still to this day, I can hear Melissa say, "I don't have time for tornadoes."

Nothing Else Matters

I learned the hard way that men are different from women. Yes, I read the book *Men Are from Mars: Women Are from Venus*, but that came out too late to offer much help early in my marriage. What I mean is that some things matter supremely to women, but not to men.

Men worry if there's no food in the house or if the roof leaks or if the car won't start or it has a flat tire. They don't care about clothes or shirts or ties or shoes or their hair, and not even how they look. But not women!

The hair matters most of all. Appropriate clothing is essential. An attractive hairdo is important. Nevertheless, nothing, I say it again, nothing in this world is more important to a woman than shoes. Yes, shoes. Nothing is more important than shoes.

Well, actually there is one other thing that is more important than shoes—and by now you must have guessed it—color. Color to a woman is everything. It's more important than food or drink or shelter or even such mundane things as health or the condition of their teeth or even the education of their children.

It is simply unthinkable for a woman to send a child to school with mismatched clothes or to have mismatched colors or something that doesn't pick up on the décor of everything else. This is a scientific fact and you can look it up.

However, I didn't know it when I decided to buy my beautiful new bride her first ever avocado colored dishwasher for our new home. It did not matter to me that our kitchen color was aqua. Like who cares?

I had saved my nickels and dimes for weeks and at the end of six months had a pretty good nest egg and just over $100 to purchase the surprise birthday gift. I was excited—nearly ecstatic about what I was doing. I could visualize the hugs and kisses and compliments and praise that she would heap upon me. It was a big, big day for me.

When the sales clerk asked me what color I wanted, I was insulted. Color? What difference does that make? What matters is that it's a dishwasher and she will be pleased.

Well, to make a long story even longer, I managed to sneak it into the kitchen, put a big ribbon on it, and a note telling her something like "surprise" or "Happy Birthday, my darling."

I had her come to the kitchen, blindfolded her, and told her I had a gift that would make her overjoyed with glee. When the moment arrived, she took of the blindfold and exclaimed, "Oh, honey…Wow! How thoughtful." Later that day the bomb fell: She said gently, "Did they have any color besides avocado? All our other appliances are Coppertone and the wallpaper is aqua and it just doesn't fit the décor of the kitchen…but how thoughtful."

Well, I settled down, took it back and finally got the right color. I knew the color had nothing to do with how well it worked. Oh, well.

It reminded me of the day I bought her a new car. She trusted my judgment about cars and whatever I got was fine.

Again there was evident the big difference in men and women. A man would ask if it's a four-door, stick or automatic, V8 or V6, stereo, CD player, cruise control, et cetera. But not women.

I took the car home, drove it into the driveway, went into the house, and announced that she had a new car. Not a word was said about what kind it was or how much it cost, or if we could afford it or how much our payments would be. She wanted to know one thing and one thing only. What color is it? I tell you from first hand experience: nothing else matters.

◆   ◆   ◆

Ah, Marriage—It Is Special!

In my present work as a chaplain, I am discovering a very large number of retirees who have no thought or interest in getting married again. Yes, most of them have a deep and lasting relationship with someone after they have experienced the death of their first mate. But marriage for them presents too many complications.

Those that I know stand in sharp contrast to the man from Beirut, Lebanon, who has now been married sixty times. According to a story that appeared in a 1966 publication of the *New York Times*, Muhammed Ahmad Issa may hold the world record for "most wives" in a lifetime. Fifty years old at the time when the story first appeared, Muhammed took a new bride every six months.

On December 31st at precisely 5 p.m. he kisses his current wife goodbye and gives her 50 pounds as a payoff and 10 pounds a week for nine months. Oh, yes. He is required to give her a two-hour notice. Wow! Then at exactly 10 a.m., January 1 he marries his new wife—you guessed—until June 30 at 5 p.m.

Muhammed claims he got the six month itch soon after his first marriage, and after all these years he continues to scratch that itch.

Over the past few years, we have continually read much about frequent marriages by both celebrities and ordinary folk. It is at once sad and humorous.

Whether I worked as a pastor or as a chaplain, I began to discover that marriage, in and of itself, does not solve problems. Perhaps that is why so many older Americans choose to stay single after their mate has died.

Friends? Yes. Companions? Yes. And always with a light touch and a sense of the sacred. Without both those expectations a marriage runs quickly into trouble.

5

Life in the Church Is a Scream

It was obvious that this "blue-eyed blonde," who in fact was a hazel-eyed brunette, saw a lot more in this good old boy from the deep south than what was justified.

She was later to confess that she fell in love with a "southern gentleman" and even though he had a lot of rough edges when we got married—a little polish would bring him around. "A diamond in the rough" is how she described me. I never saw the diamonds—only the rough edges—but, oh, how I was determined to become all that she thought I was.

I deeply respect my wife and her struggles in life before I met her. As a child, she suffered from polio and had to learn to walk a second time at age 14 when her legs and one arm were affected. The doctors pronounced that she would probably never walk again. However, she was determined and even forced herself to mount the stairs at her three-story school when she was at last able to return to school.

When a teacher told her she would never be able to catch up with the other students after being gone for months and would fail that grade, she turned her fury into further determination and passed courses with flying colors.

When we were dating, I showed up at her house one day with a Pat Boone record to play for her. She was so excited thinking that I had bought it for her, I let her keep it and only told her the truth about it later. She jokingly used to accuse me of marrying her just to get my record back.

We were married and six years later began our work as the pastoral family in Winston-Salem, North Carolina. It was a suburban church in Pfafftown. Our Regional Minister hinted at how "lucky" I was to be called to this particular church since it was considered the "plum" of churches in my home state.

My seven-year pastorate there was to be among the best and most enjoyable of my thirty-five plus years of ministry. The good experiences outweighed the bad. The joys were far more numerous than sorrows, and at every corner, there were serendipities, laughter, surprises, and even a genuine embrace of my "foreign" born wife. Everyone could tell she wasn't from North Carolina because she didn't have the "South in her mouth."

Ah, I was soon to learn that life in a parish church is a scream.

We loved the years we spent in Winston-Salem. In those days, we had many visitors. One day, a couple spoke to me about conducting the wedding for their daughter.

The date was set and fifty or so wedding guests showed up for the 2:00 p.m. wedding. All were there—the mothers and fathers, grandparents, brothers and sisters, the groomsmen and the groom.

Everyone was there except the bride and her maid of honor.

We waited fifteen minutes. I then started going to the sanctuary every few minutes to announce that the bride was on her way.

When she finally arrived one full hour late, the parents were in tears and the groom had started a search party.

She sauntered into the church parlor nonchalantly and said, "I just couldn't get my hair done to suit me."

Well, I have known for years that hair was important to the ladies—and this was all the proof I needed.

The parents of the young bride never got over their daughter's actions. Finally, out of embarrassment I think, they dropped out of the church.

However, even my own wife was never too sick to get her hair done. One Saturday, she woke up deathly ill. I think her fever was something like 167 degrees. She looked like death—weak, shaky and had a raspy voice. I asked why on earth she was out of bed and she stated that she had a hair appointment at the beauty salon and that would make her feel better. Besides, she just had to look presentable for the Sunday morning worship service.

I protested loudly but to no avail. She got dressed and through what seemed like great anguish of body and mind, drove herself to the beauty salon for a shampoo and set, dried with one of those old fashioned electric machines.

She was gone half a day and then walked into the house all beautiful, happy, cheerful and totally restored to health. Even the fever was gone. I saw it but I didn't believe it. Well, I have believed in beauty salons ever since. I think it's that machine they used on top of their heads. Apparently, it gets so hot that the fever doesn't have a chance. I thought, some day the doctors of America are going to discover those machines and there won't be any more fever.

I recall the incident because several people mentioned how lovely her hair looked on Sunday. After all, I learned early that among the list of life's highest priorities, hair is at the top of the list. How could I have been dumb enough not to realize that earlier?

That reminds me of something funny I heard about being dumb. A good-natured elder told me the following:

Bill was a great athlete and the star quarterback for the football team but he was flunking math. The coach said Bill would have to miss the game Friday unless he could pass a simple math test. Huddled with all the players and Bill, the coach said, "Okay, how much is six plus seven?"

"Thirteen," blurted out Billy.

The coach groaned in relief as though he had been hit below the belt. Whereupon the other football players said, "Ah, come on, coach. Give him another chance."!!

Dr. Joe Wick was perhaps the first person to awaken in me the important role of humor in the life of the parish. He said to me once, "If you are going to survive in the church, you need a light touch—and if possible, develop a sense of humor." Somehow, some way I knew it was true.

The year before we moved to Winston-Salem, I heard Dr. Joe give a talk to our soon-to-graduate seminarians. In those days, religion was serious business, heavy and almost burdensome. No one laughed in church.

However, Joe gave his talk—and it was funny—really funny. We all stifled our laughter at first, pretended not to be laughing. After all, this was a chapel, a place of "divine worship," whatever that meant, and no place for humor or laughter. We felt so guilty.

Finally, we could stand it no longer. Chapel or no chapel, worship or not, Joe was funny and we laughed. That's been forty years now, but it marked a turning point for me. I think that it helped me to take everything seriously except myself. When I look in the mirror even today, and stare at this "body" that God has created, I know that even the eternal God must have a sense of humor.

One day I looked in the mirror at the bulging midriff and chubby cheeks and asked God, "Lord, what have you made?"

I seem to have heard him say: "I didn't make that...that was made by McDonald's hamburgers."

Dr. Wick's admonitions were to serve me well whether in humor or in the more serious side of ministry. Some things had to be learned rather painfully—like our attitude toward people who are older than we are.

In those days, I was young—twenty-six, I think—when I began to serve my first full-time pastorate. Anyone sixty-five or more was a part of the "over the hill gang." I think that I assumed, erroneously, that if they were sixty-five or more, they were somehow severely handicapped. I assumed they couldn't see or hear or walk or think rationally or intelligently. It proved to be most painful.

I recall making a pastoral call on George who, at the time of my call, had just turned sixty-five and was newly retired. He walked with a cane because of a severe limp. But there was nothing wrong with his brain. I was young and assumed the worst about George. I felt certain he couldn't hear—so I'd best talk loud.

I almost shouted my responses to his questions. After three or four episodes of loud jugular projections, George asked me softly, "Rev, why are you shouting?"

I was stunned. I was embarrassed. I was speechless. "Well," I stumbled, "I figured that you couldn't hear."

"Because I'm crippled," he queried, "or because I'm sixty-five and retired?"

I still remember it and when I do, it still hurts.

Why do we assume that if someone is retired or sixty-five or seventy-five or eighty-five they are no longer coherent? Ouch!

In my very first full-time pastorate, there in Winston-Salem, North Carolina, every Sunday seemed like Easter. We were new in the church and the expectations were high. Back then, the ladies wore hats and there was lots of excitement in the air—which always seemed to put extra pressure on this young, anxious, nervous new pastor and his wife.

Sundays were a time when the ladies especially had to present their best side. It was even truer for the pastor's wife. Everything was watched, observed and scrutinized—including her dress, her hair, her manners, or even her culinary skills when we attended the monthly pot luck dinners.

She had the burden of being a Yankee married to a "southern gentleman," as they said. I recall the extra pressure that rested on her shoulders. Always, she had to prove herself. She was under the gun. Good enough for those southern ladies just was not adequate for a Yankee. After all, when we moved there, the Civil War had been over only one hundred years and those southerners weren't about to forget.

I remember our first pot luck all-church dinner. It seemed to Janet and to me that everyone was anxious to find out what dish this pastor's Yankee wife would bring.

Young John, about twelve, stood in line behind us and watched, with his mother, as we placed our dish of Yankee food on the serving table next to theirs. John asked his mother what our dish was. His mother responded, "I don't know but it looks and smells like hell."

That was my Yankee wife's introduction to our southern hospitality.

To our surprise, young John took a large helping—and ate it all. He went back for a second serving and then a third. His mother, now embarrassed, came to us and said, "Well, I guess you heard what I said…"

"Yes," we responded.

"Well, my son likes it and maybe sometime I can get the recipe for it."

Ah, sweet vengeance. We loved it.

Speaking of vengeance, I recall one of my earliest lessons in learning to be a pastor—stay humble.

Helping to Keep the Preacher Humble

Back in the early days, we were called "the preacher." I was never offended by the word but sometimes I said, "You can call me 'Pastor' or 'Reverend' or 'Mr.' or 'Dr.' or just plain 'Don'." Actually, I think I like that last word best of all.

One day we got a phone call from Dottie and Bill (I won't dare give you their real names) and they wanted to invite the preacher and his wife to visit their farm. (The minister's wife didn't actually have a name in those days—just the "preacher's wife.") This was hard for my wife who was so well educated, polished, proper, urbane, and independent—in sharp contrast to the country boy to whom she was wed.

As I recall Bill and Dottie wanted us to come and stay several hours and help them dig up a large field of sweet potatoes. When they say large, I think it was actually a garden plot of about twenty feet by twenty feet but big. They said, "Bring your old grubbies as you'll get dirty."

When we get through, they inferred later, we'll give you some potatoes to take back to the parsonage.

We worked; we perspired and we longed for quittin' time. When the time came, Dottie, an aggressive, take-charge lady who gave all the orders kind of like a drill sergeant, barked out, "Now we have to separate the potatoes into three piles—the A, B and C group which is the culls."

Well, the culls were long and stringy and had no food value. Standing there, I knew that Dottie would give us at least a bushel or two of the premium A group, or at the very worst, lots of the B group. I was excited—but wrong!

To our stunned disbelief, she directed us to take a small bucket full of the culls—the "rejects." She smiled big and broadly, hands on hips, and said, "Since you are a country preacher now, we thought you might want to plant these in your very own garden behind the parsonage."

Different people have different ways of expressing their feelings but I felt then, as I do today, that she wanted to make sure that her preacher remained humble.

I must tell you that we went home and immediately dumped the culls in the trash heap and then, tongue in cheek, thanked the Lord that we were counted worthy to suffer for this lesson in humility.

I have asked myself repeatedly if this writing is exaggerated or fanciful. I checked with the "boss," my wife, and she said, "Print it—that's exactly how it happened." She also added a humorous twist that I had forgotten. Since it was only 11:30 on a Saturday morning, there would be no lunch for us as Dottie had a hair appointment and Bill always went to have lunch with the boys.

If there was anything about this and other types of episodes that had an ironic twist, it was this. Twenty years later, Dottie was in a hospital at death's door, but still clear-headed and articulate. A call from her husband said that she urgently needed to see me. I arranged to go to the room where she lay as a patient.

She told me that she wanted me to conduct her funeral service—because I knew the real Dottie. I made no promises saying, "Well, why don't we wait. Let's talk to Bill…"

I prayed, patted her hand, and left. Unfortunately, I did know the real Dottie.

When I got to the car, I was disgusted at myself. I really intended to ask her, "Why didn't you give us any of those nice sweet potatoes?"

Then I remembered that the Lord said "vengeance (getting even) is mine." I wanted to get even for him, but I did not. Yes, we gotta help keep the preacher humble.

With all the human challenges and problems, that particular congregation proved to be one of the most joyful places we ever served.

I began early in my first church to deal with people's handicaps. Some of the handicaps were physical, most seemed to be emotional, relational, social, and, on occasion, mental. Perhaps the biggest hurdle I had was trying to help an alcoholic. Alcoholics, I came to see, were masters at playing games, and the games were designed so that the alcoholic would always win and I would always lose.

My friend Jess who was a recovering alcoholic kept advising me not to rush in too quickly and not to give help—that, in fact, nothing would help until they "hit bottom."

I didn't believe it. I could do anything and everything at that young age of twenty-six and serving in my first full-time parish, I was "all things to all people," or so I thought.

Alcohol? No problem. I still remember the visit. Randy came by with an order from an official—Go to a detoxification unit or go to jail.

Well, Randy knew that if he went to jail there would be no alcohol. His only hope was to get someone to drive him two hundred miles to the only Detox Center located in the eastern part of the state. He pleaded, begged, and cried until finally out of sympathy I said, "Okay. I will take you to the Detox unit on one condition: You will drink no alcohol of any kind during the four hour trip." He readily agreed, got in the car, and off we went.

Not even an hour had passed when his games began…telling me how desperately he needed just one tiny drink. "If I don't get something I think I will die…Oh, my God, I'm going to die…"

The trick worked. One drink and one drink only I said to him with firm determination. It worked. It really worked—for about 30 minutes. Would you believe it if I told you that I bought five bottles of beer for that con artist during that four hour trip?

I stopped off to see my mother on the way home and when I got home the next day, Randy had already left the Detox Center and actually beat me home. I had a lot to learn. However, that experience reminded me of a man from my youth.

It Will Be a Miracle If He Ever Changes

That's what they said about Rufus. I'm not even sure after sixty years if that was his real name, but I do recall he was "hopeless." He was mad about everything. He seemed worried, uptight, and distantly hostile. No, he never went to church that we knew of and he spoke few words. We only saw him occasionally and when we did see him we tried to avoid him for he was dirty, smelly, bearded, and "strange." We knew that he "drank."

That's what we called it when people drank too much alcohol back in those days.

But something happened. Once they held a big tent revival in a little town not far from where I lived, and Rufus (or Fred or Joe) went. When the invitation was given (so I was told by my Daddy), I heard how Rufus went forward and accepted Christ as his Lord.

Then the most amazing thing happened at church. The following Sunday a stranger went forward at the end of the church service to become a member of the church. No one knew him. He was clean shaven, well-dressed, neat and had combed hair.

When the pastor gave his name as "Rufus" there was a stunned gasp that could be heard across the length of the sanctuary. People seemed to be in a state of shock. No one—I say it again—no one believed it was Rufus. After all, he was called our "town drunk" and drunks can't change. I will spare the reader all the other things that were said about him. I recall even my own saintly mother joining with others and saying as we gathered in the church yard, "Well, I see it but I don't believe it."

The ways of God are strange. No person and no situation are beyond the pull of the spirit—and we stand in awe of the Spirit's power to create miracles.

Handicaps—that's the point I'm trying to make. Some are worse, more severe, than others. However, we never give up and we never stop believing in the innate worth of human personality, regardless of their problem.

I read some place that we all have handicaps of one kind or another. Alexander Hamilton was illegitimate. John Milton was blind as was Homer who gave us *The Iliad.* Ludwig Beethoven never heard some of his greatest symphonies because they were composed after he had lost his hearing. Franklin Roosevelt was a four-term president despite his wheelchair. Charles Steinmetz who taught the world more about electricity than all other scientists put together had a head twice the size of a normal man's head. Helen Keller showed unmatched courage despite both blindness and deafness.

I recall my mother saying, "Judge not according to appearances." In the final analysis, the inner being, the soul, matters most. No one need stay the way he is. People can and do change. Even the alcoholics about whom I have spoken can and do change.

Through the work of Alcoholics Anonymous (AA), literally millions of men, women and youth have achieved sobriety, even though they all confess to being a "recovering alcoholic." The Twelve-Step Program is one of the finest programs ever devised by man, matching and often exceeding the work of physicians and medications in achieving sobriety.

Handicaps are not without their humorous side.

Three teenage boys got a job selling Bibles—one with a speech impediment. Billy stuttered terribly but at the end of the day had sold 40 Bibles, far more than the other two, to the astonishment of the boss. "How on earth did you do it considering your severe handicap," he asked.

"I...I...I...went to the do...do...door and said, Do you want to buy a Bible or want me to re...re...re...read it to you? Everybody bought one."

◆　　◆　　◆

It's a proven fact: laughter is healthy and laughter is life. Dozens of prominent psychologists, physicians, behavioral therapists, and pastors are telling us of its positive effects.

I recall the study mentioned earlier, done by Dr. Susan Kunkel at the University of Miami's Gerontology Center. She said that people who are positive, upbeat and who laugh heartily are happier, healthier and more hopeful than people who are negative and who rarely laugh.

Advanced years do not have to be the end of life. In addition, humor is everywhere, even among the imperfect saints at church.

So You Think You Are Perfect?

A pastor said to the congregation, "No one is perfect. If you think you are perfect, please stand." To the shock of the entire congregation, old Billy Ray stood. The pastor said, "Billy Ray, do you mean to tell this congregation that you think you are perfect?"

"No, sir," said Billy Ray. "I'm standing in for my wife's first husband." Yes, indeed, now there was a perfect man.

Marriage is the butt of many jokes. One who made many people laugh was Rodney Daingerfield, who only a year before he died added a note of humor about his wife and their marriage. He said, "My wife and I sleep in separate bedrooms; we dine apart and we take separate vacations. We're doing everything we can to keep our marriage together."

Columnist Lewis Grizzard said of his marriage, "I don't think I'll get married again. I'll just find a woman I don't like and give her the house."

Well, our ideas about marriage and the family begin early. For that matter, our ideas about everything else also start when we are young. I remember teaching Vacation Bible School one summer at our church. I had, as I recall, the five-year old kindergartners. One student stood out. His name was Marty. Our topic was God's forgiveness and how we all may ask for God's pardon. I told them that if we got dirty on the outside, we could use soap and water and wash away all the dirt. But what do we do when we do bad things and are all dirty inside...then what do we do?

Little Marty raised his hand and exclaimed excitedly, "I know, I know. Teacher, I know."

"Yes, Marty. What do we do when we are all dirty inside?" I asked.

"You swallow the soap."

Ugh. Boy, this soap tastes good.

Well, the central theme of these pages is to encourage readers to laugh and to make positive, affirmative responses in the face of all our hurts and disappointments.

However, central to my work as a pastor and as a chaplain is the great power of the spiritual world. It may be called by different names: worship, praise, presence, love, compassion, thanksgiving, prayer. If the spiritual world were not effective, people would have abandoned it long ago. After all these years as a pastoral leader, I still do not know how it works or why it works, but why do people pray? Because it works.

I was with Dr. Robert Schuller at the Crystal Cathedral in Garden Grove, California, a few years ago. He spoke to us of prayer and its efforts. He said that when we pray, sometimes the answer is "no," sometimes it's "grow," sometimes it's "slow" but sometimes it's "Go!"

Dr. Schuller added that prayer is not so much "getting" something or even of "giving" something, but of establishing a relationship with the eternal God. A relationship with the living God becomes the primary focus of prayer.

It is true with healing. There are many different kinds of healing. There is the healing of memories, social healing, the healing of our emotions, the healing of broken relationships, physical healing, and spiritual healing.

Clearly spiritual healing is the highest and best. If a person is tuned in to the eternal or, to use Ralph Waldo Trine's book title, *In Tune with the Infinite*, then all other types of healing become secondary.

I have seen people struggling with some critical ailment. I have been with them when we prayed for complete healing of the body with no visible results. Yet, repeatedly they have said to me, "I may not be healed...and that's okay. God is so good. I am okay whether I'm healed or not." That is spiritual healing.

It is abundantly clear that many prayers for healing are never visually manifest. We begin our spiritual healing when we can genuinely say that God's perfect will—and our intimate relationship with Him is adequate for our every need.

Author Rosalind Rinker wrote a book on prayer whose central thesis was that prayer is relationship.

Sometimes I believe that everybody prays, depending mainly on their need to pray. E. Stanley Jones used to say, "Even atheists pray...if they are desperate enough." Jones told of a Japanese fisherman and his crew who were hopelessly lost at sea. They went for several days without food and two days without water. When they were finally rescued, the reporters asked them what they did. They said, "We did the only thing we could do. We prayed."

Did it work, they asked.

"Well," they said, "we were rescued, weren't we?"

Dr. Alexis Carrel once wrote:

> Prayer is a force as real as terrestrial gravity. As a physician, I have seen men, after all other therapy failed, lifted out of disease and melancholy by the serene effort of prayer.

It is the only power in the world that seems to overcome the so-called "laws of nature."

The occasions on which prayer has done this have been termed miracles. Nevertheless, a constant, quieter miracle takes place hourly, in the hearts of men and women who have discovered that prayer supplies them with a steady flow of sustaining power in their daily lives.

Frank Laubach called prayer the *Mightiest Force in the World.* This man who, it is said, taught more people how to read than any other person in history, was the author of the Laubach Literacy Program. His world-wide theme became "Each one teach one." In this remarkable little book, he shares several experiments with prayer which help the reader to know that prayer is a dynamic force. It is the best book I ever read on the subject of prayer.

Both the serious side and the humorous sides of prayer have surfaced in my work as a pastor. I still recall my first experience as a camp counselor in eastern North Carolina. We had about a hundred or so junior high campers. The director was in the habit of calling on one of the young people to give a spontaneous prayer before each meal. Today he called upon Tommy Lee who had never prayed in public before.

Tommy Lee prayed nervously, "Lord, we thank you for all the grass..." then hesitantly, "and the bushes and the trees. We thank you for everything and for the flies and frogs and the mosquitoes and all the rain..."

He continued in this vein a full minute until the counselor stepped in to rescue him saying, "Yes, and thank you for Tommy Lee and for everybody here. Amen."

Surprisingly, Tommy smiled big and seemed to be comforted by the not-so-justified thought that he had done well.

Little by little, I was learning the good effects of humor. Dr. Richard Laliberte said that, in a word, laughter makes us feel good, lowers our anger and stress levels, and makes friends out of enemies. He says that laughter is the social glue that is often more effective than medications. You can't be mad at someone very long when you are both laughing at something funny. It's true—even in a church setting.

Dr. Howard Bennett, in the *Southern Medical Journal* (Dec., 2003) said that humor has the potential to relieve stress in patients and medical personnel as well. He added that humor gives patients an opportunity to forget about their pain, if only for a brief period. It puts all parties at ease by calling their attention away from the pain or the thing feared.

No Laxatives, Please

A man was waiting for his wife in a drug store. He bought a big cigar and started puffing away. The pharmacist said, "Sir, you can't smoke that cigar in this store."

"But I just bought it in this store" the old puffer protested.

"Sir," responded the pharmacist, "we also sell laxatives, but you can't use them in here either."

No, I never used that story in church. Alas, some anecdotes just aren't meant for Sunday morning.

Everything seems to happen at your first pastoral assignment—at least it seemed so for me. Sad things, happy things, shocking things, and funny incidents.

We had an "elderly" lady in the parish that seemed to me at the time to be ancient. I think she had reached the ripe old age of seventy—what can I say, I'm close to that now.

However, one Sunday in worship dear Eliza's mind was some place else. In our denomination, we serve the sacrament of communion—complete with broken pieces of bread and small glasses of wine. It's passed along each of the rows to each worshiper, who in turn takes out a piece of bread and removes the tiny cups with the wine.

Exactly the same procedure is used to collect the tithes and offerings—except that worshipers put things in the plate.

One Sunday Eliza was sitting on the back row and reached for the offering plate—now full to overflowing with money: ones, tens, and a few twenty dollar bills. She reached into the plate and took out a handful of money—held it before her eyes for a moment—realized what she had done and then disgustedly put the money back in the plate and said to the people sitting around her, "Isn't old age wonderful?"

Her husband practiced medicine for years in Winston-Salem. He and Eliza owned a large house that had a huge yard of green grass which had to be mowed regularly. D.C. often used his riding mower to cut the grass himself.

One Saturday he was wearing his overalls, a scruffy old hat and gloves. A lady in a chauffeur-driven Rolls Royce pulled up alongside the curb and motioned for this bedraggled yard man to come. D.C. pulled up alongside the Rolls Royce. The window in the back seat went down and a sophisticated lady asked, "Sir, how much do you charge?"

D.C. responded, "Well, this lady here," pointing to his own house "lets me sleep with her."

I later asked D.C. if the story were true, but he said "No." Eliza, however, told us it was true. When I get to heaven, I will ask.

That reminds me of something I read about heaven.

It seems Bishop Fulton J. Sheen was giving a sermon on Jonah and the whale. A heckler in the crowd yelled out, "Hold on, Bishop…How do you know that a whale really swallowed Jonah?"

"Well, I don't know," said the Bishop. "But when I get to heaven, I will ask."

The heckler retorted, "Ha! What if there's not a heaven?'

"Then," said the Bishop, "you can ask."

Life in the church is a scream—whether you are Protestant, Catholic, or what not.

Al Smith was a Catholic and it was he, not John Kennedy, who was the first Catholic to run for president. The year was 1928. Al Smith was giving a talk and a heckler wanted to embarrass him and yelled out, "Come on, Al, tell the folks everything you know…it won't take very long."

Al's quick response was, "You stand and I'll tell them what we both know and it won't take any longer."

It was Easter Sunday as I recall, a very big day for any pastor. The sanctuary was packed to overflowing with many visitors and many of our twice-a-year members. As pastor and preacher for the occasion, I was anxious to do well. I recall all the preparations—the extra hours I spent writing out every single word of the sermon.

When I stood in the pulpit to deliver the sermon, I counted thirteen pages. I got past page one, two, and three, and came to a splendid quote from Abraham Lincoln on page four. I swept my hand from left to right across the wood leaf of the pulpit—accidentally sweeping all thirteen pages off the pulpit onto the floor. They floated through the first four rows of the worshipers as though in slow motion. The Easter sermon stopped, and we waited until someone would gather the pages and return them to me. I was young and nervous and nearly petrified by what had happened.

Alas, our elder for the day, Berger, assumed it was his rightful duty to help this nervous pastor. He stood, straightened his tie, pulled down his coat on the sides, cleared his throat, and moved with the speed of a snail to recover the sermon pages. It took him the better part of an hour—or so it seemed.

Desperate to find something appropriate to say, I settled on this. "I noted that George Flynt had gone to sleep. I had to do something to wake him up. The rest of you may now go back to sleep."

It defused the tension I was feeling. We laughed about that incident for months. Several people kept asking, "Did you do that on purpose?"

Life in the church is a scream…and sometimes I think we couldn't survive without humor.

Early in my ministry, I wondered what the Bible had to say, if anything, about humor or laughter. I was shocked by what I found. The *Old Testament Book of Proverbs* says: "A merry heart does good for the soul."

Ecclesiastes 3 says:

> "For everything there is a season, and a time for every matter under heaven:
>> a time to be born, and a time to die;
>> a time to plant, and a time to pluck up what is planted;
>> a time to kill, and a time to heal;
>> a time to break down, and a time to build up;

Then, the clincher: "…a time to weep, and a time to laugh."

The writer went on to say that God "has made everything beautiful in its time; also He has put eternity into man's mind…"

It is the will of God for people to rejoice and to enjoy all that is good—all the days of their life.

I had read these passages dozens of times—but I had never read them from this new perspective.

I like what Job 8 says about God—"He will yet fill your mouth with laughter."

Alternatively, Proverbs 17:22 "A cheerful heart is a good medicine, but a downcast spirit dries up the bones."

If we don't allow ourselves to laugh a little in the fierce battle that so many people seem to be fighting, there won't be any time left when the battles are fought and won or lost. "...this is the day which the Lord has made; let us rejoice and be glad in it." Psalms 118:21.

Now, I had my "proof" that humor was a justifiable topic for inclusion in a Sunday sermon. But how to weave it into the fabric? I didn't have a clue.

As a pastor, we are often called upon to assist with community projects. Once our clergy met with Billy Graham at a private luncheon. His Crusade was coming to town and he wanted our support.

The Crusade was held and we attended practically every night. After the final hymn on closing night, I wanted to take my wife to the stage to meet Billy Graham personally. By the time we got to the stage, he was gone. But Cliff Barrows, the brilliant Crusade Choir Director, remained to greet any and all who had helped with the Crusade.

We liked Cliff a lot and he had an impressive, almost electric personality. I said, "Cliff, I want you to meet my wife, Janet." He held out his hand and she tried to respond. For whatever reason (we still do not know what happened), she tried to speak but could not. I watched. She moved her mouth but no word came out. Finally, her lower jaw began to move up and down reminiscent of a fish in a bowl feeding.

Cliff seemed to understand. My poor wife obviously had some type of oral paralysis. He then took my hand and patted it as if to say, "Don, you really have my sympathy."

Memories—how funny and sometimes, how embarrassing.

◆   ◆   ◆

Her name, as I recall, was Kay. She was an active and dedicated member of our church in Independence, Missouri, until I came along.

It was fall—October—and time for the Halloween Festival at our church. Each family brought food or drink to share with all the others at the big dinner. Kay brought a large jar of lemonade and put it in a prominent place in the kitchen. I did not know that she had made it and never even saw her standing there, watching, listening.

I drank some of it, made an awful face, and shouted, "That's the worst lemonade I ever tasted..."

Stung by her pastor's cutting response, she declared, "Thanks, Reverend, I made that lemonade and I won't forget this..."

Help! What to do to save face and keep her from dropping out of the church? I responded, "Hello, my name is Rabbi Horowitz from Kansas City. I understand you have a pastor out here who is always sticking his foot in his mouth!"

Kay laughed and added, "Okay, you're off the hook—this time." Ah, life in the church is a scream.

A fellow at our Independence church had a delightful sense of humor. It was his anniversary. He and his wife shook my hand after the Sunday worship service. I congratulated him and told him that he had really done well—getting a lovely lady like that. He smiled and said, "We got married for better or for worse. I knew then I couldn't do any better and she couldn't do any worse."

Is Honesty the Best Policy?

A man asked his wife what she wanted for her birthday. She said, "Well, dear, may I be honest?"

"Of course," he responded.

"I really want a divorce," she stated.

His quick response was, "Well, I hadn't intended to spend that much."

I learned early that there were certain experiences, anecdotes, and humorous illustrations that might be perfectly acceptable with the guys on a golf course but were not appropriate for church. Always, my wife was the final judge of what humorous story would or would not be used. On a few occasions, the borderline humorous quotes were used to the dismay of certain members. An example of one of these is the following:

> Once upon a time a handsome honeybee
> Fell in love with a butterfly he met in a tulip tree.
> He said, "I love you madly
> And want to share your life.
> Let's fly away together
> So you can be my wife."
> She shook her head in sorrow.
> "No no no no," cried she,
> "For I am a Royal Monarch's daughter
> And you're just a son of a bee."

Well, actually, I did not tell that on Sunday, but it sure made me laugh when I read it. I did use, at the encouragement of my mother-in-law, the three humorous cards she sent to Janet and to me on our tenth wedding anniversary. The first card said, "The Local Geodetic Survey Diggers announce the discovery of a volcano under your house which may cut loose in the near future. May we have your advance permission to dig in the ruins?"

The second stated, "Congratulations. In honor of your recent accomplishment, the Horseback Drum and Bugle Corps will stage a parade in front of your home Sunday at 4 a.m. A special salute by the 85th Howitzer Battalion will follow."

The third noted, "You have been selected by the Air Pollution Bureau to test an all new asbestos muzzle and smog control headgear with built-in nose-guard and teething ring pacifier, designed to prevent you from smoking or biting people while trying to quit. This apparatus comes with your choice of neon red plumes or moose antlers on top."

The Fear of Being Embarrassed

I do not know what it is about human beings but I never met a person who liked being embarrassed. To be humiliated, disgraced, or made fun of in private is one thing—but when it is done in a group, in a social setting, it becomes more painful than what people can endure.

No one likes to be put down or embarrassed in front of his friends or peers. Quick thinking can and does sometimes save the day—I called it, at the time, "divine intervention."

In church, standing in line greeting people as they left, a prominent attorney said to me on my very first Sunday there, with a little smile, "I think you are a con artist..."

I said as a quick return, "Sir, it takes one to know one...Welcome to the club."

On board ship recently, I read the story of the captain of a battleship who steered his vessel dangerously close to an aircraft carrier. The admiral of the fleet sent him a telegram which was handed to the captain while he was surrounded by his staff of officers. "Well, read it," he said to the ensign who held the telegraph.

"But sir, it's personal..."

"Read it out loud, ensign," said the captain.

It said, "You idiot. You nearly ran into my aircraft carrier. I will have you given a dishonorable discharge the moment we get on shore."

Embarrassed? No. Quick-witted? Yes. The captain, wanting to save face, said, "Ensign, I have been waiting for this telegram all day. Go below and have this message decoded immediately..."

I am sure that people who are often "on guard," afraid of being embarrassed, will find it far more difficult to laugh and play and have fun than persons who are not so concerned about what others think or say. Wouldn't it be great if we could live for one full day without fear, giving ourselves permission to love and be loved, to listen and really hear, to laugh and to cry as the occasion demands—and to feel what it is to live fully, freely and joyfully.

One reason, I believe, that people do not laugh is based on how they view the world and their own life. It is sad to talk with people who are not free to live their own life but try to fulfill the expectations of other people. Very often young people grow up trying to fulfill the dream of a father or a mother who pressured them to pursue a certain career path. That behavior is usually destructive. Rarely does it reveal a person who is relaxed enough to laugh or even to enjoy his life.

How Do You Erase the Scars?

My very earliest memory of actually listening to a sermon by a pastor in church occurred when I was eight.

As I recall, it was the simple story of a young lad about my age who was always doing bad things and getting in trouble. Every time he did something bad, his dad would drive a nail in the old barn door. After a few weeks, the entire barn door was filled with nails. The boy felt ashamed of himself and decided to change.

His dad said, "Every time you say you are sorry and do something good, I will pull out one of the nails in the door."

It worked fine, and within a few months, all the nails had been removed. The father took the little boy with him to watch the last nail come out. As he did, the boy began to cry.

"What's wrong, son? Aren't you happy all the nails are gone?" inquired the father.

"Yes, Daddy," he responded, "the nails are gone, but the scars are still there."

I have not thought of that story in years. Now as I look back on my life and consider the pain of my childhood, I too can say, "Yes, I lived through them, and often with great anguish; they are gone, behind me, but the scars are still there."

I thought I had overcome them—that those awful experiences no longer affected me, but recently that proved not to be true. My son's suicide made me go soul searching once again. The scars remain.

In our 46 years of marriage, I had never experienced anything quite like it with Janet. It started out so innocently and well-intentioned. We were to meet in the theater aboard our cruise ship and get our tickets and bus number from the tour guide. It seemed simple and clear. We were at port in the Hong Kong harbor. There are twelve decks on the ship. The theater was up toward one of the top decks and our cabin was on deck three.

I last saw Janet on the elevator, but it was too crowded. I decided to wait for the next elevator. After about six or eight minutes they announced that the elevators were not working and I would have to walk.

I tried to forget about the pain in my knees that often came when I climbed the steps. I headed up all sixty-six stairs, got to the theater very late, and I could not find Janet anywhere.

In lapsed time, we were separated about thirty minutes and due to my failure to communicate clearly, we missed the first nine excursion buses. Finally, the Chinese security guard, using his own two-way phone, made contact, putting us back together on the tenth and final bus.

When she finally saw me after a long thirty minutes of not knowing what had happened to me, she began to weep, almost uncontrollably, and shake and try to tell me...

"I thought I had lost you...that you had had a heart attack or stroke and had died..."

It brought back suddenly and painfully all the anguish and despair of hearing the news that our son had died only a few months before. She indicated what I knew to be true: the thought of losing two members of her family so close together was more than she could bear. Terry Waite, who had been held by terrorists in Lebanon for over four years, was with us on board ship. His presence there brought to life the very real prospect that I might have been held by terrorists—a thought that would be frightening for Janet. We knew that Americans were often the primary target of these terrorist groups and we knew we were not exempt.

When I finally saw Janet, I fully expected her to be angry and irritated but not grieving, and I was already thinking of how I might apologize. However, when I saw the tears—and the deep grieving, I was touched by the depth of her emotion, her commitment, caring and love.

The picture that presented itself was two-fold. The first was the depth of her love for our son who had left us so recently and secondly the depth of her love for me. When I considered it, I too was overcome with emotion.

Why do we take for granted the love that comes to us daily from our mates or our children? We are so made that any threat of life that comes to people we love is an unbearable nightmare. Often it issues forth in tears, and a revelation of how deep our love really is.

I would like to tell you that we soon turned this frightening episode into something happy, even humorous, but so far, the humor of it has not surfaced. I shall not soon forget the picture of anguish that showed on my wife's face.

For whatever reason, when I thought of the depth of my wife's love for our family and for me, I thought of the depth of the love of God for the whole created order. How does one describe it? The refrain we often sing in churches is:

> O Love of God, how rich and pure
> How measureless and strong
> It shall forever more endure
> The Saints' and Angels' song.

◆   ◆   ◆

What is it about the spiritual world that seems to touch people at the deepest levels of their life? Time and space prevent my sharing other dramatic evidence of the Spirit's power—like a middle-aged man deep into the drug culture, who attributes his turnaround to the love and counsel of family and friends, but especially to intercessory prayers for him. Prayer works and studies seem to confirm that fact.

Some know the name of Dr. Pitirim Sorokin, a Harvard University professor, who researched and wrote a compelling article about religious convictions. In particular, he wanted to know what effect prayer, Bible study and religious beliefs had on one's marriage.

What he discovered surprised even Dr. Sorokin himself. He found that the average of all divorces in America runs something like one out of two marriages. But where the husband and wife read the Bible and regular family prayers are offered, the dissolution of marriage drops to a staggering one out of one thousand.

The world of the spirit is far more powerful than what even pastors and chaplains have ever supposed. I have learned so many good things about love and faith, that I now realize love is one of our most powerful motivators. In fact, our wish to please and respect others may run so deep that we don't please ourselves.

On several occasions, I have met physicians or attorneys or pastors who said, "That's what Dad did...and I'm supposed to do it, too."

I recall a father who had three sons. The older two boys both went to Yale, and it was assumed but never discussed that the youngest would also go to Yale. The parents unknowingly added to their third son's woes by saying, "Now when you go to Yale..."

No one ever asked if that was where he wanted to go to college, or even if he wanted to go to college.

One day out of pure frustration, the young fellow began to cry. His parents were concerned. His older brothers who had come home for vacation from Yale were concerned.

"What is wrong?" they all asked.

He queried, "Dad, do I have to go to Yale?"

There was silence and then a burst of laughter.

Then hugs, big hugs, and this exclamation.

"Heavens, no, son. You can go anywhere you like and if you don't even want to go to college, that's okay too."

Well, once he realized that he was free to choose his own dreams, his own life, his own college, he decided that he really wanted to go to Yale and that is what he did.

You can't live another's dream unless it becomes your own. You can't be free when you are bound by another's wishes, hopes, expectations, and dreams. Rarely can people laugh or be genuinely happy when they are not free to pursue their own dreams.

I have watched people with great interest and am finding that laughter and humor requires a relaxed mind-set and that people who are always so serious and heavy (and heaven forbid, morbid) are simply not free enough to incorporate laughter into their mind-set. Someone said, "Take everything seriously but yourself." If we aren't able to laugh at ourselves, we very well may be moving in a downward direction.

The world is still celebrating the life of St. Francis of Assisi. He was the son of a wealthy merchant named Pietro. Born in 1182 A.D. he had placed upon him high demands and impossible expectations. He was inducted into the military to help fight against "his own brothers and sisters" who lived in the towns around Assisi. He watched and listened as feudal lords and nobles went often to battle or war, killing or wounding people with no feeling of guilt. It was staggering and overwhelming to see the blood, the death, and destruction of human life. He felt a deep sense of futility.

One day on his way to battle, walking in the streets of Assisi, he was transfixed by a vision. There came to him a sense of guilt about all the killings and equally by the luxury of his own family's life style. Born into wealth, he had anything and everything he could ever want, except for one thing—peace. He laid down his sword; walked through the streets giving everything he owned to all the poor people he met. All his own money he gave to the poor and needy, and much of his father's money he also gave away.

He began to preach and teach and to identify with the poor of the earth. Everything he owned he gave away with only Lady Poverty as his closest friend.

People responded. Hundreds, thousands, and in time quite literally hundreds of millions of people have been drawn to this gentle giant who now was truly free. It was this saint who gave us the prayer:

> Lord, make me an instrument of thy peace!
> Where there is hatred, let me sow love;
> Where there is injury, pardon;
> Where there is doubt, faith;
> Where there is despair, hope;
> Where there is darkness, light;
> Where there is sadness, joy.

O Divine Master, grant that I may not so much seek to be consoled as
to console;
To be understood as to understand;
To be loved as to love.
For it is in giving that we receive;
It is in pardoning that we are pardoned;
And it is in dying that we are born to eternal life.

The whole of the life of St. Francis of Assisi became a symbol of optimism and love, of peace and joy. He was, at last, one with the world, with himself and with his Creator.

Humor generally does not and cannot emerge from people who aren't free. It is, as after-dinner speaker Dr. Joe Wick said about the mark of a healthy mind. People who are mentally and emotionally sick do not laugh.

God grant us the serenity to relax enough to stand outside ourselves and embrace all of life—both the sad and the truly funny. Then and only then will we be free.

Anyone Can Do It—If They Want To

I have long been intrigued in my church work with how the least likely people rise to prominence when they are called upon to help. I've heard it said, "It doesn't take much of a man to be a leader, but it takes all of him."

So often the most unpromising people in the church and in history can and do become the most celebrated. God can and does take "nothing" and from it, makes something. It is true in business, in science, in politics and it's true in the church.

Think about the man who started the world-wide program called "Sunday School" in all of our churches about 1780. His name was Robert Raikes, the least likely candidate in England to do anything that could be called "religious."

Raikes was described as arrogant, pompous, and vain. This unlikely man told his long-suffering friends that he was "self-made" and proud of it. He seemed always to be preoccupied with his dress and appearance. It seems that Raikes was far more concerned about external appearance than he was with internal depth.

He did attend church on Sundays which may have been his one redeeming quality. His "dress" on Sunday mornings was a different story. He would often wear very formal tuxedo-like clothing that consisted of a deep blue or black coat with silver-gilt buttons, cambric frills and cuffs, and snow-white stockings stretching down from his britches. His closest associates and "friends" agreed that he was insufferable, and they called him a "buck." Some gave him the nickname of "Bobby Wild Goose." Could God use someone like that?

However, this same man came up with an idea that was so big that today, 225 years later, people are still celebrating the life and work of this "most unlikely saint." Already Robert was a successful business man in his own right, and helped his father operate a lack-luster publishing house in Gloucester, England.

In 1780, Raikes was berating a group of skid-row boys in a slum of Gloucester who seemed bent on trouble. A lady appeared in the middle of the mob scene and defended the troubled youth. She explained to Raikes that the youth were uneducated, poor and couldn't even read. "What will you do about that," she asked.

"Why don't they go to school and learn," Raikes asked.

"They can't," came her reply. "They work twelve hours a day, six days a week. And besides, schools are only for middle class children."

"Then we will teach on Sunday and start a sort of Sunday school." The British parliament had recently given permission for the use of the Bible on Sundays in a classroom setting.

A lady teacher named Mrs. Meredith of nearby Sooty Alley agreed for pay to use her home to teach these hopeless ragamuffins. "But," she added, "It is a useless venture as no one will come."

To her amazement and to Robert Raikes' delight all twelve invited youth came to learn to read and especially to read the Bible. Soon there were fifteen on Sunday, then fifty and then seventy-five, so many in fact that other meeting places had to be found. In a few short years, by 1788, the number of youth attending Sunday school in Great Britain soared past 250,000.

When the great John Wesley and his brother Charles, founders of the Methodist Church, heard about this new movement among England's youth, they gave their blessing to the idea. By the time of John Wesley's death, there were more than 500,000 youth attending Sunday school classes in Great Britain alone.

The payback for Raikes came in having to use his own publishing company to print hundreds of thousands of booklets for all the children. Raikes became very wealthy and the idea of "Sunday School" was born.

Today there are hundreds of millions of children all over the world who meet on Sundays as a part of Robert Raikes' idea.

God can and does use anyone, anywhere, anytime to bring hope and life and love to a broken world. The light does shine in the darkness and the darkness has not overcome it.

In light of this surprising, almost shocking revelation about Robert Raikes, one wonders what could have happened had Jesus used a "consulting service" to choose his twelve helpers.

TO: Jesus, son of Joseph
Woodcrafters Carpenter Shop
Nazareth 25922
FROM: Jordan Management Consultants
Dear Sir:

Thank you for submitting the resumes of the twelve men you have picked for management positions in your new organization. All of them have taken our battery of tests; and we have not only run the results through our computer, but also arranged personal interviews for each of them with our psychologist and vocational aptitude consultant.

The profiles of all tests are included and you will want to study each of them carefully.

As part of our service and for your guidance, we make some general comments much as an auditor will include some general statements. This is given as a result of staff consultation and comes without any additional fee.

It is the staff opinion that most of your nominees are lacking in background, education, and vocational aptitude for the type of enterprise you are undertaking. They do not have the team concept. We would recommend that you continue your search for persons of experience in managerial ability and proven capability.

Simon Peter is emotionally unstable and given to fits of temper. Andrew has absolutely no qualities of leadership. The two brothers, James and John, place personal interest above company loyalty. Thomas demonstrates a questioning attitude that would tend to undermine morale. We feel it is our duty to tell you that Matthew has been blacklisted by the Greater Jerusalem Better Business Bureau. James and Thaddaeus definitely have radical leanings, and they both registered a high score on the manic depressive scale.

One of the candidates, however, shows great potential. He is a man of ability and resourcefulness, meets people well, has a keen business mind, and has contacts in high places. He is highly motivated, ambitious, and responsible. We recommend Judas Iscariot as your controller and right hand man. All of the other profiles are self-explanatory.

We wish you every success in your new venture.

Sincerely,

Jordan Management Consultants.
Source unknown

Anyone, pastor, chaplain or lay leader, can point a person in the direction of a loving and forgiving God and it may have lasting impact. The late great British Bible scholar John Barclay told just how this works. He said that an 18th century Bible salesman was accosted by a robber-thief on an old rocky road in Italy. The robber not only stole his money but demanded that he start a fire and burn all the Bibles. The salesman began to pull one Bible after another from the suitcase, ready to throw them into the fire. He hesitated and asked the robber if he might read one last verse for his own memory's sake, of course.

"Yes, read one verse," the robber said.

"God so loved the world that he gave his only son that anyone who would believe would not perish but would have everlasting life."

"Don't burn that one," said the robber.

"Come unto me all who are burdened and I will give you rest," he read from the next Bible.

"Don't burn that one," the thief said.

"Beloved, let us love one another; for love is of God," he read from the third Bible.

"Don't burn that one," came the response.

Finally, no Bible was burned and the thief left, apologizing for the disturbance.

Years later, that same Bible salesman was visiting the monks at a large monastery. A middle-aged monk came up to him and said, "Were you robbed of your money and forced to burn your Bibles a few years ago?"

"Yes," said the salesman.

"Well, I am the man who robbed you…When you read those passages from the Bible, I was ashamed of myself, my life, and the life of crime. I changed from that moment 'til this and am now a monk here."

No matter how dark the night, how desperate the situation, we need to know that there is someone who cares for us and loves us and forgives us as though he had none other to care for.

Humor is not just jokes or even funny stories. It's really a sense of perspective about life and learning how to have meaningful fun and joyful moments the older we get. As we learn to put all things in perspective, and view them from the long-term point of view, even life's tragic events can be faced and embraced.

What is perspective? It's standing outside ourselves and seeing the long view, and it helps us know that we aren't really in charge of very much. The world's future rarely depends upon what we do. We are an important part of the equation but we aren't the entire show. So being able to laugh at ourselves and the sheer folly of some of our actions is one of life's most healing revelations.

Some writers tell us that even stress management depends on humor and one's positive mental attitude. Joel Goodman reminds us that "Stress is not an event, but a perception of an event" and humor can be used to alter our perceptions, our attitudes and our approach to situations.

I remember the story of another potentially embarrassing situation that could be fixed by quick thinking and humor.

Years ago, the actress Eve Arden was on stage when the phone on the set rang during a live performance. Looking shocked by this unscripted intrusion, she stared at the leading man and knew immediately that he had staged this ploy to get a laugh. Not to be outdone, Eve answered the phone, turning to the leading man, and said, "It's for you…" Yes, indeed.

Think again of our ongoing debt to Prime Minister Winston Churchill of England, who in the darkest hours of the war never lost his disarming sense of humor.

Once he went for dinner to a large English home as the guest of the distinguished hostess. Winston loved the dinner, so much that he asked for a second helping of the breast of chicken. The hostess quickly corrected him and said, "We call it 'white meat'."

The next day Churchill sent an orchid to his hostess with an attached note which read, "I would be most obliged if you would pin this on your white meat."

Carl Simonton, M.D., whose breakthrough work was in aging and visualizations, is also a strong believer in laughter and playfulness. Dr. Simonton said, "Laughter and play are mandatory—not elective. Belief and emotion play significant roles in all aspects of health and illness."

Sometimes we use humor to give bad news to others. I love this letter from a college student to her parents.

Dear Mom and Dad,

Am really sorry that I haven't written or called during these first eight weeks at college but life has been full and exciting. And yes, I do go to church, almost every Sunday. Only missed 3 times last month.

Met a really neat guy named Rupert my first week at school. I like him very much even though he is about thirty years older than I.

The car battery went out and what with two flat tires, I just decided to walk, except when Rupert could take me. That worked fine until they took him away last month.

The good news is that I'm planning to come home for Thanksgiving. Rupert thinks he will be out of jail by that time and I am really anxious for you to meet him. Hope his old car will make it.

The other really good news here is that it looks like you are going to be proud grandparents about next June the first. And, early congratulations to you.

Must run for now.

Love, Lucy

P. S. Dad, I was just kidding about the dead battery and the two flat tires—and also kidding about Rupert and the "baby."

But I did get a "D" in chemistry. Altogether, it makes a "D" look pretty acceptable, don't you think?

Lucy

The Rev. Dr. Bill Alexander of Oklahoma City was probably the best known after dinner speaker in America for about twenty years. He left audiences ecstatic from his brilliant speaking ability and his lively use of humor. No one left his speeches bored.

Once in Texas he went into the restroom before going on stage. He met another man, a Texan, in the restroom who, not recognizing him, said, "I hear we have to sit and listen to some preacher after dinner. I hear he is totally boring."

"Yes," said Dr. Bill, "and I hear he has nothing to say..."

Well, after he finished speaking, the packed audience gave Dr. Bill a longstanding ovation for his brilliant speech. Even the Texan whom he met in the restroom was clapping. When the noise ceased and Dr. Bill was leaving, the Texan held out his hand, smiled, and said, "Pardner, we were both right."

Readers aged fifty or better will doubtless remember the name of Norman Vincent Peale. He wrote the second most popular book of the twentieth century, *The Power of Positive Thinking*.

In that book he told of moving away from the negative, cautious, fearful world of his youth that was devoid of humor, joy or cheerfulness, into a world of bold positivism.

Dr. Peale said that he grew tired of being afraid, angry, depressed and overly cautious. He wrote that he decided to change his pattern of thinking and that little change made all the difference. It happened in college, on the steps leading to his classroom.

Shy by temperament, Dr. Peale confessed that he was so frightened as a young man that he could hardly speak his name. When a teacher or a professor asked him a question he was terrified and often sat there frozen, paralyzed.

Once a professor who believed strongly in God asked him what was wrong with him and said, "Don't you have any faith in God?"

It stung; it hurt—cutting him to the core of his being. He ran out of the classroom crying and for some reason stopped on the steps leading down. There, in that spot, in that moment, there came to him a vision of a bright, cheerful, confident young man who could do anything and everything that he wanted to do. All he needed to do was to change his way of thinking from fear to confidence.

He later stated to a group of pastors that he began to act as though he was not afraid, with confidence and warmth and an outgoing manner that would prove to be a key to his enormous success. The clincher, he said, was when he began to replace negative thoughts, words and deeds with something positive. Then he completely erased the word "impossible" from his mind and from his dictionary. By the time he was forty, he was well on his way to being one of America's most gifted speakers and most-read authors. In the years that followed, Dr. Peale wrote hundreds of articles, a dozen or so books, and sold more than 30,000,000 copies of these books.

I was privileged to hear one of his compelling sermons given at the great Marble Collegiate Church in New York City. Always people left there feeling better about themselves than when they came in. They left with hope and confidence and positive feelings about their problems and their future.

Dr. Peale always pointed to the power of God to help us and to the power of positive thinking, but his humor seemed to humanize his sermons and make him "for real."

He told of an editor-owner of a newspaper who advertised for a young boy aged twelve to fourteen to do afternoon deliveries of the paper. The pay, the ad said, was good and nearly two dozen boys got in line to get the job. The very last boy in line was twelve and knew that he had no chance of getting the job unless he did some quick thinking. He wrote out a note and went quickly to the front of the line and gave it to the editor's secretary. It said: "I am the red-headed, freckle-faced boy who is last in line. Do nothing till you talk to me!"

Well, the secretary and the editor both laughed and yes, that freckle-faced boy got that job. People who heard Dr. Peale tell that story laughed and hundreds since have also enjoyed it and other stories of optimism and self-confidence.

Dr. Peale's greatness never went to his head. He remained kind, positive and deeply compassionate the rest of his life. After all, greatness is a relative term as Dr. Peale came to learn when he flew to California to preach for Dr. Robert Schuller at the Garden Grove Community Church.

In the very early days, Dr. Schuller's ministry began at a drive-in theater. There on Sunday morning he set up his microphone and organ on top of the projection booth, and using the public address system, he spoke a message that could be heard in each parked car.

Today's guest was the world-famous Dr. Norman Vincent Peale. Dr. Schuller introduced him to the very large crowd, people who had come specifically to hear Dr. Peale. His memorable introduction went something like this as Dr. Schuller cleverly began, tongue-in-cheek:

> I want you to welcome today a man whose name is renowned all over the world. Many of you have read his great book. This man has touched more lives, saved more marriages, and brought more hope, joy and inspiration than any man I know. And that man, that incredible man, is with us today hoping to give you the keys to a whole new world.
>
> You all know him—for his name...is Jesus of Nazareth...and here to tell you about him is...Norman Vincent Peale.

People were still laughing long after the sermon was over—and Dr. Peale was much impressed by the imagination and positive boldness of this young pastor named Robert Schuller. Years later I asked Dr. Schuller if this story were true and he said, "Every word of it!"

Positivism, optimism, hope, attitude and laughter—they all play ball on the same team—and they see something good about everything.

My Baptist pastor friend in Florida told me how the Baptists are able to take disasters and turn them into something hopeful and positive. He told me about a fierce flood that swept through one small town taking almost everyone away. The only ones left, he said, were a Baptist preacher and two Baptist deacons. They got together and organized a church, and set a goal *of six at Sunday School!* Now that's optimism.

Dr. Dale Matthews practices Internal Medicine in Washington, D.C. He is the co-author with Connie Clark of a book entitled *The Faith Factor: Proof of the Healing Power of Prayer.*

He noted that persons who participate in religious services of worship have lower rates of cancer, heart disease and serious illness. They have a speedier recovery from serious illnesses, have lower frequency of depression, anxiety and mental illness, have an enhanced ability to cope with life-threatening terminal illnesses, and have less pain and greater tranquility than persons who live outside a religious community.

Then like other researchers before him, Dr. Matthews stated that these religious-oriented people have a much longer life expectancy.

Do spiritual things matter? All the evidence says yes.

A similar study by Dr. Harold Koenig of Duke University published in the *Southern Medical Journal* in October, 1998, found that the length of hospital stay was directly related to religious beliefs.

The researchers studied one's faith as it relates to one's stay in a hospital. It is perhaps hard to believe the conclusion that they came to. They found that persons with no professed religious affiliation stayed an average of 25 days and persons with any religious affiliation averaged only 10 days per hospital stay. The overall study was done by Dr. Koenig and Dr. Harold Bentson of the Harvard Medical School. Its findings are compelling.

America has had few spiritual giants like the remarkable Dr. Horace Bushnell. Once Dr. Bushnell was ill and went to a mountain resort to recover. At that retreat was also the man who was the pastor of novelist Mark Twain.

During one of the periods of fellowship, it was suggested that one of these two pastors should pray. Dr. Bushnell volunteered.

Mark Twain's pastor later recounted this incident and added: "When Dr. Bushnell was praying, I was afraid to put out my hand lest I touch (the hand of) God."

That is effective praying and it is the kind of praying that helps you and me to sing in the face of life's most devastating events: "It is well; it is well with my soul."

Laughter Will Often Find You

Once you open yourself to laughter, you begin to discover that you don't have to go looking for it; it will find you.

The remarkable Barbara Johnson, who has become one of the most popular speakers at women's groups and church events, wrote about joy: "Sometimes I don't find joy; it finds me."

So, too, with humor. Once we give ourselves permission to laugh, we will find joyful, even hilarious celebrations we never even noticed before.

Barbara Johnson told about the lady who was obviously very nervous about having to introduce her at a women's gathering. Barb had written two best-seller books including "...So Stick a Geranium in Your Hat..."

The nervous lady had practiced the introduction a dozen times or so. But when the big moment came to introduce Barbara and her great book, the lady said, "We are so glad to have Barbara Johnson with us. She's written a book and in that book there is a chapter called...."

Her face got white as her memory failed her. She had forgotten her entire introduction, but continued on, "There is a chapter called...so stick a geranium in your cranium..." Barb said that she laughed so hard she could barely begin her speech. The incident proved to be one of joy and hilarity for everyone, including the lady doing the introduction. Humor will often find you.

You owe yourself the joy of buying Barb Johnson's book. If you don't laugh and cry, then we need to talk. It's called *Pain Is Inevitable But Misery Is Optional So Stick a Geranium in Your Hat and Be Happy.*

One other incident is too good to pass up. Barb calls it "Doing Something Outrageous." She told about a pastor who had been feeling tired, discouraged and depressed. One day he said to Barb and her friend, Marilyn, "What I really need is a visitation from the angels."

An idea was born. It was outrageous, outlandish, but oh such fun as they prepared to grant the pastor's wish.

They borrowed two white baptismal robes from their church, complete with heavy weights. A picture in Barb's book shows them standing at the pastor's door, wearing halos and white robes. Can't you hear them say to the pastor as he opened the front door, "We are the two angels that you prayed for yesterday...?" (Johnson, p. 78)

Barb's husband didn't think it was funny and only wanted to know if the two robes had been returned to the church. To be able to laugh, we must allow ourselves the freedom that says, "It's really okay to laugh."

It is difficult to understand why there are some people who don't laugh at anything. We all react differently to life's experiences. In a time of loss or sorrow, some people give up and lose their will to live. They never seem to see anything healing or wholesome or redemptive in the bad things that happen to them. How unlike the creative genius Thomas Alva Edison!

On a cold December night in 1914, the huge Edison industrial plant in West Orange, New Jersey, was destroyed by fire. The loss was estimated to be in the millions of dollars. Edison and his partners were only insured for a fraction of that amount due to the mistaken notion in those days that concrete buildings could not be burned or damaged.

Edison was sixty-seven at the time, an age when most men would have been crushed by such a disaster. At the height of the raging inferno, he clutched his son Charles by the arm and said, "Find your mother and bring her down here. She'll never see such a sight as long as she lives."

Later he said about the loss, "There is great value in a catastrophe like this. All our mistakes have burned up. Now we can start over again."

I do believe that our retirement years could prove to be the best years of our life if only we would set our minds to the joyful task of making it so. Even if there were no medical evidence to show that laughter makes you healthy, just think of the positive good feelings these and other people have who have learned how to laugh, and what an inspiration they are.

He's Called Albert or Albrecht or...

Albrecht Durer lived and died five hundred plus years ago and yet his paintings, etchings, drawings and wood carvings are among the most highly valued pieces of art of any other artist from Germany.

When my friend Sam, who lives in Sun City, Arizona, invited me to visit, he took me to see one of the very rare and priceless original etchings done by Albrecht Durer. I cannot adequately describe the feeling of awe and inspiration that swept over me as I stared at this original masterpiece. When I heard the story of Durer's life and how his most famous piece of art work, "Praying Hands," came about, I was touched as never before.

Of all the great art creations of Durer, none has brought him more fame or honor than his "Praying Hands." Almost everyone has seen this masterpiece.

What many don't realize is that those are the hands of a real person, Durer's closest friend and his roommate. He was much older than Albrecht and he wanted more than anything to be an artist. But when he began to look at some of Durer's finished works, the old man saw greatness. He decided to give up his own career so that Durer could pursue his.

There began a period of several years when the roommate worked at menial jobs, scrubbing floors, washing dishes, washing and ironing clothes, and cooking food. His money bought food for himself and young Durer and paid for Albrecht's art classes as well.

Finally after ten long years of working, Durer's paintings and wood carvings began to sell in the market place. Now, at last, his closest friend could go to art school, but now it was too late. He had grown old; his hands were scarred, wrinkled and cracked. His joints were swollen; muscles stiff and the old veins in his hands were protruding. He had surrendered his career that another might blossom.

One night Durer watched in amazement and wonder as his old friend folded his hands in prayer before retiring for the evening. As he knelt and prayed, Durer quickly did a sketch of the hands on a canvas. He was to write later, "I knew I could never put back the lost skill of those hands but I can show the world the feeling of love and gratitude that is in my heart for what he did for me...I will paint his hands folded in prayer—that the world will know that he gave up his life so that mine would blossom."

I've often thought and said that tears and humor are so closely entwined as to be inseparable. When I read this, I had tears, but they were celebrative, joyful, victorious tears and I felt like saying, "Yes, yes, yes! Albrecht Durer, you have made my heart sing!"

◆　　　◆　　　◆

I've always loved this letter given to me by someone years ago.

DEAR LORD,

SO FAR TODAY I'VE DONE ALL RIGHT. I HAVEN'T GOSSIPED, LOST MY TEMPER, BEEN GREEDY, NASTY, SELFISH OR OVER-INDULGENT. I'M REALLY GLAD ABOUT THAT.

BUT IN A FEW MINUTES, GOD, I'M GOING TO GET OUT OF BED, AND FROM THEN ON, I'M GOING TO NEED A LOT MORE HELP.

AMEN

Someone else gave me this memo—from God.

ATTENTION ALL:

DO NOT FEEL TOTALLY PERSONALLY IRREVOCABLY RESPONSIBLE FOR EVERYTHING. THAT'S MY JOB.

LOVE, GOD

The Pope Has Arthritis

After we get over the shock and grief of the death of Pope John Paul II on April 2, 2005, we may be able to recover our humor. At that time, the following story may be enjoyed.

When we lived in south Florida, my friend Terry told us about a bedraggled old pauper who got on a city bus and sat down beside a priest. The old man was dirty, smelly, and unshaven—a perfect contrast to the young, neat-looking priest.

The gaunt old passenger asked the priest: "Father, what causes arthritis?"

Seeing an opening to give a lecture or a sermon to the old bum, the priest said, "Why arthritis is caused by sin, filth, dirt, smoking, alcohol, and wild women. Why do you ask?"

The old man said, "Well, it says here in the paper that the Pope has arthritis."

When Rongg Is Right

The Rev. Dr. Ray Montgomery of Indianapolis, Indiana, once told a story that verifies that "fact is stranger than fiction" and in this case, with a note of humor.

Luther Wright and Herman Rongg appeared before federal judge Leon R. Yankwich in a case that is almost beyond description. Each man claimed ownership of a patent. The Judge attempted to moderate the dispute, declaring, "Well, one of you must be wrong."

"That's right, your honor," declared Herman Rongg. "I'm Rongg and I'm right." But Luther Wright interrupted.

"He's wrong, your honor. I'm right and Rongg is wrong."

The Judge couldn't quite make it out, but he offered his legal opinion.

"Well, you both can't be right. After all, right is right and wrong is wrong." But largely upon the strength of a letter Wright wrote to Rongg, Judge Yankwich at length terminated the Wright-Rongg dispute by ruling: "Paradoxical though it may appear, in this case Wright is wrong and Rongg is right, and I so enter judgment."

No, it wasn't a laughing matter to Wright and Rongg, but it was hilarious to everybody else.

◆   ◆   ◆

After a year or two or three at a new congregation, a pastor finds himself being called upon to do all sorts of things, not the least of which is "entertaining" at church parties. I recall one joyful party held during the season of advent over at the Union Hills Club where I read this anonymous piece to the obvious delight of those present.

The Agony of Agnes

December 25
Dearest John,

I answered the door today and the postman delivered a partridge in a pear tree. What a thoroughly delightful gift. I could not have been more pleased!

With deepest love and affection—Agnes

December 26
Dearest John,

Again today the postman brought me a beautiful gift from you. Just imagine, two turtle doves! I am delighted at your thoughtful gift. They are absolutely adorable.

All my love—Agnes

December 27
Dear John,

Now I really must protest. Three French hens? I don't deserve such generosity. They are just darling, but I must insist—you've been TOO kind.

Love—Agnes

December 28
Dear John,

Today the postman delivered four calling birds. Now really, they are beautiful, but don't you think enough is enough? You're being too romantic.

Affectionately—Agnes

December 29
Dear John,

What a surprise! Today the postman brought me five gold rings—one for each finger. You're just impossible, but I love it. Frankly, all those squawking birds were beginning to get on my nerves.

All my love—Agnes

December 30
Dear John,

When I opened my door this morning there were six geese a-laying on the front porch. So you're back to the birds again! I can't sleep through the racket and the neighbors are complaining! Please stop.

Cordially—Agnes

December 31
John:

Seven swans a-swimming? What kind of lousy joke is this? I've got bird droppings all over the house and the noise is unbearable. I'm a nervous wreck. Stop with the birds now!

Sincerely—Agnes

Jan. 1
Okay, Buster!

I think I prefer the birds. What the hell am I going to do with eight maids a-milking???? It's not bad enough having the dumb birds and now these milk-maids—and they had to bring their damned cows with them! The lawn is a mess; the house is a mess. I'm warning you—lay off!!!

Agnes

Jan. 2
Hey, Knucklehead!

What are you, anyway—some kind of sadist? Today there are nine pipers play-ing. Except they are mostly chasing the milkmaids. The cows are upset and stepping on the birds. The whole place is in an uproar and the neighbors have started eviction proceedings against me.

You'll get yours! Agnes

Jan. 3
You Rotten Jerk!

Ten ladies dancing? And I don't know how they call themselves ladies. They were messing around with the pipers all night long. Not only that, the cows have been sick all night, and the Board of Health is threatening to condemn the place. I've given your name and picture to the police!

One who means it! Agnes

Jan. 4
You Miserable Goon!

Eleven lords a-leaping, eh? All twenty-three of the birds are dead, by the way; they were trampled to death. I hope you're satisfied, you rotten vicious swine!

Your sworn enemy! Agnes

Jan. 6
Dear Sir:

This is to acknowledge your latest gift of twelve fiddlers fiddling, which you have seen fit to inflict upon our client, Miss Agnes McHolstein. The devastation was, of course, total, and Miss McHolstein is now at Happydale Psychiatric Hospital. Should you attempt to visit her, the attendants have instructions to shoot on sight. Enclosed please find a warrant for your arrest.

Yours very truly,

C. Montrose Fenster
Crapster & Fenster, Attorneys at Law

◆   ◆   ◆

Another source of humor is the large number of church bulletins and newsletters that contain typos or misprints. Some of the better ones that I have come across include:

"Ladies of the church, don't forget the rummage sale. It's a chance to get rid of things around the house not worth keeping. Don't forget your husbands."

"Miss Mason sang, *I Shall Not Pass This Way Again* giving obvious pleasure to the congregation."

"For those of you who have children and don't know it, we have a nursery downstairs."

"Barbara remains in the hospital and needs more blood donors. She is also having trouble sleeping and requests tapes of Pastor Jack's sermons."

"During the absence of our pastor, we enjoyed the rare privilege of hearing a good sermon when Rev. Stubbs supplied our pulpit."

"The Rector will preach his farewell sermon after which the choir will sing *Break Forth Into Joy.*"

"Mr. Benson and Miss Carter were married Oct. 24 in the church. So ends a friendship that began in grade school."

"Members of the Overweight Group will meet 7 p.m. Wednesday. They are asked to use the double wide doors to get in."

"At the evening service tonight, the topic will be 'What Is Hell?' Come early and listen to the choir practice."

"Ladies Bible Study will be held Thursday at 10 a.m. All are invited to stay for lunch after the BS is finished."

A church secretary typed in her weekly newsletter: "The Low Self-Esteem Group will meet Thursday at 7 p.m. Please enter through the back door."

"Please place your donation in the large envelope—along with the deceased person you want to remember."

"The ladies of the church will have cast off clothing of every kind. They may be seen in the basement on Friday afternoon."

"Eight new choir robes are needed due to the addition of several new members and the deterioration of some older ones."

"Tonight at 7 p.m. there will be tryouts for the choir. They need all the help they can get."

◆   ◆   ◆

Humor! How can something so simple have such far-reaching impact? Wisdom and knowledge are not confined to the scholars and intellectuals alone. If researchers, including reputable physicians and PhDs tell me that through the therapy of laughter, I may actually improve my health, I am inclined to believe it.

I soon began to realize that I don't have far to look to find stories, jokes and anecdotes that not only make me laugh, but make me feel joyful, upbeat and happy. It seems to me that even if laughter turned out not to be therapeutic, at least it has improved my outlook, my thoughts and my feelings. Consider this:

Two sisters inherited a ranch in West Texas but knew nothing about ranching. A neighbor said, "If you are going to succeed in the cattle business, you've got to have a bull."

"Where do we get a bull?" they asked.

"Oh, look around—in the paper—you'll find something."

Presently they saw an ad for a bull for sale in a town one hundred miles away. The older sister said, "I'll go see the bull and send you a telegram if I like it."

She said to the rancher, "How much is the bull?"

"It's $599.00," he said.

"Oh. I only have $600 and I have to send a telegram to my sister who has the truck and trailer."

"How much is a telegram?" she asked the man at the office.

"One dollar per word," he said.

"Oh, well, then send it to my sister and say "Comfortable," she intoned.

"Comfortable?" he asked. "Whatever could that mean?"

"Well, my sister is a little slow and when she sees it she will read 'Come for t bull.'"

A boss asked his employee, "Billy, do you believe in life after death?"

"Oh, yes, sir. Why do you ask?"

"Well, about two hours after you took off work to attend your grandfather Johnson's funeral, your grandpa Johnson came by here looking for you."

An attorney said to his client, "I was sure sorry to hear about the big fire down at your plant last night."

"Quiet," said the client, "the fire is not until tonight..."

Our work in the church has introduced us to all sorts of worship services, rituals, rites, ceremonies and prayers. Some of the funniest and most enjoyable experiences have been reading or listening to the prayers of children. Here are a few of my favorites:

Dear God: Are you really invisible or is it just a trick?

Dear God: Did you mean for the giraffe to look like that or was it an accident?

Dear God: Thank you for the baby brother, but I think you got confused because what I prayed for was a puppy.

Dear God: I think about you sometimes—even when I am not praying.

Dear God: My brother told me about being born but it doesn't sound right. They are just kidding, aren't they?

Dear God: Instead of letting people die and having to make new ones, why don't you just keep the ones you already have?

6

The Church and Impossible Situations: Money, Race and People

Money

It might seem far-fetched to some readers to say that the topic of money can become an impossible situation for young and inexperienced pastors. But there are pastors who live in fear of a few members in the congregation and avoid talk of money at all costs lest they offend these people.

How vividly I recall the stern admonition given to me at my first full-time church: never talk about money from the pulpit. I still remember the exact wording: "Money is a subject we never talk about here."

Money—that was the first impossible situation I faced. I couldn't believe all the advice I got from several of our church leaders.

One said, "If you're doing your job, the money will come."

Another warned me, "One pastor talked about money from the pulpit…finally they asked him to leave."

I had been warned. Never mention money from the pulpit. It was a Mt. Everest no one could climb! What was I to do? When you are a pastor, you learn very early that it takes money to run a church. Of course, I believed in prayer and faith and love and service—but early on it occurred to me that those things alone wouldn't pay the bills.

The second thing I began to discover was that those who screamed the loudest or protested the loudest were often the poorest stewards in the church. There were some exceptions, of course, but over and over again, I was to learn that those who objected the loudest to any talk about that forbidden word "money" gave the least.

Obviously many of them did not give because they didn't have it to give. A few others would make a big annual pledge—but never pay it. I think it salved their conscience.

What to do? What to do? I happened upon an idea that would defuse all the anxiety about the talk of money. I would continue to use it over the next 35 plus years—with positive results.

Here is what I decided. When it came time for the morning offering to be received, I would do or say something that would make the congregation chuckle or—heaven forbid—laugh.

It was risky and I knew it, but with red ink showing, I had to take the chance.

I still remember. I told them this:

Fanny Crosby is a name familiar to all of you. She wrote most of the old gospel hymns we sing here on Sunday morning. When she was quite young—and could still see—she went with her father to a little country church where Mr. Crosby was to be the guest preacher. When the morning offering was taken, Fanny noticed that her father put into the offering plate a fifty cent coin.

At the close of the service, the elders came to see Mr. Crosby saying to him: "It is the custom in this church to give the guest speaker whatever money is collected in the offering plate." They gave him the total offering which was fifty cents, the same fifty cents he himself had placed in the offering plate.

Seeing and hearing this, Fanny said to her father, "Father, if you had given more, you would have gotten more."

A soft chuckle—almost a laugh—was heard throughout the sanctuary, and I knew I had hit upon an idea that just might work.

It is safe to say that following my very first "success," a humorous approach to the subject of money, I tried to share something humorous about money over all the years that followed.

Our church in Sun City, Arizona, was located directly across the street from the Catholic Church. They have about five thousand members and we, fewer than one thousand. But sometimes the big guy finishes last, especially if you have a sense of humor.

One Sunday three strangers—all women—came to visit our church. Just as I stood to give the sermon, the three of them stood up and walked out.

Okay, I've had my feelings hurt before. I've had people walk out on me before. However, their exit created more of a feeling of curiosity than hurt feelings. An elder brought me a note as we sang the closing hymn. I asked the congregation to be seated—and mentioned that the ladies got up and left because they had heard me preach before...who can blame them, I added.

"And now the truth: they came to the wrong church. They were looking for the Catholic Church across the street...but thank God they stayed through the morning offering. The Catholics got their heart but we got their money."

I'm quite sure God has a sense of humor.

One Sunday I said, "Money talks" and then added: I heard about a pastor in Florida who got a call from a lady whose pet cat had died. Seems she wanted Rev. Jones to perform a "last rites" ceremony for the cat. He hesitated and said that Baptists were not in the habit of doing funerals for cats. Why didn't she call the Methodist pastor? She called and was told, Methodists don't do funerals for cats...Why don't you call the Presbyterians? She did and they told her she really should call the Baptist pastor.

Once again, she called Rev. Jones and in an irritated tone of voice said, "I can't find anyone to do a funeral service for my cat. I fully intended to give $1,000 to any pastor who would do the service."

There was a moment of silence and then this from Rev. Jones. "Mrs. Smith, why didn't you tell me your cat was a Baptist?" After all, money talks!

Speaking of cats makes me think of my colleague in ministry, Dr. George Tolman, who declares that the following story is true.

Seems the great Hollywood actor Charles Laughton hated cats—especially his wife's pet cat. Once Mrs. Laughton took a two-week vacation—alone. While she was gone, Charles used the occasion to get rid of his wife's cat…buried him under the family's large rose bush in the front yard.

When Mrs. Laughton returned, she asked her husband if he had seen her cat. He pleasantly responded, "Honey, I haven't seen that cat in two weeks."

She announced that she was giving a $500 reward to anyone who could find her cat. Charles said that he himself would add another $500 as a reward. Then the neighbor heard about Charles' most generous offer he said to him, "Considering how you hate cats, I'm surprised that you would make such a generous donation to find the cat. How do you explain it?"

Laughton responded, "When you know what I know, you can afford to be generous."

I used that on Sunday just before we took up the morning offering. Did it help? I don't know, but I was sure of one thing: people who can smile and chuckle and even laugh about money will give more than those who give out of guilt or duty or obligation.

A very rich man was visiting a new church and stood to confess how much he needed prayer. He said he gave thousands of dollars to ridiculous causes. Then he added, "I must stop giving all this money away."

"Yes, Brother Jones, and we will have very special prayer for you and your problem right *after* we take up the morning offering." My thoughts exactly.

Ah, life in the church is a scream—especially when it comes to money—which makes me think of George Bernard Shaw.

Shaw once visited the palatial estate of newspaper mogul William Randolph Hearst in California. He looked around in astonishment at the extravagance and said, "This is probably the way God would have done it if only He had the money."

A little boy, on his way to church, was given two dimes—one for the Lord and one for ice cream. He slipped on the sidewalk and watched one of his dimes drop down the open water drain. "Oops," he said, "there goes the Lord's dime."

Quite by accident, I came across a story about Andrew Carnegie. It seems that Mr. Carnegie gave the money to build the spectacular Carnegie

Hall in 1891 and continued to subsidize it for years after it was built. The amount of money involved was substantial but Carnegie never complained.

Eventually he decided that it would be better to broaden the base of support. Accordingly, he instructed his secretary to go out and find matching funds. In only a few hours, the secretary came back with the money. While Carnegie wrote out the check for his half of the money, he gave his male assistant a lecture saying, "Now see how easy it is to get money if you only ask." Then he paused and asked, "By the way, who gave the matching money?"

"Your wife, Sir," came the reply.

Humor helps to soften the approach to asking for money from the members of a congregation. I have used all the following "soft sells."

A man was accosted by two street muggers. He fought them off bravely but was finally subdued. They found only a dollar bill in his pocket and said to him: "Old timer, you mean to tell us that you put up a fight like that for only a dollar bill?"

He responded, "I wasn't fighting you for the dollar in my pocket but for the $500 in my shoes."

It's time for the morning offering.

◆   ◆   ◆

Two elders were canvassing the entire congregation for financial commitments for the church budget. They approached one well-to-do lady and gave her the pledge card. She wrote on it $50 and asked if that was okay. The elders responded, "If that's the best you can do..."

She took the pledge card back and added another zero left of the decimal point making it $500. "Is that okay?" she asked.

They said, "If it's the best that you can do."

She took the pledge back and added yet another zero left of the decimal point, making it $5,000. She then added, "And that's the best that I can do."

Some say we give money to God for many different reasons. We give to meet a need. We give out of obedience to the Bible's teachings. We give because of our own emotional involvement with another person. In addition, who knows, maybe people give to be better prepared for the second coming of the Lord or the Resurrection.

A street preacher asked a well-dressed man on the street if he was ready for the Resurrection. "Well," asked the man, "when is it?"

"Sir, the Resurrection could be this hour, tonight, or tomorrow."

"Well, please don't tell my wife. She will want to go all three times."

It's time for the morning offering.

♦   ♦   ♦

A nasty, mean, self-centered man learned that he did not have long to live. He said to his wife, "Put all my money in a bag and put it in the attic...I will take it with me on my way to heaven."

The wife laughed but did as directed. After the funeral, she went back to the attic and there was the money. She chuckled and said, "I told him he should have put it in the basement."

It's time for the morning offering.

♦   ♦   ♦

The Internal Revenue Service got an unusual letter from a citizen with a $500 check enclosed. The attached letter said, "I owe the government a lot of money from past taxes and haven't been able to sleep since then. I enclose $500 toward the debt—and if I still can't sleep, I will send you the rest."

It's time for the morning offering.

♦   ♦   ♦

Obviously, people are impressed with financial clout, with bigness and with power. I remember years ago when anyone from Texas seemed to do their fair share of boasting.

I heard about a trip to Australia made by a group of Americans with one tall lanky Texan who was forever boasting about how big things were in Texas.

The tour guide said, "These tall buildings..."

"Aw, those aren't tall buildings," said the Texan, "not compared to what we have in Texas."

The guide said, "Now these large cattle..."

The Texan said, "Heck, they aren't large cattle...not like what we have in Texas."

Presently a kangaroo went jumping across the old dirt road and the Texan was frightened. "What in the world was that?" he asked.

The guide said, "You mean you don't have grasshoppers in Texas?"

It's time for the morning offering.

◆   ◆   ◆

Once I used a light-hearted story that really was far-fetched. I served as a trustee on the Lexington Seminary Board. My friend Harry, a long-tenured trustee, told me this.

We are all sons and daughters of God and he said the things we can do for each other and for God are amazing. We are not unlike these thoroughbreds here in Kentucky.

Once a trainer was out walking his race horse and had gotten a long way from home. A neighbor in his truck recognized him and offered him a ride home. "The old racehorse can just tail along," he said.

They got up to twenty-five miles per hour and the driver said, "That horse is right on my tail."

He got up to fifty miles per hour and said, "That horse is still on my tail..., but, say, his tongue is hanging out."

"Is it hanging out the right side or the left side?" the owner asked.

"Why, the left side."

"Then stay in your lane...He's getting ready to pass."

It's time for the morning offering.

Well, that's enough about impossible situations with money and how I incorporated humor into the morning offering. Since researchers have found that humor relieves pain, I simply applied that rather revolutionary anesthetic to parting with one's money. Somehow, it seemed to work.

Race

The controversial topic of money in the church has caused problems for a lot of pastors. But however serious the issue was for me, it paled in comparison to the issue of racial equality. I raise this topic convinced that pastors in every generation must do and say what is right and not just what is popular.

Sometimes pastors must break the mold—shatter old stereotypes that are no longer effective. Yet, pastors are often intimidated by strong lay leaders in the church. Repeatedly I have known pastors who lived in fear—they seemed afraid of their own shadow. Many never took a stand on anything that mattered. Yes, they were forceful and positive on such things as patriotism, courage, sacrifice, motherhood, and ethereal topics like faith and love and peace. However, they were always nervous and on guard on anything specific—or heaven forbid—controversial.

I don't know why it is that so many pastors think they have to please everybody, making everybody happy. Some of them are what we in seminary came to call "sweet Jesus" pastors. They seemed to me to deal with platitudes, innocuous comments, and statements that never hit the vagus nerve. People left bored, but not stirred.

I am not arguing for pastors to become offensive or divisive or hostile or defiant. Why can't they be kind and gentle, fair but firm? Why can't we say with softness and gentleness, "I greatly respect Mr. Johnson's position on this matter, but I see it a little differently"? Take a stand. Be open, honest, gentle, but always kind. If someone wants to know what we think, why can't we tell them? Is it fear of being dismissed or fired?

Once I was embroiled in the hot debate about racial equality. I was, after all, a southerner who grew up on prejudice and racial superiority, but now, at my first church, I no longer believed in racial superiority, and said so—at great cost. I will explain how that event happened.

It has now been sixty plus years but I can still hear my mother tell me these words—"Your Daddy is wrong: the 'colored people' are not inferior."

The year was 1945 and I was seven and in the first grade. One of our "colored" neighbors had failed to carry through on a project with my father. I still recall how my father, whose deep-seated racism was always in evidence, offered his cutting, insulting remarks about the "colored" neighbor who, he said, was "inferior and not really human...why, they don't even have a soul..."

If he had said that on Saturday, on the town square, where all the "white" folks gathered, they would have applauded his words. Prejudice was so deep-seated in our little town that anyone saying something nice or kind about our African-American neighbors would have been booed, hissed or even viciously attacked by the white majority.

However, it was not so with my mother. There at our dinner table, with all my brothers and sisters present, my gracious mother declared, "Eck, you ought to be ashamed of yourself. God made the "coloreds" same as he made you and me. They have a soul—same as you and me...Children, don't pay any attention to your Daddy because your Daddy is wrong."

I cannot adequately explain how I felt. For whatever reason I knew that my mother was right and that my father was wrong. I never shall forget it.

Mother then lovingly chided our father by telling him about the brilliant Booker T. Washington and George Washington Carver—and other "coloreds" who had risen to prominence. She even told my father something he did not want to hear...that many of the soldiers fighting in the war are colored. "They are dying so that we can live..."

My father smirked and added, "Woman, you are crazy."

At church, my mother mentioned the controversial topic that had surfaced at our home. She then told her adult Sunday school class that she thought the "coloreds were as good as me" and that they could accomplish as much as "white folks" if only they were given the chance.

There was, my mother told us later, a loud, strong voice of protest coming mainly from the men in the class. One man in particular said to mother, "Why, Sarah, I don't know how you can call yourself a Christian and think like that."

My mother said to him, "Mr. J., it is because I am a Christian that I do feel that way." I never saw courage more graciously present than in the words that fell from my mother's lips. I would never forget it.

This vivid experience empowered me later through the most frightening episode of my entire career. The memory of it is fresh and still painful. The year was 1969 and the issue that surfaced in our community and in the church as well dealt with busing the underprivileged children from the inner city to the suburban schools. There was also a side issue that in some ways was more explosive than the issue of busing. That had to do with hiring a "colored" teacher at the local school where our son attended.

I recall giving a sermon titled "All Are God's Children." I knew that it might not be well received. I felt it could be explosive and far-reaching in its after-effects. In the sermon, I told the congregation that as a child from the deep south, anything my close friends and family believed was what I believed. I told them that I used to espouse the cause of racial superiority—and the inferiority of the colored people.

With little or no thought to what I was saying, I used to mouth the same emotionally charged racism that I had heard my father preach. Our resentment of the "colored" was never rooted in truth, or in facts or anything even close to accuracy. When I was growing up, racial putdowns and sarcasm met the approval and even applause of my friends. But then I added that I had changed—slowly, painfully, but definitely.

I told them about the episode around our dinner table, and the soft but gentle rebuke of my mother toward my father's racism. That night I began to change. I knew my mother was right—maybe not scientifically or clinically, but at the level of my deepest consciousness. I knew we were all one and that the great eternal God was God of all of us.

I then said the most dangerous thing I ever said in all my thirty-five plus years of ministry. In that southern community, surrounded by two hundred people whose resentment and even hatred were more akin to fear than to enlightenment—I said, "We are all made of the same blood by the same great God." I then told them I supported equality of education for all

people—even if that meant busing children. That was the "nail in the cof-
fin" so to speak. But even that was not without its lighter side.

After church, Chistopher and his mother were driving back to our
house. She said to him, "Christopher, your daddy stood ten feet tall this
morning!"

His six-year-old eyes widened because he took her statement literally,
and he said, "He did? Really?"

She explained to him that she meant his daddy had done something
that not many people would have the courage to do. "Your daddy is very
brave," she told him.

The days that followed were the toughest days I ever lived through.
Two families dropped out of our church immediately, declaring that the
preacher had become a full-blown "Yankee" with no love or respect for his
Southern heritage. I was given the cold shoulder, ignored, and quickly
became the topic of lots of small group conversations. Some said I had
gone berserk; others that I had been reading too many books with too
many wild ideas. Two very prominent members told me that I should just
stick to "preaching the gospel" and leave all that racial stuff alone.

In retrospect, I know now that the only reason I was not dismissed or
fired as their pastor was that I was, after all, still a good ole' Southern boy
who would eventually come around to the "truth."

The issue of busing and employing a "colored" teacher soon had to be
dealt with in our community. I was determined to support both—regardless of the cost. I knew that we are "all of one blood" and that truth and
justice and fair play could and would somehow win out.

The auditorium was jam packed for the called meeting of all parents,
teachers, and school administrators. I estimated that there were over 500
adults there to cast a vote of "consensus" about busing and hiring the colored teacher. Five hundred to one, I thought, as I took my place toward
the front of the auditorium. I wanted to be seen and in no way to hide.
Moreover, yes, I would stand to vote for the resolution, even if it meant
the end of my life.

I cannot adequately describe the powerful emotions that were present in that room. I thought of it in terms of being near a powder keg of high explosives—and any trigger, any trigger at all, would set it off.

I sat there determined but shaking and frightened because several dozen members of my church were at the gathering. I felt that if I voted against the busing and the hiring as most of the crowd would do, I would never be able to live with myself. In addition, I would be seen as a weak and pathetic pastor who could be talked into anything. Moreover, I would almost certainly lose more members and perhaps the emotional support of the whole church.

For whatever reason, I thought of Martin Luther whose protest against the Catholic hierarchy in 1517 put his very life in danger. When he met with the Council of Bishops, he defended himself saying that, "I can do no other. God help me. Here I stand."

I knew that I was no Martin Luther or even Martin Luther King, but I was a follower of Christ and I was running no popularity contest. When the no votes were called for, every single person in my line of sight stood. When they were seated, the call for the yes vote was given. Trembling I stood, alone, looking around the crowded room to remove any doubt about who I was, and sat down.

How I survived is still a mystery. I tried hard not to create any more divisions or alienation among my parishioners, but the "damage" had been done. However, for whatever reason my ministry became empowered.

I have never regretted my words, my actions, or my decisions. I knew then and I know now, "God has made of one blood all who dwell upon the earth."

We really needed some humor to lighten the mood. Therefore, the next Sunday I said something to the effect that it had been a very interesting week. I added that I felt like an overworked tea bag. I added that a famous person had once said, "You don't know how strong a tea bag is until you put it in hot water." There was muffled laughter and I somehow knew that the worst for me and my family was over.

Take a stand—whether it's money or race or justice or service or even how to read and interpret the Bible. However, always be kind and gentle and loving to all people—regardless of how "wrong" they might be or how "right" you might be.

I suspect that there are far too many clergy who live by the dictum "to get along, go along."

Always we must be in touch with reality, get our heads out of the clouds, and deal with the specifics of life, not the theoretical abstracts.

I'm reminded of the story that surfaced about Sherlock Holmes and his sidekick, Dr. Watson, a few years ago. Seems they went camping overnight in the countryside of England. They cooked supper, pitched their tent, and went to bed. About 2 a.m., Sherlock awakened Dr. Watson saying, "Wake up, Watson, and tell me what conclusions you draw by what you see..."

Dr. Watson looked up and said, "Ah, the stars twinkling, the vastness, the universe—a wonder to behold."

Holmes said, "Watson, you idiot, someone has stolen our tent!"

If I could give even one word of counsel to clergy, it would be, "Be yourself"—do not feign piety or religiosity and do not play the role of pastor. Talk in your normal tone of voice and do not preach in pious vocal tones. Preach the same way you talk to your friends. If your congregation is offended by your "humanity" perhaps you should change careers.

Once during the heat of the racial issues in my church someone suggested that I should be careful, worried, and a little more fearful. I laughed and recall saying, "Do I look worried to you? After all, I can always sell cars."

Well, okay, that might have been a little haughty or even arrogant, but I refused to give in to fear or to intimidation even when dealing with the hot topic of race.

People

Let's face it: every congregation has at least one "impossible" member. No matter what you say or do, it will prove to be the wrong thing. Pray that you never have to deal with persons who have risen to the level of first-line church leaders, but who are plagued with major emotional or mental problems. It requires all the skills you possess to manage.

I shall not soon forget the ordeal of dealing with Miss Daisy. I was new in the church, young, naïve, confident, and overly cheerful. I had never before dealt with a serious emotional or mental disorder. But Miss Daisy would soon awaken me from my naivete. At first she was lovely, warm, gracious, and wonderfully excited about her new pastor. But that was soon to change.

One day in the church office, she was full of praise, happy, joyful and smiling from ear to ear. Suddenly, she became a different person, a scowl came upon her face, and she began to shout epithets at me and others in the office, calling us names sailors would be embarrassed to use. I was stunned, speechless, noticeably shaken and wounded. She stormed out of the office and slammed the door behind her.

I soon learned that Miss Daisy would prove to be a bigger challenge than what I would ever be able to resolve.

I also recall the man who taught me much about controlling one's temper—another one of my "impossible people."

It was probably a mistake as I look back on it. But it seemed the right thing to do at the time.

I asked our church board for money to help a desperately poor woman find a place to live. She was in an abusive situation and urgently needed to escape her husband's harshness and cruelty. The board readily agreed and the money was given.

But the real problem was just beginning. A man in the church didn't agree with sending the money or helping the woman get back on her feet. He blamed me for it.

He came by the church, marched straight back to my office, and began to yell and scream at me for giving the help. His face was red; his fists clenched, and then came the accusing, threatening finger in my face. He was so animated I was afraid he would have a heart attack. He yelled even more, was bold, blustery, loud—the secretary, who seemed about two miles away, said she heard him yelling.

What do you do when someone is "in your face," when someone verbally attacks you, yells at you, embarrasses you, or even threatens you?

How do you handle anger from other people directed at you, or how do you handle your own anger—which is usually the real issue.

Well, whether right or wrong, I decided to listen, without interruption, until the accuser was completely drained of energy and emotion. Oh, I wanted to fight back, to argue back, to defend myself, to explain myself, and worst of all, to interrupt him before he was finished.

Whether right or wrong I do not know. But, I decided to stand, appear to be relaxed and receptive, and listen. Is it easy to do this? No! It may be the hardest thing people ever have to do. Who wants to be attacked? Who wants to be mocked, ridiculed, made fun of? No one! But I learned early that there is a time and place for everything under the sun. There is a time for speaking, and a time for listening.

This was no time for talking. Why? Precisely because Bill was not in a listening frame of mind. He had his emotional basket full to overflowing with barbs and rocks and stones—and he was bound and determined to unload the whole thing on me.

For nearly thirty minutes, I had my every weakness exposed. I was accused of being stubborn, pigheaded, defiant, arrogant, lazy, and only interested in playing golf. I was pushy, controlling, intolerant, impatient, and totally unworthy of the high salary that I was paid. He then told me that I was the highest paid pastor in the Sun Cities and that I wasn't worth anything. I did manage to ask him how he knew that I was the highest paid pastor in the Sun Cities, to which he said, "I have friends in high places."

Then he stopped talking and began to smile…smile! At a time like that? Yes, he smiled and then, to my very great surprise said, "Well, really this is no big deal…"

I thought, really, no big deal. He had dumped all his garbage on me and there really wasn't anything left. I do recall saying to him as he wound down, "I don't believe you left out anything…except that you told me once that I am way overweight—let's add that to the list."

Come to think of it, that may have been the reason he began to smile.

How to handle anger and hot tempers and impossible people? That is the question. For me, three or four responses seem to work:

1. Let the angry person talk without interruption. This "silence" on your part may be the hardest thing you ever have to do, but it does work.

2. Listen to what is being said, noting the topics mentioned and the things said.

3. Never rush to defend yourself. If possible, find some point of agreement.

I said to Bill, "Well, actually you are right on target on several of your points, and I will do my very best to change them. Now my weight is another matter—that may take me a while to turn around...but I really blame you and Lucy for that since you are always inviting us out to dinner."

He laughed again.

4. Thank your accuser for telling you. What? Thank them? Yes. Thank them.

5. Ask if he or she has time to go over the list of complaints and then, objectively, briefly describe only the facts, the data, and the confirmed decisions by the board, et cetera.

6. If any agreement is reached, you have found a friend. If not, he will respect you for your time and for your ability to listen without judgment or condemnation of him.

Does it work? For sixty-five years plus, I have found that it does.

He Brought His Gun to Church

It was the most frightening experience I ever had in my forty years of pastoral work. We lived in Florida and served the church in Plantation. I got a call from some lady whom I did not know. She talked about turning her life around and allowing God to help. We prayed and then hung up the phone.

Next day I got a call from some man whom I assumed was her husband. He wanted to know exactly what she had told me.

I asked who he was and he would not say. I gave him nothing about the phone call except to say she requested prayer.

Then the shocker! He told me that he would be coming to church the next Sunday and was going to bring his gun and kill me during the worship service. I felt powerless, helpless. How does one deal with impossible people?

Suddenly the work of pastoral ministry took on a whole new meaning. It was now a life and death issue. I didn't know what to do or which way to turn. Had my life in the church come down to this? I began to see the headlines in the Ft. Lauderdale newspaper:

LOCAL PASTOR SHOT WHILE DELIVERING HIS SERMON

I happened upon a brilliant idea. I would call the Board of Elders and have two of them stand at each of the doors. That way the headlines would read:

LOCAL CHURCH ELDERS SHOT WHILE GUARDING THEIR PASTOR

The newspaper story would then describe how the pastor courageously escaped, and at least his life was preserved.

Imagination! How real it can be.

Well, we did post the Elders at all doors, and I gave the shortest sermon of my entire career.

I'm just now coming to realize that's why everyone told me that sermon, eight minutes long, was the best sermon I ever gave. Life in the church is a scream.

And, no, the would-be shooter was never heard from again.

7

Life as a Hospital Chaplain Is Also a Scream

Who would have ever thought that in this world of medicine, x-rays, catheters, mammograms, blood tests, MRIs, surgeries and bed pans there would surface the topic of humor? As improbable as it might appear, those humorous anecdotes have come to me here more than any other place in my career.

And forget the idea that docs and nurses and techs are too serious to laugh. They laugh—but they make sure that it is appropriate humor.

Consider the enormous resource of our three thousand plus volunteers and the hilarious stories they tell and the articles they clip out for me to read at our hospital. Consider too that some of the most popular books on the market today were written by physicians—and most of them are probably available in a public library.

A volunteer gave me a quote by Erma Bombeck. She laughed as she read it. I laughed when I heard it…and in more than a dozen talks I have given through our Speaker's Bureau, others have laughed.

Erma wrote: "Asthma is a disease that has practically the same symptoms as passion—except that asthma lasts longer." She added, "I rather enjoy the sound of asthma. It's the closest thing to passion I've heard in years."

Another volunteer said, "Anyone who looks like the picture on their passport is too sick to travel."

Dr. Harold Bennett wrote, tongue in cheek: "If you've got your health, you've got everything. If you don't have your health, sooner or later your doctor will have everything."

A man complained about a $1,000 bill from his anesthesiologist for putting him to sleep. "That's ridiculous," shouted the patient. "It only took you 30 seconds to put me to sleep."

"Actually," said the anesthesiologist, "it only cost $20 to put you to sleep. The other $980 was to make sure you woke up."

Chemicals and Humor

Why all the fuss about humor? In a word, it works! Therapists agree. Psychologists agree. Chaplains agree. And a growing number of physicians agree: Laughter is good medicine and people love to laugh.

All I really knew before my research began was that when I laughed, I felt good. Sometimes I felt good for two or three hours. Little did I know that there is now scientific data that shows exactly what happens when we are positive, cheerful, upbeat and especially when we laugh heartily.

Dr. Candace Pert, a psychopharmacologist at Rutgers University, was among the first researchers to speak of a substance known as neuropeptides. She noted that there are many types of these peptides—created by the tissue of the brain—when people are happy, joyful, positive and especially when they laugh.

You will recall that a neuropeptide is an opiate-like substance that gives a person a feeling of euphoria and well-being. These peptides—their names and their number are many—encephalins, endogenous morphines (endorphins for short) permeate the blood stream and neutralize the poisons and various toxins that make us sick. Hearty laughter produces an abundance of these peptides which in turn render powerless toxic chemicals and "killer cells." They also have the effect of raising the level and strength of our immune system, warding off the body's tendency to grow weak or frail.

Dr. Pert stated emphatically, "Laugh and live!" She added that laughter may be the most important single ingredient in modern health—even more important than many of our medications.

Dr. Joan Matthews Larson has given us helpful insights about these peptides. She stated that the human brain transmits thoughts and creates emotions in part by means of neurotransmitters that load and fire and reload continually (Larson, 1999).

Communication within the brain and the rest of the central nervous system occurs by means of chemical messages that are then exchanged through our neurotransmitters. The proper function of our brains and emotions depends upon an adequate supply of these vital natural substances.

Neuropeptides continually circulate and communicate through our brains and bodies. Receptors for these peptides and transmitters reside in the brain and the endocrine system, spinal cord and even the immune system.

The pitching and catching of these chemicals in the brain and body generates behavior and all the necessary physical changes that behavior requires.

Dr. Wilder Penfield at Montreal's McGill University discovered nearly 90 years ago that stimulating certain areas of the brain would automatically produce different stored memories producing emotional reactions such as crying, laughing, and anger. These various peptides that are thereby produced by humor have the effect of neutralizing many of the toxins that tend to make us sick.

Norman Cousins may have been the first to validate this statement by Dr. Pert. Readers may remember that Cousins was the editor of *The Saturday Review of Literature.* In 1965, he was stricken with a type of collagen disease (spondylitis ankylosis) and suffered almost unbearable pain.

A long-term patient at the Johns Hopkins University Hospital in Baltimore, he wondered if anything could be done to end the brutal pain and to give him a glimmer of hope.

While in this state of mind he came upon a book by Dr. Hans Selye called *The Stress of Life.* In that book Cousins read that prolonged negative thoughts and feelings lower the body's immune system and open the door to disease. He read that dealing with unresolved stress, fear, worry, and anxiety puts the body in a defensive posture, as though to ward off any threat or danger. This stress on the human body can be and often is a positive thing for people. However, if prolonged, where worry and stress continue unresolved for weeks or months, the body produces negative chemicals which can and do make us sick.

Is there any possible way to counter these toxic chemicals—these poisons—in the blood stream, Cousins asked himself? His pain continued and seemed only to get worse. Then a serendipitous event occurred. He called it a "miracle discovery." One night in that hospital room he watched a T.V. show called *Candid Camera* with Allen Funt. Cousins began to laugh and then laughed more heartily at all the funny, hilarious episodes unfolding before his eyes. He laughed for about an hour—and then made the discovery that was to bring him complete healing: for over an hour after the laughing episodes, his pain almost totally disappeared. He slept for the better part of two hours without pain.

He was puzzled, then amazed, then excited and then ecstatic. The crazy thought came to him: could there be a relationship between the laughter and the decrease in pain?

It was only a question but how timely it proved to be. The pain returned to his body. Then the thought came to him: Why not watch more funny movies or TV shows and monitor the results of my experiment?

Over the next eight weeks, Cousins rented anything and everything that he could find that was funny. He watched every episode of *Candid Camera* shows—including all the old ones which he rented. He watched the Marx Brothers, Red Skelton and anything else that would make him laugh.

To his astonishment, a ten to fifteen-minute segment of laughter would inevitably result in one to two hours of peaceful and pain-free sleep.

His physicians were alerted. He talked to the hospital counselors about what was taking place. They decided to measure the blood sedimentation rate before and after the laughing episodes. To their surprise, there was a five-point change in the sedimentation rates. This continued to drop to healthier levels. Ascorbic acid (Vitamin C) was added to his daily diet with good results. Each day showed progress.

Cousins said of the experiments: "What I discovered was that a strong will to live plus active participation in the treatment program—and all the elements together led to my complete recovery."

The end result of this therapy of laughter was that Norman Cousins was completely cured. He went on to become a leader doing extensive research with many published reports on the effect of humor on one's health.

He lived another twenty-five years and died in 1990, leaving behind a whole new world of possibilities. Readers unacquainted with Cousins will find his major books in most public libraries. They are: *Anatomy of an Illness, The Celebration of Life* and *Head First.*

The skeptic will say, "But that is only one example—and it does not mean that laughter will work for me..."

Yes and no. It is all in the experimental stage. However, dozens of studies are being done and the overwhelming amount of evidence shows that "humor works." In my recent research, I have come upon the names of dozens of well-known researchers including psychologists, therapists, counselors, and physicians who seem to be of one mind: people who have discovered humor tend to be healthier, more positive and upbeat than those who don't laugh. The reasons are becoming increasingly clear.

I think of Dr. L. S. Berk who described how laughter increases immune globulin A which protects the body, especially in respiratory infections. It also activates key components of our immune system and helps to ward off toxins.

Dr. Paul McGhee entitled one of his articles "Humor as Survival Training" and stated that it reduces the body's "killer cells." It also reduces the stress hormone called serum cortisol and releases nitric oxide which helps the blood vessels relax.

Life as a chaplain introduces you to people and to situations you might never know otherwise. As chaplains, we recognize culture and religious diversity and respect the traditions that patients bring to our medical center. We are ecumenical, meaning world view. Yes, we have our own deep religious faith and denominational ties but those are less important than the patients' needs and wishes. A chaplain never imposes his or her beliefs onto a patient out of respect for that patient's beliefs and rights.

We are learning, sometimes painfully so, that a number of our patients do not want a chaplain to come by. One patient yelled, "Get out! I can't afford the doctors, let alone a chaplain. Get out!" Of course, there is no fee of any kind related to the chaplain's visit but that patient wasn't interested in anything related to our work.

Another patient responded, "My God, a chaplain. I didn't know I was that sick." Not a few patients associate chaplaincy with death or "last rites" and want nothing to do with either. We respect their wishes.

We do our best to make our visit and our presence as non-threatening as possible and we learn what works and what doesn't work. My chaplain supervisor often introduces himself by saying something like, "I'm the chaplain and am making the rounds today and wanted to say hello to you."

My general comment is something like, "I'm the chaplain and just wanted to say hi." If there is a positive response from the patient we go deeper, relating only what might be helpful to the patient.

On several occasions, I have been asked to visit Jewish patients. I used that introduction, "Just wanted to say hello..." and almost without exception, that opening results in a healthy conversation with several patients asking me to come back again.

It is important to note that we go only when and where we are welcomed. We know that we are not the main thing at the hospital. No one actually comes to our facility hoping to see a chaplain. They do come hoping to see the doctor or nurse or technician or to get a procedure performed. We are not the main thing, but we are an important part of the healing team for many patients.

It is increasingly clear to us that patient healing is sometimes blocked by negative emotions. If patients are frightened, anxious, worried, depressed or without hope, often the very best thing for them to do is to talk with someone about their fear or anxiety. Chaplains are good listeners and often can help the anxious patient find deep spiritual resources that lead to healing.

Holistic medicine is pointing increasingly to treating the whole person. We are learning that any medication or treatment that does not consider the patient's emotions, his attitudes, thoughts, and feelings will result in slower healing. In fact, your attitude, your thoughts and your emotions can actually block the work of many medications.

It works in practically every sphere of life. People who have a chance to talk about their fear, their worry, or even their anger often find a degree of healing in the process.

I still recall an angry patient who came to the hospital through our Emergency Department. His ailment was not life-threatening and so, on a very busy day in the Emergency Room, he sat in the admitting area for two or more hours. I went to check and discovered that every bed in ER was in use—every doctor and nurse overwhelmed by the twenty or so more critical patients. I told the angry patient what was happening and then asked him about himself. Well, that was the key. He began by berating the hospital, the staff, the nurses, the doctors, and I listened. Nearly yelling at the start, his voice began to soften and lower as he began talking in conversational tones. He described the great pain in his abdominal area and seemed extremely tense, serious and obviously in much pain.

For twenty minutes I listened to him rant and rave but increasingly with less intensity. I told him that the doctors and nurses knew that he was waiting—that they had not forgotten him and that he would get excellent care. I then told him I wished there was something I could do to relieve the pain.

In a very calm voice, he said to me, "I think you already have. I think I was so uptight that it actually made my pain worse. I feel better...and I am thankful."

The psychological factor is such a powerful force in healing, as is one's spiritual foundation. Those who are rooted in a deep faith in God get well sooner, are sick less often and stay as a patient fewer days than those who have no spiritual or religious roots.

When we lived in Florida, we learned of one patient's faith that was most impressive. The nurse and doctor gave her the bad news that she didn't have long left to live. The nurse stayed around to comfort the patient—thinking that she would surely be very upset and crying. As it turned out the nurse sat down beside the elderly lady's bed, held her hand and herself began to cry. It was the patient who offered comfort and consolation to the nurse, taking her hand, patting it and saying, "Now, honey, don't you go worry yourself…We are safe in God's love…and everything's going to be all right."

◆   ◆   ◆

I once had an experience as a chaplain that made me appreciate my own good relationship with my mother. Before I tell about the experience at the hospital, let me tell you about my own family.

My older sister once said, "I was always Mother's favorite…" Strange that she would say that because that is what I heard my older brother say, "I always knew that out of nine children, I was Mother's favorite."

I recall once, years after all nine of us were grown and gone from home that we gathered for a family reunion. The unlikely topic of conversation turned out to be which of us was Mother's favorite.

At the end of the one-hour discussion, each adult child explained with great passion why he or she was Mother's favorite. Well, being a pastor and all, I knew I was her favorite. Suddenly it occurred to each of us, but was articulated by my older sister. She said, "Do you realize what has happened? Mother had the ability to make each one of us feel that we were special and loved and cared for as though she had none other to love."

When she died just a few years ago, it was noted that Mother had the rare and wonderful gift to make each of us feel, really feel, that we alone were the most important person in her world.

Now, let me tell you about the experience I had with a mother in the hospital. I went to see a terminally ill lady who refused to die because she and her adult son were at bitter odds with each other. The son and mother hadn't spoken to each other in fourteen years. I talked to the nurse who explained that the son was in the Visitor's Lounge waiting for his mother to die but refusing to see her because of a long-standing disagreement.

I asked the son if it would be okay if I went in to see his mother. He nodded yes. "Is there anything you want me to tell her?" I asked the son. There was a long pause and then this:

"Well, well, ah, well, you can tell her that…well…that I love her."

I was astounded by this apparent breakthrough and repeated what he had said. "So you want me to tell her that you love her?"

He stood up and said to me, "No, I think I will tell her myself." Eureka! He went into the room. I stood watching and listening at the door.

He said, "Mother?"

She said, "David?"

They hugged; they embraced; they cried for about five minutes. It was the most powerful reconciliation I had ever seen.

I waved goodbye to David and went back to the office. One hour later the nurse called me to say that the mother died shortly after I left—but that she died at peace.

I learned then that healing may come through medications and surgical procedures but often the deepest and most far-reaching healing is relational, social, emotional, and supremely spiritual. Chaplains may not be the main thing but our presence is a positive force for good. What an inspiration it is to us.

One of the great rewards of being a chaplain is getting to meet clergy from all sorts of denominational backgrounds. I have especially benefited from knowing a number of priests from the Catholic churches in our area and trying to identify with those priests at a time of unparalleled crisis in their church.

I have had the privilege of spending time with leaders in the Presbyterian, Methodist, Lutheran, Episcopal, Disciples, and Baptist churches. Often they share information about their work and sometimes stories about their people.

One Baptist pastor told me about a remarkable lady named Lottie—Lottie Moon to be exact. She was tiny, less than five feet tall but high spirited, feisty, opinionated, articulate and brilliant.

Lottie was born into wealth in 1840 in a southern, aristocratic family in Virginia and boasted that they owned 54 slaves. The shame of that did not dawn on her until after she became a Christian. For whatever reason, this daughter of enormous wealth decided to become a missionary to the people of China. Her conversion to Christianity was deep, lasting, and real.

She served nearly forty years in Ting Chow and Pingtu. She was not at once embraced by the Chinese people and herself suffered hunger, persecution, ridicule, and scorn—still she persisted; giving anything and everything that she had to the less fortunate people in her town. Always she spoke of the love of God and the model of Christ in the New Testament.

Through her passion for the Chinese people and her great compassion, the long-term results of her life were astounding. For one thing, she won over a brilliant, young Confucian scholar named Li Show Ting. When given a copy of the New Testament, he scoffed and ridiculed Lottie, but he did respond to her love and care and to her brilliant mind. In time, Li Show was baptized into the church—and in his ministry which was to follow, baptized more than 10,000 persons into the Christian faith.

But that, said my Baptist pastor-friend, was only part of the story. In December, 1887, little Lottie Moon asked for and got permission to take up a Christmas offering in all the Baptist Churches in America. The money would help to send more missionaries to China and to help feed and educate the poor.

The first year's offering totaled $3,215, enough to train and send three new missionaries to China. Then my friend added, "We have now taken up a special Christmas offering every year since 1887, and to date Lottie Moon is responsible for raising $1,500,000,000 (that's 1 ½ billion) to help the underprivileged of the world."

Ah, chaplaincy. One day I'm going to write a book about this amazing work.

What does a chaplain do? I asked that question of our Volunteer Chaplains shortly after I began my work as staff chaplain in Sun City West.

"As little as possible..." was the quick retort of one of our tenured chaplains. We all laughed and I quickly rephrased the question: "Well, what are chaplains supposed to do?" The response from Katie was immediate, but unhurried: "I don't think it's what we do so much as who we are and what we represent. Our role," Katie added, "is more being than doing." I thought of the psychiatrist Paul Tournier's book titled *To Do or To Be.* How timely she was.

I was amazed at her insight and almost shocked by this and numerous other insightful revelations about what chaplains do and don't do. I knew early on that we had a team of volunteer chaplains capable of making a genuine contribution to our patients' therapy and to their healing.

Someone said, "Wisdom comes with age." I was to learn that this same lady, Katie, who chaired the Chaplain's Committee, was already eighty-six and still going strong. She is, by almost any standard of measurement, a remarkable lady. She has taken many graduate-level courses offered to clergy and clergy-types. She has had more work in clinical pastoral education than many of our ordained pastors. She is a brilliant organist, having been the lead organist at several large churches. She is kind, deeply caring, and beautifully compassionate.

In addition, her pastoral skills are second to none. It was no surprise to me that before I came on board three years ago as staff chaplain, Katie managed all the volunteer chaplains with great skill. But still the question went unanswered. What does a chaplain do? Perhaps I can best answer it by telling you what I do or have done.

I visit patients in our hospital who have requested a "chaplain visit." My first two years here I averaged about fifteen to twenty pastoral visits during each four hour period on the job. The Volunteer Chaplains (we currently have fifteen) each give three to four hours a week visiting patients in our hospital who have requested a visit. Together we average between forty and fifty calls a day. I now make twenty to twenty-five visits a day.

We are there to listen (how powerful it is to listen), to care, and to share something of the world of the Spirit when it is appropriate.

We are a spiritual presence. We do not so much solve problems as we listen to them with kindness and understanding. We offer hope in the face of so much sadness and we communicate, less by words and more by a caring presence. We are just beginning to learn the healing power of presence and compassionate listening.

Not long ago, one of our chaplains told of visiting a patient who couldn't talk. Not a word was spoken in many days. Jean noticed that he seemed restless, agitated, distressed, very tense and "in knots." She explained who she was and he nodded. She asked if he would want her to offer a brief prayer for him. He nodded approvingly.

She asked the eternal God to come into the room, thanked God for this patient, and asked that God's peace might flood his being and make him whole. She noticed a sense of relaxation in his hands, then his arms and face.

As she left the room, the "speechless" patient said to her, "Thank you for your prayer..."

Howard Bennett, M.D., professor of Clinical Pediatrics at the George Washington University Medical School, declared that the following humorous ad appeared in a publication with its rather unorthodox way of advertising for a physician:

ACADEMIC PHYSICIAN NEEDED

We're a big sprawling hospital in a seedy part of town. We haven't matched in three years and our physician in chief just quit to go to law school. Are you an academic doc who is ready to deal with motivational atrophy, turf battles, cost overruns, sneering, pimping and the occasional food fight? If so, this could be the match of a lifetime.

I don't think that any such ad ever appeared in a newspaper but imagine the fun and laughter a group of educators, physicians and nurses might have just reading this ad.

"Lighten up!" the psychologist said to me. "Slow down. You're in such a hurry and you are soooo serious. Where's the fire?"

Her words stung—but they worked. I had been speeding down the Interstate Highways at a breakneck speed. I was tense, and in a mad rush to get on with whatever came next. My haste was especially obvious in the Sage Unit where I gave a thirty-minute talk to twelve or fifteen patients who have experienced some type of emotional trauma. The therapist, Johanna, was there watching and waiting to see what I would do or say.

On my fourth or fifth visit, I rushed into the Sage Unit to give my talk on "spiritual things" with little or no thought to what those patients needed. I was serious and heavy and determined to tell them about God's love.

I wanted to tell them everything I knew. But, as someone said, "It won't take very long." Aargh!

To be perfectly honest, the group seemed relieved when my serious talk was ended—and so was I. Something was missing. Johanna spotted it instantly when she said: "Relax, Reverend. Where's the fire?"

A week later, I made one of the most important discoveries of my 40-year career—I discovered the place of humor in the Sage Unit of a hospital.

There was an older man in a wheelchair who was somber, sad, down and out, and almost out of touch with reality. I spoke on the love of God and told how we were all chosen by God but there was no response from him. I then closed the session with the group by telling a couple of really funny jokes. The older man in the wheelchair laughed heartily, opened his eyes, took my hand, and said, "Damn, I'm glad you came."

When one combines the ingredients of humor and spirituality, positive things can and do happen. It isn't a theory; it's a fact!

Chaplains and clergy alike learn early that knowledge alone is rarely adequate to meet the diverse needs of patients or church members. In the Bible, the author of First Corinthians spoke of wisdom and knowledge working conjointly—and one without the other is often ineffective. Think of all the "geniuses" who never used their brilliance to enhance the health and happiness of other people.

Any one of our nurses, doctors, or chaplains may have vast knowledge on how to bring about health, healing, and wholeness, but if they never use it to that end, it is of little value.

A friend said of our ability to read: "Those who don't read (or won't read) are no better off than those who can't read."

In my work as a hospital chaplain, I joined the Speakers Bureau here. In the past three years, I have given about seventy-five talks in the greater Phoenix area on the topics of health and humor, positive attitudes and the upbeat life of our 90,000 retirees in the Sun Cities.

The key phrase is and must always be: appropriate humor. When a chaplain or a pastor, rabbi or priest combines humor with spiritual moorings, positive things happen. Moreover, it's exciting to see and hear.

Chaplaincy teaches us much about the world of the spirit. When a person is able to align himself or herself with a living, loving, forgiving God, healing of the mind, the emotions and the spirit often takes place—even if there is no obvious physical healing. It is not infrequent when full restoration of health occurs. It is as if a desert wasteland has come to life.

Two hundred miles northeast of Los Angeles is a desolate baked out gorge appropriately named Death Valley. It is the lowest geographical point in the U.S.A., dropping some 276 feet below sea level. It is also the hottest place in the country holding the official record of 134 degrees. Streams flow into Death Valley only to disappear in the searing heat and only a scant two inches of rain falls on this barren wasteland each year.

However, a few years ago an amazing thing happened. For nineteen straight days, rain fell on that bone-dry earth. Suddenly, almost overnight, all kinds of seeds lying dormant for months or even years in the hot sand burst into bloom. In every direction could be seen all the magnificent colors of creation in the flowers.

In this Valley of Death, there was life. In a world of heat, dust, wind, and sun sprang up a mural resplendent with all colors of the rainbow.

The thought occurred to me repeatedly that something like that happens when a person reaches out and in a symbolic way touches the hand of God. The wellsprings of God's love and grace reach us, touch us and renew us. The Old Testament psalmist says at moments like that, "He restores my soul." When that does occur a desert becomes a garden, illness yields to health, beauty transcends the ugly, love outwits and outlasts hate, and despair gives way to hope.

In my ministry of forty plus years both as pastor and as chaplain, I have seen men and women alike come to life as they discovered for themselves the amazing world of the Spirit. In the final analysis, spiritual healing is the thing that matters most—and you find it in the most unlikely places.

I confess that after all these years serving as a pastor, and more recently as a chaplain, I still know so little about the world of the Spirit. I choose to believe. I choose to walk by faith and I choose to assert the positive affirmations of life instead of doubt, fear, and indecision. Yet, still the ways of

God are beyond me and sometimes strange and amazing things happen that defy explanation.

One such event occurred in Swan Quarter, North Carolina—only a few miles from the place where I was born and raised. The people in Swan Quarter are still talking about what they call "the ways of God."

The year was 1876—only eleven years after the Civil War ended. A group of Methodists wanted to build a church and desired to place it on the highest hill to avoid certain flooding that was common in that little community.

When the land owner of that piece of property was approached about selling it, he said, "Absolutely not!"

However, the little frame church was built on a less desirable lot of low-land and was proudly dedicated "to the Glory of God" on September 16, 1876.

Three days later on September 19, it began to rain. It continued to rain hour after hour, day after day. It rained so much that severe flooding set in. Incredibly, the little church was lifted off its foundation and began to float down Main Street to Oyster Creek Road.

Then an astonishing thing happened. There at that juncture, the little chapel seemed to be guided by a mysterious hand. It took a ninety-degree turn, moved uphill to the exact piece of property they had tried in vain to buy. On that spot, the little chapel came to rest.

When the land owner came, he waded through the water to see for himself. The sight so overwhelmed him that immediately he decided to deed the property to the members of the little Methodist Church.

Chaplaincy helps us approach all people as though they are sons and daughters of God. It is such a temptation to treat people differently according to their social standing, education, or financial clout. We are drawn to people who are educated, polished, erudite and tend to turn away from people who are not. It is a rare and gifted leader or pastor who truly values all people equally and who has no favorites. That is always the aim and intent of each of our chaplains—all are equal and worthy.

We saw that modeled in the pastoral work of W. S. Abernethy, pastor of the Calvary Baptist Church in Washington, D. C. When the distinguished Charles Evans Hughes served as Secretary of State, he attended Dr. Abernethy's church.

One Sunday at the close of the worship service, three people went forward to be accepted into the membership of the church—one, the honorable C. E. Hughes, the second, his mother, and the third, an unknown man from China who had recently emigrated to the states and was a man no one knew.

I am so pleased by what W. S. Abernethy did. Dr. Abernethy, sensing the feeling that some members would want to elevate Secretary Hughes and denigrate the poor man from China, spoke a word that came from God. He said, "You have all come to present yourself to Christ at the foot of the cross. Let it be noted that at the foot of the cross the ground is level. Yes, all are equal before God because all are sons and daughters of the eternal God and God has no favorite sons."

◆   ◆   ◆

You don't have to be a pastor or a chaplain to find funny things in life. I came home one night and asked my wife Janet to sit down while I read something funny—the names of country songs which were supposedly recorded in hopes that they would sell. Well, I was raised on country music and had laughed at some of the songs like: "Does Your Chewing Gum Lose Its Flavor on the Bed Post Overnight?" and "I Got My Education Out Behind the Barn" and "Rockabilly, Rockabilly, Rockabilly Rock."

But these new "love songs" which someone handed to me for a good laugh were even better. Janet and I laughed heartily then and much since. Here are a few of our favorites: "Her Teeth Were Stained but Her Heart Was Pure," "I Liked You Better Before I Knew You So Well," "I Wouldn't Take Her to a Dog Fight 'Cause I'm Afraid She'd Win," "My Wife Run Off with My Best Friend and I Sure Do Miss Him," "If I Had Shot You When I Wanted To, I'd Be Out by Now," and "I Just Bought a Car from the Guy That Stole My Girl, but the Car Don't Run, So I Figure We Got an Even Deal."

I hear that country music is major business in many parts of America. However, if these songs are in fact real songs, then I suggest that we pray for the songwriters and for those who can't laugh at what their pen has produced.

Speaking of songs and music prompts me to recall what our choir director told us a few years ago. It seems there was a husband who never felt well, and always complained to his wife about feeling bad. He had the habit of stopping off at the tavern on his way home from work and overindulging. His wife yelled at him and said there was nothing wrong with him except going to too many taverns and bars.

"Besides," she said, "go to the doctor and find out what is wrong."

Next day the old drunk went to see the doctor and not wanting her to know the truth came out and announced to his skeptical wife that he had really bad "syncopation."

The wife went home, looked up the word "syncopation," and began to laugh. It said, "syncopation: the irregular movement from bar to bar."

Another husband complained to his wife that he was inferior to everybody—not as intelligent or handsome—"I'm just inferior."

His wife protested, "You are not inferior; you just have an inferiority complex. Let's go see the doctor."

When he walked out of the psychiatrist's office, the wife said, "Well, what did the doctor say?"

"He said I do not have a complex—I really am inferior."

There is an article about another inferior guy who was called a "geek" in Dave Barry's recent book. This is from a piece called "Why Abe Was a Geek."

> Getting the right school supplies is crucial to your child's chances for success in life. We all remember the tragic story of Abraham Lincoln whose family could not afford school supplies so he had to write on a shovel with a piece of coal. This meant that if young Abe saw a cute girl and wanted to pass her a note in class, he had to hand her this big gross filthy digging implement, sometimes with worm parts stuck to it, and she'd go Ewwww!

> In addition, all the others kids would laugh at Abe. (It did not help that he was the only boy in the fifth grade that had a beard.) As a result, Abe had low self-esteem and was so desperate for popularity that he became president. Unless you want that kind of thing to happen to your child, you had better get the right kind of back-to-school supplies. (Barry, p. 65)

Groucho Marx used to kid about being inferior. He wrote a letter of resignation to the Friar's Club in Hollywood saying, "Please accept my resignation. I don't want to belong to any club that will accept me as a member."

You Are Not Worthy

Another form of feeling inferior can be aroused by the "you are not worthy" game.

A rather intimidating man who belonged to the church I served was interested in history and not much else. He was an officer in the U.S. Military and had a very enviable record both in the military and academia.

I went to their home for a short visit after becoming their pastor. As soon as I entered the house, the game of "you are not worthy" began. He had just finished a six hundred page book on some strange, far away province in China and wanted to know if I had yet read it.

"No," I said.

"Well," he responded, "I don't know how you can consider yourself to be an educated man if you haven't read this book!"

It worked. I felt totally intimidated. Suddenly many of the most painful memories of my childhood came rushing back. Perhaps I am not really worthy to be the pastor of this great church, I thought. He then mentioned three or four other books about strange, out of the way provinces, mostly in China, and found to his utter dismay that the new pastor had not read them either.

I then (out of spite, I think) mentioned four or five of the books that I had read recently, and had the gall to ask him if he had read any of them. "No," he said.

He got the point as I had grown tired of the bullying tactics. I suggested upon leaving that he stick to China and I would stay with the books on health, humor, and religion and we would then give each other a comprehensive exam. Surprisingly, he laughed and promptly invited me to become a member of his Rotary Club. We became good friends and I was just a little proud of myself for standing my ground. I grew a little that day.

Life is strange. Just when you think that you have finally arrived, someone pulls the rug out from under you, and you start over again. I'm learning that there are few plateaus, only mountains to be climbed.

In recent years, I have met a number of people who seem overly proud of their academic credentials and their career accomplishments. The games they sometimes play I recognize immediately. "You are not worthy" is one they also play all too often.

They mention to you the things that are of interest to them and then pass judgment on you—depending upon your verbal and emotional response. If you disagree with them, even for valid reasons, then you are reminded that you are not well-educated or lazy or even a few marbles short of a full bag. Trying to defend yourself with these people is useless. You lose, no matter what you do or say, unless you conform to their image and idea of what is important and what is not, and if you do "go along" you lose big time.

God help us to be kind but to gently disagree with any and all when it is timely to do so.

Humor, Heaven and Hell

A story is told about an old mountaineer who woke up dead. He was taken to a funeral home with no evidence of being alive. And yet there in the funeral home, he came to life and fully recovered. The reporters asked him how he knew he was still alive. He said, "Well, my feet were cold and I was hungry."

"How could you tell by that?"

"I figured if I were hungry I wouldn't be in heaven and if my feet were cold I wouldn't be in hell...So I must still be alive."

The Red Hat Society

It happened at our hospital in the lobby near our chaplain's office. I heard this rather boisterous bright happy laughter and went to the lobby to see. There were twenty to thirty beautiful ladies all decked out in spectacular lavender colored dresses and bright red hats. They were laughing and having a really good time.

When I stood before them, they looked at me. I held up my hand and they all listened as I said, "I'm the chaplain here…I don't know what you had to drink but I'd sure love to have some of it!" What a group!

Humor has been described as a "clash of values." It is saying the opposite of what is expected. It is often found in contrasts—doing or saying things that are unexpected—and at times joyfully preposterous.

Dr. Sigmund Freud recalled that humor is a sharp contrast to what is expected—a surprise. He then added, "We are so made that we can only derive enjoyment from a contrast…and very little enjoyment from the normal state of things."

One of the dullest evenings we can have is to sit around a dinner table and agree with everything that is discussed. Conformity leads to inertia and boredom—because no one is required to think. Humor shocks us into a fresh and exciting new reality. People who are laughing don't go to sleep while humor is in the air.

The packed audience who came to hear Mark Twain speak roared with laughter when, speaking about doctors and the medical profession, he said: "It's amazing how little harm doctors do when one considers all the opportunities they have."

Dr. Howard Bennett added a note of humor when he said, "A doctor is happy at least twice in his life: the day he hangs his diploma up and the day he takes it down."

Judy Gold wrote a funny quip after her visit to the Emergency Room in a southern hospital. She said, "There's no hurry down there. I saw a plaque over the door that read: Time heals all wounds."

An irate movie star said to his wife, "I'm going to fire our chauffeur. That's three times this week I've been in an accident with him driving and

I was nearly killed." His wife said, "Oh, honey, do give him one more chance."

Many writers and songwriters have written about humor. Irving Berlin sent a telegram to comedian Groucho Marx on his seventy-first birthday saying,

THE WORLD WOULD NOT BE IN SUCH A SNARL
HAD MARX BEEN GROUCHO INSTEAD OF KARL.

Even William Shakespeare would write on the value of a jester or jokester saying, "a {humorist's} success lies in the ear of him that hears it, never in the tongue of him that makes it."

Colette, the French novelist, wrote, "The total absence of humor renders life impossible."

W. Somerset Maugham, British novelist, said, "Impropriety is the soul of humor."

J. B. Priestly, another British novelist, added: "{Humor} comedy, we may say, is society's way of protecting itself..."

Will Rogers wrote, "Everything is funny as long as it's happening to somebody else."

◆   ◆   ◆

An older man in the retirement community went to see the doctor. After a careful examination, he said to the patient: "I want you to take two red tablets every morning with a glass of water, take two blue tablets at noon with a glass of water and two of these green tablets at night with a glass of water."

The patient asked, "Doc, exactly what is wrong with me."

"You're not drinking enough water," came the doctor's response.

♦   ♦   ♦

A man asked the pharmacist if he had a quick cure for hiccups. The pharmacist asked him to lean over the counter and proceeded to slap him briskly across his face.

Startled the customer asked, "Why on earth did you do that?"

"Well," said the pharmacist, "You don't have hiccups any more, do you?"

"No," said the man. "I never did but my wife out in the car still does."

♦   ♦   ♦

A patient in a hospital said to the doctor: "Doc, you say I have pneumonia but sometimes a patient gets treated for pneumonia but dies with something else."

"Relax," said the doctor to the nervous patient. "When I treat you for pneumonia, you die with pneumonia."

♦   ♦   ♦

Was It Albert Einstein?

There's a wonderful family called Stein.
There's Gert and there's Epp and there's Ein.
Gert's poems are bunk,
Epp's statues are junk,
And no one can understand Ein.

Someone asked, "Where does humor come from?" My response to him was Cleveland—no, I'm kidding. It comes from everywhere. Take for example Scott Adams who turns out cartoons and books. If you ever worked in an office or had a boss, you'll appreciate Scott Adams' new book, *The Joy of Work—Dilbert's Guide to Finding Happiness at the Expense of Your Co-Workers*. It was on the *New York Times* Bestseller List for months. I give you only a sample in a heading called "Being Funny Makes You Look Smart."

> It's an established fact that a good sense of humor is highly correlated with genius. I say this partly because I'm in the midst of writing a humor book and partly because when you say "it's an established fact," no one ever checks to see if it really is. Whether it's true or not makes no difference. All that matters is that people think humor is correlated with genius. Therefore, the more humor you bring to work, the smarter you look. In the business world, a false image of intelligence is a valuable asset for your career. In fact, fake intelligence is even more useful than real intelligence. People who are genuinely smart get peevish during meetings because they have the misfortune to understand what's going on. However, if you're only pretending to be smart, the pay is the same as if you actually are smart, and almost nothing can ruin your day.

For years, people have been reading the cartoon character called "Dilbert" created by Scott Adams. What many readers may not know is that Adams is also a prolific writer, and a master at tongue-in-cheek advice to employees. I loved his article called "Do Bad Work in Important-Sounding Fields."

> If your boss assigns you to something that won't help your resume, just ignore him and dive into a job that looks good on paper, no matter how unqualified you are. Your boss won't like it one bit, but remind him to be nice because someday he might be working for you, and he'd better not burn any bridges.... You're probably not planning to stay with your current company forever, so it really doesn't matter how often you blow things. If you don't quit after a few years, you'll be downsized in the next corporate merger anyway. So building a track record of success is a silly strategy for your career. (Adams, p. 25)

Since I work in a hospital, I am happy to know that people can sometimes have fun with the subjects of sickness and meeting one's maker. In fact, some of our big names come up with doozies—like this for example.

A star basketball player was heard to say, "I've never had major knee surgery on any other part of my body."

◆   ◆   ◆

A professional baseball team manager said, "Half this game is ninety percent mental."

◆   ◆   ◆

A young starlet said, "Whenever I watch T.V., I see those poor starving kids all over the world. I can't help but cry. I mean I'd love to be skinny like that, but not with all those flies and death and stuff."

◆   ◆   ◆

In a heated anti-smoking campaign, one young movie star said, "Smoking kills. If you're killed, you've lost a very important part of your life." Well, I would think so.

◆   ◆   ◆

Marion Barry, Mayor of Washington D.C., said, "Outside the killings, Washington has one of the lowest crime rates in the country." No wonder he was re-elected.

◆   ◆   ◆

This was attributed to Lyndon Johnson: "That lowdown scoundrel deserves to be kicked to death by a jackass, and I'm just the one to do it."

In fact, one of my favorite lines is definitely by Lyndon Johnson. He loved to drive fast. He went down to Texas during his presidency and was speeding around. A policeman stopped him and recognized him just as Johnson rolled down the window. The policeman said, "My God!" Johnson replied, "And don't you forget it!"

8

Old Age "Ain't" for Sissies

Another title for this chapter could have been "Courage" because that's what I'm going to tell you about. I'll tell you what I've found out about the courage of those who have lived a long time.

Officially, we now have a population of 286,000,000 people in America. Of that number, there are 35,000,000 of us who are 65 or older—about 20,000,000 women and about 15,000,000 men. There are 8,000,000 who are past 80 and 3,300,000 who are past 85 and we now have about 60,000 who are past 100.

Life expectancy in 1900 was 48. Today it is 76. Incredibly only 3% of these retirees are disabled. Another 2% are in and out of hospitals, but 95% of them can still get up in the morning, walk, talk, drive their cars and travel all over the world. In addition, according to the National Data Book, 112th edition of the statistical abstract, retirees own 65% of the nation's wealth.

In 2000, California had the most 65 plus residents (3.3 million) followed by New York (2.4 million) and Florida (2.3 million). Arizona, one of the fastest growing states in America, finished 23rd with only 550,000 retirees.

Ask these retirees about their keys to success and longevity and you're likely to hear them say: Find something to do; be positive and optimistic, and give yourself permission to laugh. I also read that this group of "older" Americans is the healthiest, wealthiest, and most active of any group who has ever lived. They are involved in everything. In the Sun Cities of Arizona, they are more active than ever. They serve on boards, they are volunteers, they play golf two, three, four times a week, go bowling, play tennis 'til after ninety years of age and go dancing with energy to spare.

We had an "older" member aged eighty-five who worked at our church fall rummage sale for ten full hours, moving heavy pieces of furniture and supervising a team of volunteers all day.

At day's end, he announced that he and his wife had to hurry home, take a bath and eat supper so they could get to the dance on time. I went home exhausted. The next morning, Wiff was back on the job at 6 am to help again with the rummage sale. Wow! He's no sissy.

What a story these seniors have to tell. Yes, they have problems. Yes, they lose their health, and yes, they die but they don't get old. Therein lies the difference. They are the most hopeful people I ever knew, and age has nothing to do with it. Consider Pauline. When I came to Sun City, she was eighty-two. Pauline became ill, desperately ill, not expected to live more than a day or two.

"If you ever want to see Pauline again," they said, "you'd better see her today…" I called to see if I could come by to pay my respects, say a prayer, and do a sort of "last rites" knowing she would not live.

And then the shocker! Pauline stated that yes, she had been at "death's door" and yes, I could come by for a visit, but would I mind terribly to wait four months until she got back from her world cruise? She and her daughter were leaving at 6 am the next morning to begin their cruise.

Incredibly she took the world cruise, came back home and lived another ten years. America's retirees are gutsy: they're no sissies!

Seniors can even look the end of life right in the face and laugh about it. Don Nelson told about an older lady named Mary Jones who went to the cemetery and asked to see her late husband's head stone. They looked everywhere for a George Jones, but in vain. Finally the caretaker said, "Madam, we don't seem to have a George Jones, but we do have two head stones marked "Mary Jones."

"Oh," she exclaimed, "I forgot…I had everything put in my name."

Consider the contributions of some of our older clergy, long past retirement age. A well-intentioned elderly priest and a pastor once responded to a community need. They were standing by the side of an old country road on a sharp curve holding a sign. Their sign said: "The end is near. Turn around now before it's too late."

A young motorist sped past and yelled at the clergy, "Leave us alone, you religious fanatics." Suddenly there was the screaming of brakes, a loud noise, and a big crash. Then, as a second car sped past, they yelled out the same abuse. "You religious nuts…" and then came the same screaming of brakes and the crash. Finally, the pastor said to the priest, "Father, don't you think we should just put up a sign that says: Stop now—bridge out."

The great thing is that it's the seniors who tell these stories on themselves. What about the lady and her husband who stormed into the office of a dentist? She said: "We're traveling through town…are in a hurry and I want this tooth pulled immediately…and I don't want any pain medication."

"Boy, I sure admire your courage," said the dentist. "Which tooth is it?"

The lady said, "Honey, show the dentist your tooth."

Then there was another elderly gentleman without a wife as a spokesperson who went to the dentist to have a tooth pulled. The patient yelled out, "You pulled the wrong tooth!"

"Relax" said the dentist. "I'm getting to it."

I live in a dynamic community where the average age of our 90,000 plus residents is near eighty. People ask me what it's like to live with so many "old people." I tell them we don't have "old" people and it's true. They are singularly the most active, vital, involved group of people I ever knew. As I said before, they die but they don't get old. One key to their vitality is that they are so positive about everything and they are busy and they have learned how to laugh.

They still talk about the retiree aged ninety-six who went into the ABC store and asked for a bottle of "Old Rabbit." "Don't have Old Rabbit…but I can give you a flask of Old Crow," stated the store clerk.

"Naw, I don't want to fly…I just want to hop around a little bit," said the old gentleman.

In one of Jack Canfield's remarkable books in the *Chicken Soup for the Soul* series, the author tells the humorous story of Walter Jones of Tacoma, Washington. Seems Walter was married to his first wife fifty plus years. She died and Walter remarried at seventy-five until his second wife died. Then at the age of ninety-five Walter met and married a beautiful young lady. Reporters asked him if he wasn't afraid something might happen at that age. He responded with tongue in cheek, "If she dies, she dies!"

I have loved my life in this retirement community. Someone will give you something funny to laugh about every single day, like the lady at the front desk in the hospital who said that she had finally learned how to have a satisfying marriage. "Tell us how," they said.

"Find a husband who has a little money and likes to travel. Find a man who will help you do a little work around the house, and then find a man who is...well...passionate...and make sure these three men don't know each other."

The people are hopeful, upbeat, joyful and they seem ready and willing to laugh. Perhaps that's why the average life expectancy in the three Sun City communities is about ten years longer than in other communities.

Someone told me about the two enthusiastic single ladies in Sun City who saw a new man in town. They greeted him warmly and said, "Hi, we haven't seen you here before."

"Well, I'm new in town."

"Well," the ladies said, "I'm Suzy and this is Lucy. What's your name?"

"Oh, I'm Bill," and added, "I'm from Missouri."

"Oh," they quizzed, "and what did you do in Missouri?"

"Well, I was in prison for 25 years," he said.

"And what were you in prison for?" the curious ladies asked.

"Well, I murdered my wife," he answered.

They intoned most hopefully, "Oh, you're single."

Of course, it's not only the oldest of the old who have a sense of humor. We can see it in the young old. President Ulysses S. Grant was on his way to a dinner in his honor in Washington and decided to walk. Dozens of people were invited, including a man who walked beside the president without knowing he was the president.

The man said to Grant, "I don't know why I'm going to the dinner to honor the president...I don't even like him."

The president responded: "Ah, those are my sentiments exactly."

Another young older senior was Frederick II, the long-tenured King of Prussia (now Germany). He held an official visit to a Berlin prison where

all the inmates took advantage of his presence by pleading their inno-
cence—except for one inmate. This young man readily admitted to King
Frederick that he was guilty of robbery and deserved his punishment.

The King ordered him to be released at once, saying he should not be
allowed to mingle with all those other upright inmates for fear that he
might corrupt them.

Even the author of the best-seller *Walden,* Henry David Thoreau, had a
sense of humor that came out in his writings.

His first book was *A Week on the Concord and Merrimack Rivers* and it
was a complete flop. A thousand books were printed but only 300 sold,
leaving 700 on the shelves of his own library. Not to be outdone by failure,
Thoreau wrote of this: "I now have in my library nearly 900 volumes, 700
of which I wrote myself."

It is an inspiration when anyone among us can turn failure into success,
just by the way they think. For example, "I did not burn the church
down...I only started the fire!"

Most of our retirees retain a lot of energy, enthusiasm, pride, and old-
fashioned zip despite the accumulation of years. I heard about one fellow
of 105 who was arrested and accused of taking advantage of a much
younger girl. When the old-timer was booked into court, the presiding
judge asked if he had anything to say.

"Yes" he responded haltingly. "At my current age, I just want to tell this
court what an honor it is to be accused!"

Humor in the Worst of Times

Probably no president in American history has used humor more often
and more effectively than did President Reagan. The stories that surround
his cheerful, outgoing countenance are myriad. The dozens of times that
he said or did something humorous are evidence of his deep belief that
humor really works.

Perhaps his most humorous line came after the assassination attempt.
The president, severely wounded, was told of the need to be hospitalized
and possibly to need surgery. With a big smile and a confident look,
Reagan said, "I sure hope the doctor is a Republican."

He used humor to communicate some of his most fundamental beliefs. He also found that wit, especially the self-deprecating kind, is a great way to open a speech or to get people to relax during a conversation.

His Secretary of Defense, Caspar Weinberger, stated once that Reagan's humor helped to produce some vital agreements that neither logic nor table-pounding could bring about. For example, he was opposed to government bureaucracies because once started, they are hard to stop. He said, "A government bureau is the nearest thing to eternal life we will ever see on this earth."

Perhaps President Reagan's finest humorous hour came in 1984 during the hot debates with Democratic presidential candidate Walter Mondale. Reporters asked the seventy-three-year old president whether he was too old to be president. He instantly retorted, "I will not make age an issue of this campaign. I am not going to exploit, for political purposes, my opponent's youth and inexperience."

Humor not only accounted for his popularity and high vote count, but probably accounted for a life that extended into his nineties, albeit with Alzheimer's disease.

The shocking French writer Anais Nin once said that we don't see things as they are but we see them as we are. Certainly, Reagan viewed the world through his own eyes, the eyes of a realist who believed that hope, attitude, and humor could change the nature of things. Some have called this hard-working son of a job-hopping alcoholic a near-genius. Perhaps what Thomas Alva Edison said of the word "genius" applies to Reagan: "Genius is one percent inspiration and ninety-nine percent perspiration."

Discipline, a positive attitude, enthusiasm, and a light touch defused explosive situations repeatedly for Reagan. Napoleon Hill once said that Americans are looking for a magic key that will unlock the door to the source of power, when all the while we hold the key in our hands. Ralph Waldo Emerson appreciated that as well when he said, "Every great and commanding moment in the annals of the world is the triumph of enthusiasm. Nothing great is ever achieved without it."

Some said of President Reagan that his optimism and his enlightened enthusiasm brought into being a whole new world of hope. One suspects that what worked for him could as well work for us. Let us give it a try.

Our venerable American entertainer, Bob Hope, said, "We don't stop laughing because we grow old; we grow old because we stop laughing."

It isn't the accumulation of the years that makes one old, but the loss of interest in the world around us. If only we could lighten up, find fun things to do and give ourselves permission to laugh—then we could be fit to live with.

Joel Harris, author of Uncle Remus stories and insightful tales of the South, expressed a delightful thought for older Americans. Speaking on the process of aging, Harris uttered this one-liner: "Yes, it's true I am now sixty-five and I am in the prime of my senility."

I like what Lady Astor, British socialite, said: "I simply refuse to admit that I am more than fifty-two even if that does make my sons illegitimate."

Speaking of growing older, consider Winston Churchill. He was already 65 when he became British Prime Minister. He used the power of words to motivate the British Empire to resist the Nazi onslaught, and with amazing success. He used the same articulate brilliance and humor to deal with his many detractors—including Lady Astor.

In fact, Lady Astor belonged to the opposition political party and hated Churchill with a passion. She tried desperately to humiliate and embarrass him as the circumstances allowed. Once at a cocktail party, Churchill had a bit too much to drink and Lady Astor reproached him with the words—"Sir, you are drunk and you're disgusting."

Churchill quickly retorted, "Lady Astor, you are ugly and tomorrow I will be sober but you will still be...

Okay, let's say it: "ugly."

Many will recall that President Herbert Hoover's image as president was damaged by the crisis of the Great Depression. I recall my own father's cutting comments about Hoover—and blaming everything that was wrong with America on the president. He was not a bad president. Over the years, I have come to realize that Hoover was a very competent leader, a brilliant thinker and a man who used humor to great advantage.

Hoover often had to sit at the head table for a banquet and had to listen to someone else give the message. Inevitably, if the speaker was dull or boring, Hoover would write out a note and hand it to the person seated next to the speaker. It said simply: "Your fly is open."

It always worked. The speaker stopped immediately and the president had a chance to take charge. Humor. It's everywhere if only we are on the lookout for it.

Mark Twain is considered by literary experts to be one of America's most gifted writers. His masterpieces *Huck Finn* and *Tom Sawyer* broke with established literary traditions. Doubtless, his command of the language, his gifted pen, and his quick witted responses made him a popular public figure and speaker.

Even at an advanced age, he never lost his sharpness of wit and speech.

In 1908, Twain had been lecturing in Boston. He took a train to his home…sat down beside a stranger and started to talk.

"I caught fifty pounds of rainbow trout," said Twain to the stranger.

"Well," responded the stranger, "and where are these trout?"

"Oh, I have them packed in ice in the back car," replied Twain.

"Do you know that fishing here is unlawful?" asked the stranger.

"Oh, no one will ever find out," said Twain, "and especially the game warden."

"Do you know who I am?" the man asked Twain.

"No," he said.

"Well, I am the game warden."

Silence engulfed the two men. A long pause and then from Twain: "And do you know who I am?" he asked.

"No."

"I am the biggest liar who ever lived…"

Humor. It's everywhere. We simply need to give ourselves permission to laugh…and little by little, our outlook and our health begin to improve. America's retirees: they're no sissies. How much humor they afford us.

An elderly lady had a date with an older gentleman. Her daughter called the next day and asked, "Mother, how was your date last night?"

"Honey," replied the mother, "I had to slap that old man three times."

"You mean he got fresh on the first date?" asked the daughter.

"No," said mom. "He kept going to sleep."

In addition, they are still talking about the problem some of us have with memory.

A man had a date with an older lady and called her the next day and said, "Lucy, I sure had a good time on our date last night."

"Yes, oh yes," she replied.

"We ate those steaks, drank the entire bottle of wine…, and talked of possibly getting married. Well, I'm calling today, Lucy, to ask if you will marry me."

Silence and then she said, "Well…who is this?"

Memory a problem? Yes, on occasion, but it certainly doesn't keep our retirees down. Confusion may occur, too, but that can often be laughed away.

A man burned his ear and went to see the doctor. The doctor asked "What happened?"

"I was ironing my shirt and the phone rang. Instead of picking up the phone, I picked up the iron."

"Yes, but you're burned on both ears," remarked the doctor.

"Well, they called back."

Sometimes the youngsters notice differences in retirees—whom they may mistakenly call retardees.

A granddaughter aged five was sitting in her grandpa's lap and noticed all the wrinkles on his face. She put her hands over his face as if to call attention to all the wrinkles. She asked, "Grandpa, did God make you?"

"Oh, yes," he responded, "God made everything."

Then she rubbed her own cheeks and his again, as if to compare them. She asked, "Grandpa, did God also make me?"

"Oh, yes," he replied.

"Well, Grandpa," she inquired, "Don't you think God is doing a better job now than what he used to do?"

Of course, seniors have to think about death and its consequences. For couples, there is always an inevitable question.

If I Die, Would You Remarry?

A wife said to her husband, "Honey, if I were to die, would you remarry?"

"Well, possibly," he responded.

"Would your new wife drive my car?"

"Well, possibly."

"Would she wear my diamond rings?"

"Well, maybe."

"Would she use my golf clubs?" she inquired.

Instantly he responded. "No, she's left-handed."

Sure, there are always guesses about what one spouse will do after the other dies. Guesses became known in the story of a couple, both sixty-five, when they celebrated their fortieth wedding anniversary. It happened also to be the birthdays for both husband and wife. It was so unusual, two birthdays and an anniversary on the same day. In fact, it was so unusual that a genie appeared and said, "You may each have one wish granted."

The excited sixty-five-year old wife said, "I'd like two tickets for a world cruise with my wonderful husband."

Swish. It was done and she held the tickets in her hand.

The sixty-five-year old husband said hesitantly, "May I be completely honest?"

"Yes," said the Genie.

"Well," he said, "I would like to be married to a woman thirty years younger than I."

"No problem," said the Genie. Swish! He was ninety-five.

I like what Lucille Ball said about aging: "The secret to staying young is to live honestly, eat slowly, and lie about your age."

Since I am a hospital chaplain, I know that the older you get, the more likely you are to spend some time in a hospital. Ah, the stories about hospitals will never end.

Once while convalescing in a hospital Dorothy Parker, renowned writer for the *New Yorker Magazine*, wanted to dictate some letters to her secretary without interruption. Therefore, she pressed the nurse's call button and wryly said to her secretary, "That should give us at least forty-five minutes of undisturbed privacy."

Increasingly I believe that humor is universal and it seems to matter little how rich or how poor people are. Despite trying to hide my own poverty in early years, I can make jokes about poverty. For example, a bedraggled street bum walked up to a well-dressed lady and said, "Ma'am, I haven't eaten anything in two days…"

"Wow!" she exclaimed. "I wish I had your will power."

In addition, I will not soon forget stopping at a small island in the great South Pacific Ocean. It was Moorea—situated little more than ten miles north and west of Tahiti, one of the many French Polynesian islands. Our four-hour inland journey in Moorea was aboard a four-wheel drive Land Rover that could comfortably seat four. However, the poor driver hoping for more income had seated six with uncomfortable squeezing. We six were traveling over the most rugged, dangerous paths, not really roads, that I ever saw. There were hairpin curves, treacherous thousand foot drop-offs, and jagged peaks all along the way. We were frightened.

We arrived at the "lookout" point totally exhausted by the ordeal. We were hot, sweaty, spent, and wanting intensely to get back on board ship. However, I still recall there atop the mountain, while stunned passengers stood trying to enjoy the view, three obviously dirt poor ATV drivers gathered to jabber with each other. Then this awakening. For some twenty minutes they laughed, shared their experiences and laughed some more, seeming to forget that they were lacking or needy. I left thinking about how up-tight and frightened I was—never laughing even once during the entire four-hour excursion. Perhaps it was not they who were desperately poor or needy but I. I shall not soon forget it. Humor is everywhere—even on a dangerous mountain road—if only we could relax and take it in.

When I think of that, I realize that optimism has more to do with humor than age. George Bernard Shaw was advanced in years when he spoke of humor and a positive countenance. He and others before him said, "Smile and the world smiles with you. Weep and you weep alone."

When humor and a positive countenance combine with a definite purpose in life, it becomes an unbeatable combination. Shaw also wrote that the true joy of life was being used for a purpose recognized by yourself as a mighty one instead of being consumed by grievances that the world will not devote itself to making you happy.

It's been about as hard to get humor into the courtroom where people argue over their grievances as it has to get humor into medicine and the ministry. However, we all know that serious issues can use some levity. Legal laughter may be the best of all. I'll pass along some things that have actually been heard in courtrooms.

Q. "The youngest son, the twenty-year old, how old is he?"

◆   ◆   ◆

Q. "Were you alone or by yourself?"

◆   ◆   ◆

Q. "Did he kill you?"

◆   ◆   ◆

Q. "How far apart were the vehicles at the time of the collision?"

◆   ◆   ◆

Q. "How many times have you committed suicide?"

◆   ◆   ◆

Q. "So the date of the baby's conception was August 8th?"
A. "Yes."
Q. "And what were you doing at that time?"

◆   ◆   ◆

Q. "You say the stairs went down to the basement?"

A. "Yes."

Q. "And these stairs. Did they go up also?"

◆   ◆   ◆

Q. "Can you describe the individual?"

A. "He was about medium height and had a beard."

Q. "Was this a male or a female?"

◆   ◆   ◆

Q. "Is your appearance here this morning pursuant to a deposition notice which I sent to your attorney?"

A. "No, this is how I dress when I go to work."

◆   ◆   ◆

Q. "You were not shot in the fracas?"

A. "No, I was shot midway between the fracas and the navel."

◆   ◆   ◆

Q. "Doctor, before you performed the autopsy, did you check for a pulse?"

A. "No."

Q. "Did you check for blood pressure?"

A. "No."

Q. "Did you check for breathing?"

A. "No."

Q. "So, then is it possible that the patient was alive when you began the autopsy?"

A. "No."

Q. "How can you be so sure, Doctor?"

A. "Because his brain was sitting on my desk in a jar."

Q. "But could the patient have been alive nevertheless?"

A. "It is possible that he could have been alive and practicing law somewhere."

◆   ◆   ◆

Now let me tell you about some more courageous people. Little did I know then in 1970 when we took our son to the Child Guidance Clinic in Winston-Salem, North Carolina, that that experience would, in time, unearth an almost unbelievable story about the lady who helped found these clinics nationwide.

Lillian J. Martin can teach us much about using our retirement for creativity and for fulfilling purposes. Lillian, like thousands of other sixty-five-year olds in San Francisco, retired. But then she launched into a career of such memorable adventures that retirement lecturers and after-dinner speakers often cite her as a one-of-a-kind senior citizen.

She had been a professor of psychology at Stanford University, but her academic career was colorless compared to what lay ahead. After sixty-five, she tried to enjoy the quiet fruits of retirement, but, rebelling at boredom and inactivity, she became convinced that retirees needed her challenges. She decided to set a personal example by packing her remaining days with useful effort and stimulating activity. And pack them she did.

- At sixty-eight, she became a consulting psychologist.

- At sixty-nine, she opened the nation's first Child Guidance Clinic for preschool children.

- At seventy-five, she and a friend took a trip around the world with leisurely stopovers in India, Japan, and Israel.

- At seventy-six, she bought an automobile and took driving lessons. Flunking the first examination, she passed the second and subsequently drove across the country four times.

- At seventy-eight, she opened the nation's first "Old Age Counseling Center" in San Francisco which became a kind of model for counseling centers for the elderly.

- At seventy-nine, Lillian took an extensive automobile trip through Mexico. The trip was packed with excitement and skirmishes including a robbery during which a bandit brandished a fifteen inch hatchet over her head.

- At eighty, she purchased a typewriter and taught herself to type.

- At eighty-one, Lillian took a tour through the Soviet Union traveling alone as the elderly friends who had promised to go with her backed out at the last minute.

- At eighty-two, she bought a seventy-eight-acre farm near Pleasanton, California, to do experiments with scientific farming methods.

- At eighty-six, she visited Guatemala and studied the fascinating Mayan ruins.

- At eighty-eight, she embarked on a twenty thousand-mile trip through South America using every mode of transportation from oxcart to four-wheelers to airplanes. She continued her lively pace for twenty-six years after her retirement.

- At ninety-one, she died.

Writer, columnist, and author Robert Peterson said Lillian's life should be an inspiration to all of us for she showed as few others have shown that the retirement years can be the most exciting and adventurous years of a person's life.

Old age "ain't" for sissies. Listen to Lillian's courage.

The Best Is Yet To Be

One Sunday I asked the congregation how many of them believed that the best of life is yet to be. They were asked to raise their hands. Almost all of the young people held their hands high, plus several middle-aged people. However, out of the hundred or so retirees present only one, a lady, raised her hand. Later I asked with interest why she had, at her advanced age, raised her hand.

She responded, "I raised it because you just never know when some good-looking younger man might come along and sweep me off my feet…I do live in hope."

However, the overwhelming number of responses from our older members was that the best of life is clearly behind us.

It need not be so…especially if you consider the amazing things that our retirees have accomplished after they turned sixty-five. Consider the far-reaching influence of Col. Harlan Sanders of Kentucky Fried Chicken fame.

It was my privilege to sit at table with him in San Juan, Puerto Rico, in 1965. It was an open-air sidewalk café at noon. The Colonel approached our table and sat down with my friend, Rev. Fred Warren, and me to talk.

He was at the time the most easily recognized person in America, and some said, in the world. He told us that he came home at sixty-five after his career retirement and said to his wife that he didn't feel his life had been very successful. His wife offered him little sympathy, saying to him that now, at last, he could do what he always wanted to do—cook chicken and wait on customers in a restaurant. That is exactly what he began to do.

In something like ten years, his new business ventures grew exponentially with hundreds of new restaurants opened all over the world. The Colonel lived well into his 90s and left behind a powerful testimony that the best of life just might be in front of us.

Think of Cornelius Vanderbilt who was a multimillionaire at age sixty-five. Nevertheless, he did not become a billionaire until after sixty-five. His enormous investment in the railroad business was to be his most successful venture ever—propelling him to a level of staggering wealth. However, it is not about money alone—nor even about money primarily—but about having an impact that will benefit other people. It's about doing something that matters, that seems to have been a driving force for them.

Clara Barton's life appeared to "take off" at age sixty-five, and she served as President of the Red Cross until she was eighty-three.

Evangeline Booth, free-spirited independent-thinking daughter of General William Booth, served as President and CEO of the Salvation Army's world-wide ministry until her eighty-second birthday.

Henry Lytton operated one of the nation's largest department stores until he was one hundred. And Winston Churchill became British Prime Minister at age sixty-five and again at age seventy-seven. He wrote his near-classic books on World War II and *The History of the English Speaking Peoples* late in life and won the Nobel Peace Prize for Literature when he was seventy-eight.

Paul von Hindenburg retired from the German army at sixty-four, but went back into service at sixty-seven when World War I began. Later he was president of Germany until his death in 1934 at age eighty-seven.

Arturo Toscanini conducted the New York Philharmonic Orchestra and the NBC Symphony Orchestra and other symphonies until his ninetieth birthday. Buckminster Fuller was writing with clarity, depth, and insight well past his eightieth birthday, and John D. Rockefeller ran his empire until his ninetieth birthday.

All these stories do not automatically suggest that you or I will, or can, reach such lofty heights, but they do suggest that age sixty-five is not the end, and that it is often the very best part of life. I choose to believe in tomorrow regardless of how old or how young I might happen to be.

In the last twenty years or so, a number of books have been written using the words "old age" and "sissies." In all the books that I have seen, retirees are funny, joyful, playful, healthy, and happy. In addition, when they are not totally healthy, they can still laugh about their plight. It's inspiring to be around them because they refuse to stay down very long.

One thing surfaces over and over again. America's healthiest retirees have learned how to laugh and how to accept whatever comes their way. Moreover, there are dozens of funny things that happen every day.

Different people have asked me what the funniest things I have read or heard were. I share a few of them with you.

An older lady (in Sun City, of course) was stopped for speeding. The officer asked to see her driver's license and she said, "I don't have one."

Shocked, the officer demanded, "May I see your registration?"

"I don't have one...and I hope you won't find a dead body in my trunk."

"A dead body in your trunk?" he said. "I'd better call for backup on this one." He called the sergeant.

The sergeant arrived and said, "I'll handle this…. I understand you don't have a driver's license…"

"Oh, it's right here, officer," she said.

"I understand you don't have a registration," he said.

"It's right here, officer."

"I understand you have a dead body in your trunk?"

He looked and then said, "There's no dead body in your trunk."

"What?" shouted the lady. "I bet that other officer also told you I was speeding."

◆   ◆   ◆

An elderly lady called the police to say that she was sick and tired of people speeding near her house located in a school zone. The next day she herself was stopped for speeding in the school zone. She protested, "But officer, I'm the lady who called to tell you."

"Well, Madam," said the officer, "you ought to be glad that we finally caught somebody."

◆   ◆   ◆

In Kansas City, friends there told me about the man and his wife who were stopped for speeding. The officer said, "You were doing eighty-five in a sixty-five speed zone."

"I was not," protested the man. His wife spoke up loud enough to be heard by the trooper.

"Honey, you know you were speeding…"

"Shut up," he said to his wife.

"Officer, my husband was driving close to one hundred miles per hour…"

"I told you to shut up and say nothing," demanded the husband.

"Madam, does your husband talk to you like that all the time?" the trooper inquired.

She responded, "Officer, only when he's drunk..."

◆   ◆   ◆

They tell a story in Phoenix of a man who bought a new Mercedes and was driving it at top speed on Interstate 17. He was stopped by a trooper who said, "You'd better have a good excuse for I clocked you at ninety miles per hour."

"Oh, I do," he said. "Last month my wife ran off with a state trooper and, well, I thought you were bringing her back."

◆   ◆   ◆

A story is told of an elderly Idaho potato farmer who wrote a letter to his son who was in jail. "Sure wish you were here, son, to plow up my garden. It's time to plant potatoes and I'm not able to do it."

Next day he got a letter from his son—away in jail. It said, "Dad, whatever you do, don't plow up the garden...That's where I buried the bodies."

The next morning the farmer was awakened by the police and the F.B.I., complete with a backhoe and tractor. They proceeded to plow up the entire garden—finding nothing.

Next day Dad got a letter from his son saying, "Dad, go ahead and plant your potatoes...That's the best I could do in my situation."

Sometimes we think more highly of ourselves than we ought to.

The phone rang at Dr. Johnson's house as he sat down with his family to have dinner. He answered the call, and then said, "Quick, get my medicine bag and keys. There's a young teenage boy who says he simply can't live without me."

"Daddy," said his teenage daughter, "I think that call was for me..."

So Much to Do—So Little Time

In many ways, Michelangelo was a genius. The world still marvels at his masterful hand-carved sculptures and his brilliant paintings. However, what many people do not realize is that his temperamental spirit kept him from doing far more than he did. He was so impulsive and hot-tempered that it took him years to complete the Sistine Chapel in the Vatican. At the least provocation, he would drop his brush and go to Florence until the Pope himself came to persuade him to return.

Most tourists to Italy have seen first hand his matchless mural of "Creation" in the Sistine Chapel and his statues of "Moses" and "David" and others.

However, some don't know that he left far more pieces of sculptures unfinished than those that he finished. In the new sacristy of Michelangelo in Florence, Italy, you may visit an entire hall filled with his unfinished sculptures.

Someone said, "There is all the time in the world to do what you have to do…but not one minute to waste." When you think of the impact of your own life, it might be well to reflect on the events of recent days or even years and reward yourself for all the positive things you have said and done. It might also be helpful to think of "works in progress" which could be completed by you while there is still time.

You might never become a Michelangelo or a Picasso or a Van Gogh, but you can still be yourself, which is the best gift of all. You can still give the gifts of friendship, of kindness, of a warm smile or handshake. You can give the gift of a positive word or experience. You can give the gift of a sincere compliment, or even share something funny.

Perhaps there will never be a way to evaluate the impact of your life on others. Nevertheless, one thing seems clear: when you give the best you have to other people, not even the angels in heaven could do it better.

Ralph Waldo Emerson once said that perhaps the saddest thing in this life would be not personal failure or the death of a loved one but to come to close one's life and discover that he had not lived at all.

There is all the time in the world to do what you should do…

Water Skiing Champion at 78

The hundreds of spectators at the Cypress Gardens gasp at the sight of a water-skier being yanked off a platform at forty miles per hour. Their gasps turn suddenly to smiles and then applause when they announce that this youthful athlete who is gliding across these pristine waters at Cypress Gardens is not only seventy-eight years old but he's doing it barefoot.

George Blair is a remarkable senior who doesn't know how to say "quit." His "feats with the feet" have landed him in the Guiness Book of World Records for having water-skied on all seven continents. In addition, as late as 1993, he was not only one of the star attractions at the Cypress Gardens Water Show, but he continued to ski every day, being pulled by a rope held between his teeth.

The story of this remarkable "Bonanza" George Blair is an inspiration to any and all sixty-five-year olds who have thought about calling it quits. George has at this point in his exciting life turned a near tragedy into a triumph for the human spirit.

He had a serious back injury earlier in his life which required a spinal fusion in 1955. He wore a brace from his waist to his arm pits. Once he saw people water-skiing and concluded that he ought to try it despite the restrictive back brace. He got a pair of water skis, started slowly, and went on to literally master the sport as a barefoot champ. The story of his amazing life may be found in the book by Roberta Sandler.

I recall another man named Dr. Stuart Struever. In 1968, he took a momentous drive from Northwestern University campus where he was professor of anthropology toward St. Louis where he was to give a lecture. For some reason, he got on the wrong road and got lost, but along the way, he made the greatest archaeological discovery in American history.

He saw a farmer shoveling dirt at a large mound. Dr. Struever stopped his car and began a conversation with the farmer. He noticed artifacts dug up by the farmer. It turned out to be a very old mound of Indian ruins dating back eight hundred years. He noticed the unearthed relics and recognized them as items of great worth—a treasure in a big pile of dirt—he thought.

So significant was this find that twenty years later some twenty-four buildings had to be constructed to house the ruins. The Koster site has become known all over America in its new location in Kampsville, Illinois. Dr. Struever said, "My whole life changed because I got off the main highway."

Whether one is looking for a happy spirit or for a closer walk with God or for a more positive attitude, it may mean getting off the beaten path. It's worth the effort. Treasures are all around us, but they do require a little digging.

I recall Dr. Robert Schuller addressing a group of clergy who came to see him at the Crystal Cathedral in Garden Grove, California. Among the many timely words of wisdom he gave us were these: "Inch by inch, anything's a cinch." He reminded us that Rome wasn't built in a day—and that the writing of the U.S. Constitution was a slow, painful process, often deadly dull, but with persistence, almost anything can be accomplished. Getting started, he said, is the pivotal key, and then he added: "Once begun, half done!"

I thought of the man who was one of the greatest baseball pitchers of all time. His name is Walter Johnson or "Big Train" Johnson. One day in 1920, he arrived at a ball park in Washington, D.C., complaining of a sore arm. The game he was scheduled to pitch that day was against the Boston Red Sox and it had great bearing on the pennant race. The bleachers and seats were filled to capacity.

Clark Griffith was the Washington Senators' manager. He knew that many in that vast crowd were visitors to Washington and had come specifically to see Johnson pitch. He didn't want to disappoint them. So he told "Big Train" to just go in and pitch the first inning and if the arm was any trouble, he'd be taken out.

Johnson pitched the first inning giving up no hits and sat down. Although his arm hurt some, he agreed to go back for the second inning, and then the third, and the fourth, and so on for the entire nine innings.

However, the remarkable thing is that while working with a sore arm, he pitched the only "no hitter" of his twenty year major league career—that included four hundred victories.

Take the gift you have and use a little discipline or tenacity or perseverance. You and those around you will be amazed by what you can do.
Handicaps very often serve to enhance our will and our ability to succeed.

The legendary NBA star, Wilt Chamberlain, came to the basketball
arena telling the coach he did not feel well. He would play only a minute
or two. That night he scored more than fifty points. Inch by inch, anything's a cinch.

Finding Meaning in Your Work and Life

President-elect John F. Kennedy called him to ask if he would take the job
as Undersecretary of State for his administration. He would be working
directly under the Secretary of State, Dean Rusk. His name was William J.
Crockett and when he placed a call to my home in Florida, I did not know
who he was.

He was at the time of his phone call to our home serving as the chairman of a Search and Call Committee to find a new senior pastor for the
Disciples Church in Sun City, Arizona. I was called to be the new pastor
there, and over the next five years met with Mr. Crockett on numerous
occasions to talk of the meaning of life, career, church, and family; and life
in Washington's "fast lane."

William Crockett was a supremely gifted leader, thinker, and writer and
as he told me over coffee one morning, "a pretty effective subordinate…"
He had the gifts to be mayor, governor or the head of any of our major
corporations—but always he refused to take the top job saying his gifts
were as a subordinate—serving the needs and wishes of the president, or
earlier, the CEOs. It is little wonder that his masterful book, *The Secrets of
a Dynamic Subordinate That Every Manager Should Know,* was used by cor-
porate managers and politicians alike as assigned reading for their staff
subordinates.

However, of all our long and sometimes deep communications, Bill
Crockett had a nagging feeling that his life had not added up to very
much. I was astounded.

He organized the presidents' trips out of the country and accompanied both Presidents Kennedy and Johnson on many trips aboard Air Force One.

He managed literally thousands of employees over the length of his governmental service. He was a masterful speaker who used humor to great advantage. He was a splendid writer and great organizer whose memory was uncanny.

How is it possible that someone, anyone, who has reached the lofty peaks of international acclaim in politics or business as well as making judgments that could affect the lives of thousands of employees, could possibly feel a sense of emptiness and uselessness toward the close of his life?

He was not without humor. His hearty laugh could be heard all across the room. His smile was warm and contagious. He was distinguished, proper, dignified, but so incredibly down to earth.

I mention his name in this book because he was one of the greatest churchmen I ever knew. I owe much to William Crockett for my confidence, courage, management style, and the staff management procedures that I developed.

Perhaps it was a problem, and still is, for people who have risen to the levels of greatness in their careers to know how to step down—to give it all up and start a whole new life in a new part of the world. How can we find meaning in retirement?

People desperately need to be needed. We have to have something meaningful to do with the rest of our lives. Let us assign ourselves to the task of finding creative and deeply fulfilling ways to use the skills and talents and sometimes genius that is readily available after we step down from our main career.

It can work; it must work. We are not permitted to squander brilliant minds and gifted leaders. Putting people on a symbolic shelf is, I think, tragic. People must be allowed to and encouraged to use all their talent and ability for as long as they choose.

We watched with delight, joy, and amazement at what one of those "elderly retirees" did aboard our cruise ship recently. One of our table dinner mates was a college professor, Bill, recently retired, who complained of headaches and high blood pressure. Our friend Roy, a physician and former Army surgeon under George Patton, and practicing dermatologist, was on alert. One evening at our dinner table, Professor Bill said he could not use his right hand. Dr. Roy suggested going to the ship's doctor but Bill would not agree. Dr. Roy indicated Bill might have had a stroke.

Next day the headache got worse. Dr. Roy, retired some twenty plus years, called the emergency room, and stated that he felt we had an emergency and requested a wheelchair. Roy looked like a doctor, spoke like a doctor, and acted like a doctor.

He accompanied Bill to the ship's hospital where Bill was kept overnight. Next day, when we docked in Osaka, Japan, Prof. Bill was taken to one of the hospitals in Osaka where it was determined that he had indeed had a stroke. Bill was treated by a fine Japanese neurologist (who spoke excellent English), and he was kept in the Osaka hospital for three weeks. He was finally flown back to his home in Pittsburgh, Pennsylvania, in an air ambulance and has made a remarkable recovery.

The upside of this episode is that Dr. Roy probably saved the life of one of our well-liked passengers and he himself came to life.

I wondered then, and I have wondered many times since, why isn't there a way for our gifted, skilled, and well-trained professionals to keep on keeping on—giving life and love and encouragement and leadership as long as they are able to respond.

Today I bless God for Undersecretary of State William J. Crockett and for the gifted and dedicated physician named Dr. Roy Averill. Don't hang up the shingle until you have to!

Use It, or Lose It

Someone said to me recently, "Good health is hard work." Yes, I thought, and if it came easy, everybody would be healthy. It is not an accident that on every sheet of medical "essentials" is the necessity of exercise. Muscles that aren't stretched and flexed on a regular basis will lose their strength. Brain cells that aren't used regularly lose their capacity to serve you. An older friend of ours tried to recall the name of the apartment complex where he once lived—but couldn't. He said he hadn't thought about the name, or used it in many months. Memory depends on continuous use of our minds. Use it or lose it.

Hard work? Yes. However, it is really a compliment that God left us with mountains to climb so that we might use every fiber of our being to achieve maximum health and vitality.

Dr. Allan A. Stockdale of Toledo, Ohio, was the featured commencement speaker at a high school graduation ceremony years ago in Toledo. Students still recall his stimulating message. One such student, the noted columnist Harold Hartley, recalled that Dr. Stockdale challenged the class to break away from a "getting by" mentality, urging them to use all the tools and gifts at their disposal to mold and shape their world and their life as well.

He added that it was the plan of God to leave the world unfinished. God could have finished it, but he didn't. He left the raw materials there to tease us and to tantalize us, to set us thinking, experimenting, risking and adventuring, thereby bringing us to life.

He said that the Eternal:

> Left the oil in the ground,
> The copper in the hills,
> The aluminum in the clay
> The electricity in the clouds and rivers
> The rivers unbridged
> The mountains untrailed
> The forests unfilled
> The cities unbuilt
> The music unsung and the
> Poetry undreamed.

God gave us the challenge of the raw materials, not the complacency of a finished product. He left us with plenty to do. What a blessing for our retirees.

Yes, good health is hard work but it is, in the final analysis, God's way of complimenting us by making us partners with him in creation. Struggles, yes. Down times, yes. Sorrow, setbacks, and disappointments—it is all part of the world we inherited. But let us work and laugh and love and thereby reach the loftiest heights possible, regardless of our age.

I was intrigued by a quote that came from the indefatigable Benjamin Franklin on the topic of negative and positive confessions. He wrote: "Let your discontents be your secret. If the world learns them, it will only despise you and (thereby) increase them."

Quite literally everyone has emotional and psychological sags—highs and lows. It's the common lot of all humanity. We all experience deep feelings of inadequacy and unworthiness, and become deeply disheartened. Perhaps it is well to remember that there would be no progress at all if everybody were completely satisfied with his job, his life, his family or performance. There is no such thing as perfection, but often our inadequacies are the things that propel us to new levels of achievement and who knows—even greatness.

The wish to be perfect is a powerful motivator. The 20th century probably did not know a more gifted pianist than Ignace Paderewski. Yet with all his greatness, he told a friend once that there had been only a few moments when he had known complete satisfaction, and had rarely been free from the disturbing realization that his playing might have been better.

9

Health and Humor Are Kissin' Cousins

Sir William Osler was Canada's best-known man of medicine during the whole of the twentieth century. He wrote many books including the acclaimed *The Principles and Practices of Medicine.* In America, he is best remembered for a speech he gave to the student body at Yale University called "A Way of Life," which is often given to medical school students upon their graduation.

Osler described to those students how the massive water-tight doors on an ocean liner worked to help keep the passengers safe and the ship afloat. He then drew a parallel saying that we too can touch a mental button and hear our own doors closing to shut out a crisis, or a failure, or a threat, or anything from our past that is too heavy a burden to carry.

Then in addition, we can, in a symbolic sense, close another water-tight door to an uncertain and threatening future. Then, said Dr. Osler, we are free for the living of this day. He added, "Yesterday's failures and pains and heartbreaks are far too heavy a load for us to carry into the dawning of a new day. Leave them behind…and walk away…"

Dr. Osler in essence coined the phrase "The future is now." So he said, Live today, fully, as completely as possible, and when tomorrow does come, there will be few regrets.

Robert Louis Stevenson understood this deep insight when he wrote in his classic novel *Treasure Island* that we can face almost any crisis and carry any load if we don't try to borrow tomorrow's burdens. He said that anyone can do his work, however tedious, for one day, and anyone can live sweetly, patiently, lovingly and purely until the sun goes down because that is all that life really demands.

Dr. Kabat Zinn published an amazing study which he did back in 1979. The article appears in the *Internal Medicine News,* June 2004, only a year ago under a broad heading of "Mindfulness Meditations."

Dr. Zinn uses deep breathing exercises and helps patients who are in pain to learn how to relax into their pain and try to become part of it. He stated that in his own research, these deep breathing exercises have reduced the mood disturbance by as much as sixty-five percent and the symptoms of stress reduced by thirty percent and there is a reduction in the so-called "killer cells" in the blood stream. There are, says Dr. Zinn, over 240 such programs now in existence.

Dr. Bert H. Singer did a study on negative and positive emotions as it relates to writing your life's experiences on a sheet of paper. It was done through the Institute of Aging at the University of Wisconsin.

A group of participants was asked to write for fifteen minutes on something in their life that had been frightening, and blood tests were run. He then asked the group to write for fifteen minutes on something joyful, positive, and happy, and did blood tests. To his great surprise, the blood tests from the joyful, positive image writings showed a dramatic improvement in the person's antibody response. Even if nothing else could be found about such an experiment, the positive mental exercise proved to be persuasive.

In another study done with college students, the professor gave a lecture with no "human interest" factors and nothing humorous or funny to test group A. He followed the lecture with a test and the scores were noted. With test group B, the identical lecture was given, but humorous anecdotes were added to it. The test results showed an average improvement of nearly twenty-five points total. The researchers concluded: not only is humor fun and pleasant, but it actually improves the memory in a classroom setting.

Many will recall the name of Dr. Patch Adams from the popular movie about his life released three years ago. It was he, perhaps more than that of any other medical professional, who added a touch of class and respectability to the use of humor in medical care.

Dr. Patch Adams, born 1945, attended George Washington University in Washington, D.C., for three years, then for two or three nights a week, he went to local taverns and bars to understand human behavior. "Why," he wanted to know, "do these people come here?"

He was accepted as a student at the Medical College of Virginia and for the next four years was angered when the medical school professors insisted that doctors keep their emotional distance from their patients.

No, he insisted, and began wearing a wacky colorful clown suit and a big red clown's nose which created a warm, positive response from patients, especially children. Incredibly, the most critically-ill patients laughed and began to feel better. In many cases, there was a significant improvement in the patient's health. However, for many of the terminally ill who knew they would not get well, there very often was a level of peace and acceptance not seen in other patients.

Dr. Adams told about one visit to a young girl with a large bony tumor on her face. She was obviously going to die. It had disfigured her to the level of the Elephant Man, in horrendous ugliness. He went in, talked to her, and found out her great sadness. It wasn't sadness about dying. It was sadness of why when her parents came to see her they did not stay very long, and why were they crying? Why didn't her friends visit her any more?

Then she asked Dr. Adams why it was so hard for people to look at her. She asked him, "What have I done?"

Well, he looked at this young girl and said, "We're gonna play. We're gonna have fun!" Moreover, he spent the rest of her life having fun with her. He told her about people who are serious and uncomfortable but explained that he was fun to be with and not afraid. He said that he just fits death into one of the many things that happen in life.

There were, and still are, a number of physicians who scoff at the idea of using "fun" or humor or laughter as part of the medical care given to a patient. However, Dr. Patch Adams says he's not running a popularity contest—that warmth, compassion, fun, personal attention and care are fundamental to the healing process.

In his most recent book, *House Calls: How We Can All Heal the World One Visit at a Time,* he suggests that everyone, including medical professionals and ordinary people alike, can be friendly to everyone. He said that friendliness creates the best atmosphere for healing and it feels good, too. He adds that much of what we call mental illness is really a consequence of our troubled society, one that promotes loneliness and conformity.

So deep has been his commitment to bring fun and humor to his medical care that he calls himself a clown who is a doctor.

His life has given rise to the advent of "humor carts" in many hospitals that are taken to patients who want to read humorous books or funny videos for those who want to watch something funny on their hospital TV sets.

As more studies are done on the effects of humor on a patient's health and attitude, it will almost certainly confirm that humor doesn't hurt anything and in many cases actually helps.

But, in fairness, it must be said that the so-called magical world of neuropeptides and endorphins has not created the "miracles" in health and in the healing process anticipated when they were first discovered.

One writer, Jim Parker, says the euphoria about the endorphins didn't last—in large part because researchers didn't really know what they were or how they worked. To further complicate the issue, there are now dozens of types of neuropeptides and more are being found every year. Still, Parker says these chemicals created by the body offer hope about their effect on one's health as future tests are conducted.

Neuropeptides were first discovered in 1975 by two researchers working in the field of drug addiction in Scotland. The existence of "receptor cells," part of an opiate-like substance, was found three years earlier in 1972 at Stanford University. The neuropeptides discovered by Drs. Kosterlitz and Hughes in Scotland was dubbed "enkephalin" (Greek: head) since they were apparently created by the tissue of the brain. While we maintain caution about their potential, we can be hopeful.

We've only Scratched the Surface

It is called by different names: alternative medicine, mind-body interactions, biofeedback, attitudes, and thought control.

So far-reaching is the mind's control over the body that Dr. John Basmajian at McMaster University in Canada made what some called an astounding discovery: that people can learn to control individual neurons and muscle cells that were thought previously to be beyond the control of the conscious mind. Conscious control of one's thoughts can and does regulate even the involuntary nervous system of the body, he found.

It is at least theoretically possible to control and thereby to regulate the neurological response heretofore thought to be beyond our control.

Blinking one's eyes may now be stopped or dramatically regulated by one's thoughts. Certain muscles of the body may now be moved by thought control.

The conclusions drawn from this largely theoretical experiment are far reaching and nothing short of staggering. It may in time come to mean that we can control the pain neurons and the pain centers and create relief well short of medications just by the way we think.

Jean Achterberg, Ph.D., was right on target when she stated almost matter-of-factly: "Those who think they will get better have a significantly greater recovery rate than those who think they will not get better, or think they will get worse."

The new world of positive imaging seems to be very powerful. It may be called by different names including visualization, positive imaging, and mind-body medicine. In case after case, it seems to be an effective treatment for certain types of physical disorders.

Out of my own life and experience, I recall a lovely lady who was found to have a large tumor in the abdominal tract. As I recall she had read about mental imaging and the impressive work being done by Carl Simonton, M.D. Peg's doctor insisted that he do surgery soon as he was concerned about the size of the tumor. Peg asked for two weeks, during which time she began a rather intensive four-times-a-day of mental therapy on the tumor.

She said to me with hope, "I began to see the tumor in my mind's eye…and began to talk to it the way you would talk to an offender." She told me she began to see the tumor getting smaller and smaller, and then telling it that it was dying and leaving her body. She said that at the end of the first week of these imaging exercises, she could tell by her comfort level that the tumor was smaller. She continued this self-treatment for a full two months. She went back to the physician for a report and was told there was no trace of the tumor in her body.

I saw her ten years later and she was still going strong. Does positive imaging work? I suggest you ask Peg.

Dr. Marc Barasch (in *Natural Health* 7-8, 1994) told an amazing story about a patient named Ted Lothammer who was told he didn't have long to live. Cancer had caused internal hemorrhaging and affected most of his body. The head of the Oncology Department told him he had less than four months to live. He was offered chemotherapy and told it might help him live up to a year. Ted said, "No" and then added: "You guys are wrong. I'm going to take care of myself."

Ted began an intensive program of visualization and positive mental imaging. The images he chose to use came from his childhood. He said that his house and the field around them had many very destructive brown-colored mice. The family saw these small brown creatures as the enemy but had no way to get rid of them. Ted said that he saw the cancer cells in his body as copies of those destructive brown mice, running everywhere out of control. But what to do?

One day his father did an amazing thing. He came home with two white mice and turned them loose in the house and yard. For whatever reason, the brown mice were frightened by the white mice and began to disappear. After only a few days, they were all gone. The white mice were treated as pets, fed and cared for, and the brown mice never returned.

Then Ted sat down, closed his eyes, and began to see in his mind the white mice chasing away the brown mice-like cancer cells. This he did over a period of several weeks. The bleeding stopped, the cancer disappeared, and literally years later Ted was still going strong.

Does this process of visualization and positive mental imaging work for everyone? Obviously, it does not. But is it worth a try? Is it worth a 30-day trial period? Yes, precisely because many people are helped. And it just could mean that your own health could be helped dramatically by such an exercise.

For several years now, I have been giving talks on health and humor in the greater Phoenix area. At first, there was one talk, then a second and then a third given now some 75 times in the past three years. What I have learned is that people have a genuine interest in humor, and especially how humor actually might make them healthier and give them a brighter outlook on the future.

I myself was intrigued by the thought: can my health be affected by my ability to laugh? The thought served as sufficient motivation to send me to the medical library at the hospital and to the public library in Sun City West, Arizona. What I discovered about the powerful effects of humor on health captivated my thoughts, my feelings, and much of my time in the weeks that followed.

About a year after I began speaking publicly on the positive effects of humor, I received an invitation. It was the Development Office wanting to know if I could prepare a two-hour lecture to give to the staff and employees at the hospital. I agreed to give the lectures in the summer and fall of 2004 and set about to learn everything I could about the topic.

What I began to discover was that the healing we all seek was not limited to humor or laughter alone but to anything that was essentially positive: attitude, thoughts, speech patterns, feelings and actions. Perhaps the greatest discovery was how powerful our words are. I began to learn that what we confess is what we possess—confession creates possession. That was what Norman Cousins also discovered in his recovery from the collagen disease thirty-five plus years ago. That was what Norman Vincent Peale discovered nearly seventy years ago.

We can't always control our feelings or even our thoughts, I reasoned. However, I can control what words come out of my mouth, the words I choose to speak. I may think that this is a dark, gloomy, miserable day but

I don't say that. What I try to say is: "This is the day that the Lord has made, let us rejoice and be glad in it."

I wanted, repeatedly, to say, "I am feeling rotten, gloomy, down and out, and depressed." What I said was things like, "I am beginning to feel better. It's going to be a better day. Life is a gift from God. Life can be beautiful. My life can be beautiful."

Someone said, "But isn't that burying your head in the sand? Isn't that lying to yourself?"

Well, maybe. Yes, but our body reacts as much to our actions and words as to our thoughts and attitudes. If I say positive upbeat words, in time I will come to feel them, and in time, to believe them. Confessing them helps me to possess them! I somehow knew that this was true.

Doctors Lee Berk and David Felton said, "Positive words like hope, joy, love, faith, grace and laughter have a benevolent effect upon one's emotions and are decidedly regenerative."

I knew somehow that a negative attitude could be changed into something positive and that it could begin with the words I speak. Healing, I believed, takes place as we move from negative words to positive thoughts and attitudes. I recall a quote by Dr. James Gordon who said, "Virtually every chronic illness is affected by one's attitude. Positive people are less likely to get sick and they suffer less and actually live longer than persons who are overly fearful and negative."

It was the same findings that Dr. Candace Pert found in her research at Rutgers University twenty years ago: "Feelings of pleasure, joy (laughter) start a positive feedback cycle so that good health and positive feelings lead to increased good health."

The problem I found with most of us is that we quit trying something new when it does not bring us instant relief or gratification. We should consider that most of our illnesses have evolved over many months and in some cases over many years. It will take some time for the new world of positive affirmation to do its work in the body.

Someone said to me after a talk I had given, "Chaplain, even if none of this positive stuff actually worked, it would make you feel better just by doing it."

I thought to myself. "There is a man who has learned an important lesson about successful living."

He then volunteered that he had had radical cancer surgery with very little chance to live more than a year. He smiled and added, "That was five years ago and I am still going strong."

What we must guard against is giving the impression that humor, laughter or positive thoughts, attitudes, or words alone will make people well, or take the place of established medical practices. At best this new world of joy, humor and positive thinking can only supplement, never replace, our normal medical care. This relatively new world is becoming an important part of the alternative medical approach that factor in Mind-body practices. If they didn't help at least a little, people wouldn't use them.

When Pessimism Becomes a Good Thing

I have been around people who come across as genuine pessimists. They are hard to be with. They seem to be cautious, fearful, and negative about everything. If they won the lottery, they would only complain about having to pay the taxes. If the doctor finds a tiny spot on their hand, they assume that it is a terminal illness. They are not unlike the hypochondriac who had engraved on his tombstone, "I told you I was sick."

We rarely know why pessimists get to be the way they are. Doubtless, it is a combination of factors such as a poverty background, constant put-downs as a child, unhealthy pressure to "succeed," or a dozen or so other causative factors.

Nevertheless, the truth is that they are hard to live with and just as hard to be around. One man we knew complained about everything. He had money, health, a beautiful home, a loving and devoted wife, but nothing made him happy.

It was either too hot or too cold. The music at church was too loud, the lights too bright, the sermon rotten, the soloist bad—really bad.

One might ask how anything good or helpful or lasting comes out of this type of negative behavior. Yet it does. Here is a case in point.

One night, years ago, we went to a very busy restaurant for dinner. We went there with a couple we had met a year or so before. We were told we had a thirty-minute wait to get a seat. My friend went into a furious rage at the inconvenience. He yelled, shook his fist, and waved his arms. I was embarrassed for his wife and for mine. I walked away, both to protect and distance myself from his rantings.

I began talking to three ladies who were also waiting for a table. I happened upon an idea. I was the chairman of a new speaker's bureau designed to raise money for our Alzheimer's Research Center in the Sun Cities. We needed $1,000,000 quickly to get the project of construction underway. So I jokingly said to the ladies, "You don't know where I can get 1,000,000 dollars tonight, do you?"

They laughed heartily. "Sure," said one. "I think I have that much in change in my purse..."

Another lady asked, "And why do you need $1,000,000?"

I said, "We are trying to build a new Alzheimer's Research Center to help find a cure for this awful disease."

The third lady spoke up and said, "Oh, my husband has Alzheimer's. Can you come to our church and give a talk on the project? I know some people who, I believe, can help."

That chance encounter in the lobby of the old Lalo's Restaurant resulted not only in a large monetary gift, but several ladies who took an active role as volunteers in our work.

I returned to be with Fred and his wife and found him still ranting and raving about having to wait.

However, the really good news about people who seemed to be negative by birth is that they can change. That is the best news of all.

Taking control of your thoughts, and especially your attitude, giving yourself permission to laugh, are key tools to use in moving toward health.

I was intrigued recently to discover that humor may affect, for good, even the sugar levels in our body. If you are diabetic, this study will have great appeal.

The American Diabetes Association reported on a study of nineteen Japanese patients—all diabetic. The study indicated what researchers have thought for years: negative emotions, thoughts, and feelings such as fear, anxiety, and prolonged sorrow elevate the blood glucose levels in one's body. Now, conversely, the recent study of sixteen men and three women found that positive emotions, attitudes and thoughts, and especially laughter, modify the levels of glucose by accelerating the body's muscle actions and lowering blood sugar.

In the group of nineteen diabetic patients, there was a measurable change for the better in the glucose levels after they watched a funny movie called "Manzai," according to an article in *Diabetes Care*, May 2003, V. 26, p. 1651 (2).

We are familiar with life's so-called "essentials": exercise, good diet, regular medical checkups, enough rest (sleep); but what about doing an experiment with laughter and humor? Why not find the books or magazines or tapes or DVDs that are genuinely funny and for a period of thirty days, let humor do its work? If I were a gambler, I would wager that the result of thirty days of laughter would put you firmly on a road that leads to health, plus your wife or husband will suddenly stop nagging you for they will be paralyzed by your new happy persona.

There is now almost universal agreement among researchers and health care professionals that the way we think has a profound impact upon the body. People who are negative, fearful, cautious, what some researchers call a pessimist, too often don't live as long nor are they as healthy as persons whose outlook is hopeful, cheerful and positive. These "optimists" have fewer problems at work, less pain and fewer limitations, increased energy, are calmer, happier and more at peace.

Psychiatrist Dr. Tashihiko Maruta found at the Mayo Clinic in Rochester, Minnesota, that the mind and body of a person are so interrelated that one's attitude has a profound impact on life itself. That is to say, whether a person lives or dies may sometimes be decided by that person's attitude. This was reported in the "Mayo Clinic Proceedings" published in August 2002 in *Mayo Clinic Health Information*.

Who Ever Heard of Dysthymia?

Well, not I. Have you heard of this word? These people, say the researchers, have every reason to be happy. They have money, health, nice homes, cars, family, and friends who seem to care for them. In other words, there is no loss or reverse of fortunes or starting point for their unhappiness and yet they still feel sad and dissatisfied, and may be classified as having a type of depression known as dysthymia.

Doctors are telling us that this particular disorder is less severe than a major depression but is every bit as continuous. Patients with dysthymia have symptoms like irritability, restlessness, sluggishness, and sleeplessness. It may last as long as five years but incredibly eighty percent of all patients with dysthymia improve dramatically after treatment according to the *American Journal of Psychiatry*, March 2001.

The opiate-like substances mentioned earlier called "endorphins" which are created when we are positive or when we laugh, get into the blood stream and reduce stress, lower anxiety and help lift a depressed spirit.

If eighty percent of the depressed or even mildly depressed people in America can actually feel better through positive thoughts and actions, then it ought to be worth a try. In addition, humor, ah yes, it just might be the best creator of endorphins of all.

The power of the mind to create health is getting stronger support from people inside the medical community. One recent study dealt with meditation, positive affirmation, and visualizations. The study was done by Leo Stalbach, M.D., then at Boston's Beth Israel Hospital, but more recently at St. Vincent's Hospital in Worcester, Massachusetts.

Dr. Stalbach had a packed audience of doctors, nurses, and health professionals as he showed pictures on an enlarged screen. The pictures were of lymphocytes moving like soldiers toward threatening cancer cells and then battering themselves against the walls of cancer cells. Members of the class watched in amazement as large numbers of these lymphocytes joined themselves together like a unit of soldiers in battle, attacked and destroyed the colony of cancer cells.

Patients with known cancer cells were encouraged to visualize the powerful healthy cells attacking cancer cells in their own body.

Dr. Stalbach stated that positive mental images that some patients had used with good results included blue birds in a cherry tree. The patient visualized the birds eating up the wrinkled, shriveled old cherries, (cancer cells) thus rendering them powerless.

Another patient sees a knight in shining armor hunting for armadillos (cancer cells). The knights come back from the visualized battle carrying hundreds of dead armadillos.

One patient who used the knight visualizations had pancreatic cancer and had become severely depressed. His doctor indicated to the patient's family that his death seemed imminent.

Then began the intensive sessions of visualization where the patient could see in his mind strong, bold knights with sharp metal spears destroying all the threatening cancer cells. The patient's depression began to lift and at the end of one therapeutic session, he announced that there were no more armadillos to be destroyed.

A computerized tomography scan showed that the cancerous tumor had disappeared.

"Humor as Medicine"

That title was catching to say the least, when I first read it nearly two years ago. It was written by Dr. Marguerite Guzman Bouvard, Resident Scholar at Brandeis University in Waltham, Massachusetts. She described how she had been trying to cope with three debilitating chronic illnesses: cystitis, fibromyalgia, and chronic fatigue. She describes the emotional burdens of her illnesses and said that they were more draining than the physical symptoms.

Once while waiting for a prescription she picked up a copy of *Mad Magazine* and began to read. That particular issue dealt with Moses who was dressed like a hippie and doing a boogie. She wrote, "Before I knew it, my dark mood lifted and I began giggling. That something so simple could make such a difference in how I was feeling was a revelation to me."

Dr. Bouvard discovered that laughter lifted her spirits. She tells how reading two funny books by southern writer Florence King left her laughing. One book is "WASP {White Anglo-Saxon Protestant}, Where Is Thy Sting?" and the other is "As Ye Roe So Shall Ye Wade."

She did research and found that in numerous European countries and in countries related to oppressive political regimes that it was the therapy of laughter that kept the common people going when little hope was left. She concluded that humor has a way of "surviving appalling circumstances."

In one scandalously funny quote, Bouvard told of reading what the Russian politburo said citizens should do to protect themselves in the event of a nuclear attack: "Cover yourself with a sheet and try to crawl to the nearest cemetery. Crawl slowly so as not to create panic." Now, that's funny.

My colleague, psychologist Diane Holloway, attended a psychiatric conference in Eastern Europe before communism was dismantled. Mental illness wasn't treated with psychiatry, psychology, and religion (self-searching and faith) because they were inconsistent with communism. The treatments were medicine, hydrotherapy (like Jacuzzi baths), music, art, physical exercises, and reading. She assumed that reading was to gain insight into one's condition, until she heard laughter coming from the library. Yep, the cure was humorous writings.

Laughter Even in Far Away China

They say that Hong Kong is not typically Chinese and I suspect that "they" are right. It is not like Beijing or Nanjing or any of the other major cities of China. However, don't tell my wife that it is not the real thing. I say this because we ate lunch at the world famous Jade Garden restaurant and were surrounded by nearly three hundred Chinese people who had also decided to dine there.

The Jade Garden is one of the most beautiful restaurants I ever saw. We "dined" there for the better part of two hours on two consecutive days. We were given no fork or knife, no napkin or water to drink. What we were given, along with the other customers, were genuine Chinese chopsticks—and one spoon.

The setting was magical; the food superb; the service, without flaw. Nevertheless, what I remember about this fascinating place was the laughter that came from all the people around us. Here we were in this far-away place and what surfaces is laughter. At one table, we saw a mother, father and four children—all sharing humorous experiences of their lives. At another table, there was what looked like a manager and four or five employees—all smiling, talking, and laughing.

Janet said to me, "I bet they are laughing at those two silly Americans trying to eat vegetables with that spoon." I still don't know how they can break long asparagus spears in half and eat them with two sticks.

I had seen this same joyful, happy, even hilarious response in the South Pacific among the drivers of those four-wheelers that took us to the very top of the mountain peaks only a month before. Now we were in China at noon, enjoying a splendid meal, and the primary feature was that these people had learned how to enjoy life. It was a happy moment for us and it seemed to validate the fact that humor is universal. It makes you feel good. In addition, it may very well be the "medicine for the soul."

Researchers at the University of Wisconsin found that activating the sections of the brain associated with negative emotions weakened a person's immune system in its response to a flu vaccine.

So excited were some researchers that Richard Davidson at the Laboratory for Affective Neuroscience said that, "It was the first time the brain had been brought into the picture to validate such a thought." (Good, 2003)

10

Being Poor Is Not a Disease

I love the opening lines spoken by Steve Martin in the movie *The Jerk*. "I was born a poor black boy in the deep south." Well, obviously, Steve Martin wasn't born poor, black or southern, but I was two out of those three. We were so poor we used to brag about it—a sort of humorous competition—I bet you can't beat this one.

It's especially true today. When I go back to eastern North Carolina to attend my high school reunions, we spend half the night bragging about how poor we used to be.

I recall going to school in the dead of winter wearing shoes with the soles completely worn through. I recall cutting out a piece of cardboard and fitting it snugly into the shoe, and hoping no one noticed.

And socks with holes in them. I have no memory of ever having new socks when I was a child—only socks with holes. Once in the eighth grade, I wised up. I discovered that if I turned the socks around and put the heel on top, the hole wouldn't show. That reminds me of Oprah Winfrey's line about her poverty: "I still have my feet on the ground, I just wear better shoes."

However, an eighth grader is supremely self conscious, and this plan worked only until one day when I got caught by a cute girl I liked a lot. I'll call her Nola. She announced to the whole class that Donald Gene Farrior had a big hole in his socks and turned them around so no one could see.

Boy, that hurt—and that was suddenly the end of any romantic thoughts I ever had of her. I was later to learn that it was Janet, not Nola or Pat or Joy or Jacque or anyone else, who would share my life.

We were share croppers in the little farm community of Richlands, North Carolina. No one in today's world is likely to believe it, but my father never earned $1,000 for a year's work. Fact is, he never earned $500 for a year's pay. Yet somehow, we survived. How we survived is still a deep mystery.

Perhaps it was the bartering that my father used—a sort of "this for that." I recall Daddy would work all day—got no money—but brought home a side of beef or two or three large hams in exchange for his work. It was enough to last several days—especially when the hams were smoked and salted down. Ah, memories. Today sixty years later, I still recall sitting down at the table with ten other people to eat fried country ham and grits and red-eye gravy. Those Yankees just don't know what they missed out on.

Nine children—that's what we had—plus Mama and Daddy and less than $500 a year. Survival in those days was simply a gift from God.

I recall Kathryn Kuhlmann describing her childhood in the tiny town of Concordia, Missouri. She was sort of an evangelist who was also blessed with the gift of healing. She spoke to some of the largest crowds ever to assemble at any healing service. I was on stage with her—along with fifteen thousand other worshipers in Chicago. She called out healings that were taking place as she delivered the message. Dozens of people were healed—and many of the healings were later validated by physicians. She was one of the two or three most famous preachers in American history.

I wondered about her past—and she told us. She said she was plain, red-headed, freckle-faced, and skinny—with protruding bone structure. She said she knew that she was plain and poor and had nothing except the love of God.

She added, "One day I prayed to God—Oh, God, I am nothing, I have nothing, no beauty, no money, no nothing..." Then she added, "Oh, God, can you use nothing? If so, I give you nothing." And God took that nothing and made something. Her rise to greatness is purely and simply the work of the Holy Spirit.

Repeatedly in our little communities, we see how God takes nothing and makes something. It was true of Harry Truman. It was true of Dwight Eisenhower. It was true of Oprah Winfrey—and it may be true of you. We take what we have, including our abject poverty, and give it to God.

It was true of me. I had nothing—nothing—but pride and a strong faith in a living God and a sense of humor. Above all that, I had a mother and I had an older brother and sister who believed in me when I couldn't believe in myself. Year after year, my brother and sister would come back from Indiana to spend two weeks with the family. Always they talked about my going to college—getting an education…and it happened just as they described.

My mother said to me on numerous occasions, "Son, it's no shame to be poor…" Once she coined the phrase, "Being poor is not a disease."

Early on, our family goal and my personal goal was not so much to be rich or famous—and not even to escape poverty. I think my goal was to be the best that I could be and to walk close to God wherever He might lead.

In the end, what matters in this life is not where you have been, but where you're going. Poverty and being poor is not a disease. You can and you will overcome the painful past if you choose to make it so.

Time and again young men and women break the bonds of poverty and narrow provincialism, when and only when they have a mentor, a sort of older "brother" or older "sister" who believes in them when they can't believe in themselves.

It can be a member of the family. It can be a pastor, rabbi, priest, teacher, or professor. Young people move to higher levels of achievement, when and only when there is someone to encourage them and to help them.

For me it was my mother, and then my brother, Lester, and my sister, Nan. Then along came this "blue-eyed blonde" who saw something I could not see. Then Janet's parents were there to offer whatever support we needed but never more.

In the final analysis, a mentor or a helper or encourager is one who enables you to use your God-given abilities and talents. They don't do the work for you, but they provide the inspiration and motivation for you to do it yourself.

But if I have been able to touch other lives at all, it was a gift from God.

Was I determined? Yes. Was I disciplined? Yes. Was I hardworking? Yes. Was I proud? Yes—but with all that it was the guiding hand of the Spirit that helped me "launch out into the deep."

Strange as it might sound, being poor turned out to be a blessing in disguise. Like thousands of other Americans who were able to turn their poverty into a motivational force, I never shirked from hard work. Our entire family were strangers to the "something for nothing" philosophy. We never expected handouts or "freebies" but only what we worked to achieve.

In 1956 when I began my college career at Butler University in Indianapolis, we called it "burning the midnight oil." I recall seeing the future once. I was seated at the Hinkle Field House at Butler University along with two thousand other entering freshmen. We were at orientation. The Dean of the University welcomed us and then did a memorable thing. He had us each shake hands with the person to our right then to our left. "Tell them," he said, "Goodbye...You will be missed..., but I'm here to graduate in four years..."

It worked. Over literally hundreds of nights, I sat up to read and write my papers, fully conscious of those words—"Tell them all goodbye...They won't be here on graduation day...but you will be."

I never forgot it. Moreover, I never gave up. I saw myself wearing a blue robe in the graduates' processional line, diploma in hand, and a firm handshake from the president of the university. He said to me, "Well done, Donald...well done."

Looking back, I don't know how I did it. During my first three years of college work, taking sixteen hours each semester, I worked at Bob's Marathon in Broad Ripple pumping gas from fifty to sixty hours a week.

I don't know if you have ever wanted something so badly that you were willing to pay any price to get it. That's where I was.

Some will say I was trying to escape my poverty background. That may well be true. When I returned to my home in North Carolina, people said that I thought I was better than they, that I was "uppity" and "high falutin'" and arrogant. Well, I didn't mean to be but I wanted all the education and formal training that I could get. I guess I thought that was the way to escape poverty. In addition, most importantly, I wanted somehow to talk with other people about the love of God.

If arrogance or over-confidence showed itself in my life, it was never intentional. I have identified with the characters in *Les Miserables*, the truly poor of the earth, and have tried to be as generous as could be.

We just returned from a world cruise—a 110-day venture abroad, stopping at 34 ports in 23 different countries. Repeatedly we were greeted both by merchants plying their trade as well as children with their hands out—all desperately poor. Our guide told us that if we helped even one we would soon be overwhelmed with dozens of other children and many of the very poor adults. There were reports of pushing and shoving and grabbing and pick-pocketing that sometimes left the passengers wounded, injured, lying on the ground with all their money gone—and their passports missing.

Handouts did not seem to be the answer. We had given generously to help these and other poor people but always through humanitarian agencies like the Salvation Army and the compassionate arms of our church.

A trip of any kind, and especially a world cruise, awakens one to the depths of despair, hunger, poverty, and blinding ignorance that is present in numerous countries of the world today. As painful as it is not to hand out money to each of them standing in line, in the long run it is far more effective to go through reliable agencies where the help is truly given to those in need. Helping them to help themselves is better than continuous handouts—as necessary as what those might be.

For any among us who want to break with the cycle of ignorance, hunger, or even poverty, one thing became abundantly clear. You will be criticized repeatedly, criticized by well-intentioned people who simply don't understand or who may be threatened or even jealous of your dreams and your course of action. My own response to all has been to be as kind as I know how to be. However, if you wait to get a majority vote on pursuing your dreams, you may wait a very long time.

Listen to your critics and detractors and even thank them when appropriate, but keep your own dream alive. It is, after all, your life that you are living and not theirs.

I do not speak of my own poverty background with any sense of braggadocio. There is a fatal flaw in being proud. It is, after all, one of the seven deadly sins. Yes, I had heard Dr. Ronald Osborn, professor of church history at our graduate school, tell us about the fifth century saint, Augustine of Hippo. In his *Confessions,* he goes to great length to tell of his "carnal" sins. He berates and chastises himself until, as Dr. Osborn said, "He seems to be bragging about all his sins…so we don't know if he is confessing or bragging or both."

Perhaps there is an element of truth both in what was said of St. Augustine and of what might be said of those who lived through poverty. One thing seems clear—whether bragging or confessing, one is not likely soon to forget it.

Ten cents. That's what it cost to buy a hot lunch at our school cafeteria. But ten cents was a lot of money for some people. We had nothing. In all those early years, grades one through six, I remember eating in the school cafeteria only two times. Somewhere along the way, I found a dime or was given a dime.

It is hard to describe the feeling of ecstasy I had inside of me, standing in line for lunch with my buddies and friends. I felt rich, resplendent in extravagance. I still recall the feeling. It was glorious. I recall wanting desperately to find ten cents so I could have a hot lunch each day.

However, it was not to be. What I had for the better part of six years was two molasses biscuits wrapped in a brown paper bag, and often sitting down alone, alone where I had to hide my shame for being so poor, and eating them quickly and then hiding the paper bag. Molasses biscuits. It wasn't much but it was all we had.

Some of my classmates said, "Back in those days, we didn't know we were poor." Well, maybe. Nevertheless, I knew it and it hurt deeply, profoundly, and the thought of all that still hurts fifty or sixty years later.

If there is now any sense of pride about it, then so be it. I would never wish upon any other human being those feelings and experiences. Yes, I am glad they happened to me, but no, I would not want to go through that again.

I am very hesitant to share the following information with anyone but perhaps it can help some other person—especially young people who may face the same circumstances as I. It will take a page or two to tell the story.

Poverty leaves deep scars on many people. It was especially true for me. Part of it was a social or societal consciousness that existed in our little town. There was, in those days, a system of rigid social stratification. Growing up as I did as a part of the poverty group I never felt that I quite measured up to those who were in the privileged group. We had the "haves" and the "have nots" and it seemed, in those days, almost impossible for the poor of our town to have any deep social interaction with the privileged.

The effect of that status-consciousness had a profound influence on me. Though it went against my own cultural background, I began to force myself to act as though I were a part of the "haves." There began a pattern of self-destructive behavior that has taken me close to fifty years to overcome.

I pretended to have money—though desperately poor and often hungry. I pretended that I was not hungry. Once, our school chartered a bus to take students to the State Fair in Raleigh. For the all day trip, I had a total of twenty-five cents in my pocket. My mother tried to get me not to go, knowing that it could be most embarrassing for me, but I insisted. After all, a cute girl whom I liked a lot was going and I wanted to see her, to be with her if possible, and to impress her.

I recall that my mother also offered to make me two or three of our now "patented" molasses biscuits, but I was too ashamed to even consider it. Therefore, I went for an all-day trip with no food, and no money except twenty-five cents. What was I to do for food? What would I do if I wanted to get on a ride on the Ferris wheel? I walked around the fair grounds—alone—by choice. I didn't want any of the other students to know, or even suspect, how desperate my situation was.

Finally, I knew enough to think of buying myself some lunch. There, alone at the great State Fair, I purchased a hot dog and a bottle of Pepsi for twenty cents, leaving me with a nickel to spend the rest of the day.

Different classmates would see me, greet me, and ask what all the rides I had been on were. My answer to them was not altogether a lie—but a huge exaggeration. "Oh, I think I like the Ferris wheel most...Ha—and no one got sick..." They laughed and walked off.

I would give anything in the world if only I could now reach back in time and hand that ten-year old boy a dollar. It is quite a revelation that today, fifty-six years later I feel an anguish of body, mind, and soul at the thoughts of that experience.

This vignette of my life was to be a pattern over most of the next twenty years. Repeatedly I found myself in social situations where my lack of money led to profound embarrassment, which I buried, somewhere deep in my consciousness and, later in life, in my subconscious.

Incredibly, this pattern of having to pretend or of doing something to show that I was worthy and honorable seemed to be widespread: the consequences of such a pattern can and did have devastating results.

I recall now two or three very poor people in our little town who married into an "upper" class family. While there were doubtless many factors that contributed to their actions, all three of these persons eventually took their own lives. At one point some columnist stated, in 1950 I think, whether accurately or not, I do not know, that our little town had the highest suicide rate per capita that year in North Carolina.

I am fully aware that there are often numerous causes for much self-inflicted violence. However, in our little town, poverty had to be one of the major factors.

I still do not know why or how I was able to face, and then to live through, my own inadequacies. It seems now that I never blamed others for my lack—but always myself. I thought I could change both myself and my circumstances. Early on, I made the tragic mistake of trying to "better myself." It became tragic to the degree that I placed upon myself impossible demands—a kind of rigid self-discipline. Determined, I was. Driven, I was. Goal-oriented, I was at almost any cost.

Looking back, I haven't thought of this in years. I began to use people to pretend a friendship that I didn't feel. I didn't feel like I was one of them because I had such a poor background. Therefore, I tried to be like them by pretending to be listening to them, but all the while, I was thinking about what I would say in response so I could impress them and be accepted. To say I "used" people in those days would be deadly accurate—always, it seemed, in search of the "movers and shakers" and especially the rich people that I chanced to meet. By being with them, I reasoned, I will "better" myself.

My behavior took on a sort of social pathology—a social sickness—that found me using people and feigning warmth, friendship and intimacy. It was a sort of game for me as I often recall standing outside myself as it were, judging myself, looking at myself and wondering how I was "coming across."

The renowned psychiatrist, Paul Tournier, said that the marks of a healthy personality are three-fold: creativity, intimacy, and spontaneity. It occurred to me, much later, when I was in graduate school, that I had none of those characteristics, as everything I did and said and thought seemed designed to elevate my own social status.

The ironical twist to all this was that when I had the chance for real intimacy in the years that followed, I never knew how to relax and return the love, the trust, the tenderness that such intimacy affords. That pattern was to last well into my thirties and early forties, but it did change.

I blamed myself for my poverty and now I blame myself for choosing such selfish methods to cover it up. Have there been others who did the same, felt the same or acted this way?

As painful as it may be to have little food or clothing or creature comforts, it is far worse to suffer from social or mental or emotional traumas that do not soon go away.

No One Should Be Slapped

She called me to the front of the room—and there, before all my classmates and friends, the teacher slapped my face so hard I fell to the floor. Speechless, nearly unconscious, I struggled to get to my feet and with great humiliation, began to cry.

I was a 6th grader. I came to school without having done my homework for the third or fourth straight day. When the teacher asked me where my homework was, I said that I had left it at home. It was a lie, of course, but she didn't seem to appreciate my sense of humor about it.

I remember the slap. I remember pain—real physical pain and my ears rang—and the hand print on my face was so deep I could see it in the mirror the next day.

My mother was furious. Never in all those twelve years in our family had I seen my mother so upset.

Next day she went to school with me to confront the teacher. Mother was gentle and kind—never harsh or loud or violent or even confrontational. She didn't need to be.

She said to the teacher, "I can't think of any situation, any at all, where a twelve-year old student would deserve this kind of brutality."

God, I was proud. Eureka. Yes, right on! Bells rang. Pride entered. I stood tall—held my mother's hand. It was for me more than serendipity—it was supremely a revelation. For the first time I could remember, I felt a deep sense of worth and value as a human being. I felt alive suddenly. I was somebody and not a poor "have not."

I recall that the teacher cried...apologized profusely and told mother about her own trials and tribulations.

Has it been fifty-five years since that happened? As I tell you this today, tears well up in my eyes. Emotional scars—how deep and lasting. This shows me how deep my lack of self-respect was until my mother started to help me recognize it. Thank heavens, I had always known that God loved me just as I was whether anyone else did or not.

May I never be an instrument of violence or hatred or vengeance—but of peace and joy—and when possible—even laughter.

Yes, laughter—especially when I think of how much people need support, help and justice.

Suddenly now, all these years later, it all comes back to me—and it was not without its lighter touches. For the teacher who slapped me was plain—I mean dirt-poor plain, but she thought she was beautiful!

On board the cruise ship recently while on our world cruise, I came across a story of a lady not unlike my teacher.

It seems that the renowned Rector Dr. Dick Sheppard of St. Paul's Cathedral in London told, in one of his many radio broadcasts, about a fashionable lady who went to a photographer. She was plain, but thought she was beautiful. She said to the photographer: "Young man, mind you do me justice."

The young photographer replied, "Madam, it is not justice you need, but mercy."

I think that if it had not been for a sense of humor and a sometimes inappropriate light touch, I would not have survived those years.

I read some place a quote by Sigmund Freud who said: "Laughter and joking relieves anxiety and repressed impulses on the part of people facing bad news or tragic news and often converts unpleasant feelings into pleasant ones." (From his article "Jokes and Their Relationship to the Unconscious.")

Laughter is a life-saving escape from the real world. Laughter and tears together represent our emotional extremes—and touch us at the deepest level possible. I seemed to know then, even at that very young age, that as I laughed about my pain, I felt better. Tears and laughter, more than anything else, seemed to put me in touch with the person that I really was.

While both laughter and tears may be culturally conditioned, they are found among people from every walk and rank of life, and for all of them it becomes a temporary way out of their crisis.

Gallup, New Mexico, boasts that it has the largest concentration of Native Americans (Indians) of any place in the country. Janet and I have stopped there on numerous occasions in our travels and really enjoy the laid-back, unhurried atmosphere that seems to pervade that group of Americans. I have been curious to know to what degree these and other Native Americans embrace humor as a part of their culture.

Just recently, I came across a story that is still handed down from one generation to another by the tribal chiefs in the Apache culture. The story they tell in the oral tradition says:

> The Creator endowed human beings with two legs, two hands and arms, and the ability to do everything—talk, run, walk, see, and hear. However, the Eternal was not satisfied until the two-legged creatures

could do one more thing—laugh. Therefore, people learned how to laugh and laugh and laugh. And the Creator said, "Now you are fit to live."

I recall two young African American teenage boys who lived in our little town and were actually poorer than I. I had food to eat, clothes to wear and a bed to sleep in. They had nothing. Repeatedly, I saw those young boys on a Saturday afternoon riding in their friend's car, a convertible with the top down, and talking and laughing and clapping their hands as though they had not a care in the world.

Vividly I recall saying to my friends, "Look at that. They are as happy and carefree as a lark. How can you explain it? They have nothing but they can still laugh."

It wasn't a rhetorical question because I genuinely wanted to know how anyone who possessed absolutely nothing could be that happy.

All of this is simply an attempt to share how I and others survived the poverty background of our childhood.

I think that I was beginning to learn that regardless of how dark the night, the sun also rises—as Ernest Hemingway was to tell us in his famous book. The Bible also held out for me the thought that "the light shines in the darkness and the darkness has not overcome it."

On a practical level, what this encouraged me to do was to "Hold on, hang on, never quit, never give up." I remember the words of the heavy-weight champion of the world, Gene Tunney, who was asked how he was able to keep on keeping on in some of the brutal boxing matches.

He said that his trainer and corner man told him he didn't have to fight the entire fight—just one more round.

One more round. The darkness will lift. The light will come. You can do all things—as the apostle Paul learned back in the first century world—through the hope and living presence of the Eternal God. I believed it. I knew it was true and so I pressed on—not looking for greatness but to be the best that I could be.

Somehow, in the center of all our family struggles, I felt a deep level of comfort by my spiritual roots. Perhaps it was my mother's faith in God that rubbed off on me. It is difficult to express what my faith meant to me.

It is certainly true that the wonderful new world of education, training, and pastoral ministry occurred in large part because of the spiritual roots. Mentors, yes. A light, even humorous touch, yes. A powerful will to be worthy and acceptable, yes. It was all there—but at the core were also my spiritual roots.

I discovered that humor was really the beginning of healing for both Janet and me during the last year. Perhaps it can be so for you.

In retrospect we were so distraught, so broken that we quite literally walked through the valleys of despair. Even though it has now been a year since the sudden and violent death of our son, the memory of our anguish and tears has not gone away.

Once I recall describing my anger and sense of rage about his decision not to live. I said, almost without thought, "The first thing I'm going to do when I see him (in heaven) is slap him."

My wife laughed and responded, "You'll have to stand in line…at least five other people also plan to slap him…"

We laughed heartily and long and deep. I can't explain what that did to me and for me. It was therapeutic; it was healing, it was cleansing. It was as though I took a degree of delight in "getting even" for the pain he had put us through. Then I remembered my own dictum: No one should be slapped!

I realize now that whatever healing and wholeness that did begin to emerge came about through the love, encouragement, and support of family and friends. However, a vital part of that healing must be attributed to the world of the spirit: the return to sanity, healing, and wholeness was a spiritual matter.

Recently I came across an important statement by the psychiatrist, Dr. Carl Jung, who wrote:

> During the past thirty years, people from all civilized countries on the earth have consulted me. Among all my patients in the second half of my life—that is to say, over thirty-five, there has not been one whose problem in the last resort, was not that of finding a religious outlook on life.

It is safe to say that every one of them fell ill because they had lost that which the living religions of every age have given to their followers.

I knew early on that I did not need to prove God or to debate God or to argue God. It was not something one could prove but something one could assert, believe and act upon. I decided to act as though there was a God, to act as though there was a heaven and another life when our life on earth is finished.

While my faith in those early days was utterly simplistic, even naïve and "black and white," the level of comfort afforded me by that faith was very high.

On hundreds of occasions, I recall singing those old gospel hymns which my mother used to sing around the house, with absolute assurance that I was loved by someone strong enough, big enough, and wise enough to be called my Father. It did—and it does—feel good. Like John Wesley who earlier had described his deeply moving Aldersgate awakening, "I felt my heart strangely warmed." To this day, that experience and that feeling have never left me.

It seems clear now that my behavior in those days came very close to being a frightening form of social pathology.

To the degree that I faced it, owned up to it, and found help in finding the real me, a spiritual force made the difference. There was a presence—persistent, tenacious, and unrelenting—a presence that confronted the phony me, that embraced me and loved me and forgave me and turned me in the direction of healing and wholeness. I learned first hand what St. Augustine of Hippo, writing in the fourth century world, meant when he said, "Our hearts are restless 'til they rest in thee."

Francis Thompson's *Hound of Heaven* poem helped me. It described how the Eternal God sought him and searched for him until at last he was found. It was true for me.

This is not to say that I, nor any of us, are what we ought to be, but we are at least on the road that will take us safely home.

How painful to tell you all of this. Perhaps someone can identify with it and be encouraged. Perhaps the most vivid part of these painful memories was not being slapped by my teacher or even the all day trip to the State Fair with no money, but living with an alcoholic father.

All of us have our way of escaping from a harsh reality. For me it has been humor and meaningful work. However, for my father, it was alcohol.

For the first fourteen years of my life, I lived through the frightening ordeal of this alcoholic presence. I recall that every time he earned some money, he would use it to buy alcohol. We called it "white lightning" for it was made illegally by neighbors who operated a still. Daddy would come home drunk late—9 or 10 p.m. or later, and begin to yell at my mother for not having a hot supper ready for him to eat. He yelled and screamed. Mother cried. Often she tried to reason with him—telling him he would wake up the children.

I recall lying in bed frightened, shaking, and yearning to run away. It seems pretty clear now why all my brothers and sisters decided to leave home at the earliest possible moment—several leaving home before they even got out of high school. The verbal abuse, the violence and threats I feared would destroy our family and injure me. Repeatedly, I lay there shaking, frightened.

My desire to get away from my father's near-violent behavior had the effect of getting me out of bed very early in the morning. I got up early and went to school without any breakfast, wanting so badly to escape my father's cruelty.

That pattern occurred eight to ten times during a school year—and continued over at least five of the first six years in school.

Ironically, all my teachers and the principal thought that I came to school early because I was so anxious to learn. They never suspected the real reason I came so early.

There was no money and I had the anguished pain of going all day with nothing to eat. I recall how ravenously hungry I felt. On those painful days, I still recall going out under the stairwell alone with a book in hand, and weeping about what was happening to me. When friends came by to ask if I was okay, I would just smile, pretend, and say, "Oh, sure, I'm just catching up on my reading." This is probably where the effort to pretend really started.

This same father who became a different person when he was inebriated could be so wonderfully kind and generous when sober.

It was the custom in those days for nearly everyone including young people to "go to town" on Saturday afternoon. Farmers came by the dozens to buy groceries and, before shopping, to sit around and talk. Some of the men would gather around the benches and chairs along the sidewalk to gossip about this and that. Some would stand, with one foot propped up against a building, and talk for an hour or two before shopping and going home.

My father stood, week after week, on Saturday afternoon, foot propped up against the old bank building, and talk. I would approach him and say, "Daddy, do you have any money?" Almost without exception, he would reach into his coin pocket and pull out a nickel or dime or, on rare occasions, a quarter. I never forgot it. Maybe he was pretending in front of the other fellows that he had more than he had. He had nothing—nothing—but such as what he had he shared.

I recall many years later when my Daddy died at the age of 91, I stood in our home-town church to speak at his memorial service. I told the audience that my father never bought me a car or a bicycle or a baseball glove or even a suit to wear. He didn't have it to give. Nevertheless, I added, he gave me as much as he had and that was enough.

Earlier when I became a pastor, I was invited to preach in my home town church. I was thrilled to be asked and wanted all my family to be there—sitting on the front row. They all came but Daddy. Over the next twenty-five to thirty years, I returned home to preach in my home church many times but Daddy never came to hear me.

Finally, a year or two before he died, Mother talked him into going to church to hear his own son preach. He did but with such pained resistance. I hugged him at the end of the worship service. He said in leaving, "Boy, you didn't do too bad." It was high praise coming from my dad and it was okay.

Birthdays Should Not Hurt

He told me with tears in his eyes. As I recall he was seventy-eight at the time. His first wife had died and he met and married a beautiful lady who seemed to care for his every need.

It was, he told me, his birthday and a party was held in his honor at his spacious home in Arizona. Close friends, church people and most of the executives whom he knew from the hospital board came. There were 40 or more present. He told me that each family had brought a lovely card, many flowers—and there was a huge cake which his wife had purchased.

They sang to him once, twice, three times, "Happy birthday, dear Henry." Then, with a halting, shaky voice, he said, "That is the only family birthday party I ever had. It was one of the greatest days of my life…"

I was shocked. After all he had been for many years a high level executive—one of the "movers and shakers" in his home town.

"What do you mean?" I asked, running the risk of embarrassing him. "Surely your first wife and children held a birthday party for you…"

Then through obvious pain, he told me that his first wife never allowed him to call attention to himself. Once, he said, a small cake was purchased—and hidden away until after supper. Then, a neighbor and invited guest got up, went into the kitchen and brought out the cake which Henry had purchased.

Then he told me that his wife was so angry at him that then and there she scolded him, telling him that he was extremely selfish—and only thought of his own big ego.

"That," he told me wiping the tears from his eyes, "was the last birthday celebration I ever had…until our party last week."

Some will say that it was no big deal—but if not, why did I feel a lump in my throat—and tears in my own eyes as he told his story? That kind of pain never leaves us. It sticks in the unconscious and tells us that no matter what great things we have done or accomplished, we are still nothing and certainly not worthy of having our birthday recognized.

That strikes me as being a tragedy of the first order. Simply put, we cannot survive without ego affirmation, ego stroking. The tragic message that this omission sends is that you are not worthy of love, respect, recognition and praise. Without some of that, we simply cannot survive as a human being. Besides, that harsh cruel treatment stands in perfect contrast to the teachings of the Bible that tell us we are sons and daughters of the eternal God...and therefore we are worthy.

Perhaps there are those who feel that such treatment would have no carry-over effect. Wrong. The effects of that kind of treatment are profound and far-reaching.

I recall all the time we spent with Henry and his new wife. Always he would indicate to us how unworthy he felt. It occurred to me that he had touched the lives of literally thousands of people for good. Several times we would say to him, "Oh, Henry, that is wonderful...You are such a kind and caring man..."

Instantly he would drop his head—as if in sorrow—and say, "Oh, no. That's nothing...I think my first wife was right. I'm always calling attention to myself."

Put downs of any kind are devastating and they are eternal.

A beautiful young girl was attending class at school on the first day of the fall year. The sixth grade teacher called out the name of each student and had them stand and receive the accolades of the entire class. Nancy's name was called and she stood. The teacher asked, "Are you the Nancy Jones (or Smith or Johnson) whose older brother was Sammy Jones?" Yes. Sammy Jones had dropped out of school, been arrested and was serving time in prison.

There, in front of the class, the uncaring teacher recounted Sammy's life and imprisonment and then added, "Well, I certainly hope that you don't turn out like your brother..."

She could live one hundred years and never be able to live that down. That teacher should be fired—or reassigned to the restroom detail at the school for the next ten years.

How can people be so cruel, so unfeeling, and so unkind? It hurts just telling you about this. No one, no one at all deserves that kind of treatment.

If there is any word to counter this ever-present harshness, it is the word "kindness." My mother used to tell us that kindness was just as important as the word "love." She said, "We should even be kind to the devil. Who knows? He just might change."

I recall my father and some of his amazing insights. Once I got angry at my younger sister, yelled at her, and commanded her to do this or that.

Daddy said, "Son, anger and bitterness don't make people change. If kindness won't do it, then nothing will."

Call them what you will; birthdays, anniversaries, promotions, graduations, or retirements—they are all intended to call attention to the worth and value of the person and to the value of human life.

Admittedly, many families simply can't afford to throw big and expensive parties for members of the family. As short as money may be in today's world, it was dramatically shorter in the days of my youth. Money, however, is not the issue—and big parties are not necessary. What is necessary is some kind of positive recognition that tells the recipient, "You are somebody special."

While my own youth was filled with painful memories too harsh to recall, it was not so with birthdays. One might think that not having a birthday cake or a birthday card would be painful. In my eighteen years at home, I have no memory of ever having a birthday cake or a card presented by my family to me. Surprisingly that was okay because none of the nine children had them. However, Mother and Daddy gave such as what they had: they did somehow remember to say, "Oh, by the way, this is Donald Gene's birthday" and that was enough.

The Most Painful Hurt of All

He loved his wife and children and really didn't want to leave them for a month. But duty called and so he went. It was in England—several different cities there—he was one of many trying to impress the English audience in the hopes they would do business with his parent company.

He said he quite literally knew no one at any of the social-business functions he attended. Others, he noticed, would cluster with three or four people who were obviously friends, but often he was left out—alone. He said once to me being there at all those business affairs with dozens of people all around was the "single loneliest feeling I ever had. I wanted desperately to be recognized, included, befriended," but it was not to be.

I knew this feeling he was describing. Yes, I had heard people speak of being "lonely in a crowd." Now I understand what it meant and so did he. Why did I have trouble listening to him?

Who knows why this is? In my own desperate struggle to find companionship and intimacy, I kept pushing people away—being threatened when they stood too close or when they were sharing stories out of their lives that were important to them—but not to me.

For whatever strange reason, I found myself turning away from the person who was talking to me. It was like I wanted to move on to other people whom I considered more "important." I had decided that he had little value. Of course, I thought I had little value early in my life, and I wanted to flee from that feeling. Maybe that's why I wanted to run from someone who reminded me of myself.

I reached the age of forty before I began to understand this destructive pattern. It occurred to me that I really was not listening to any of them because I did not value them, let alone love them. I was using them to get what I wanted—and nothing more. I had become an actor pretending to care and share. What did I really feel? Who did I really care for?

The revelation hurt far more than what I can tell you. I recall going to board meetings out of town where I served as a trustee or a board officer and watching the people around me laugh and joke and kid about this and that. I wanted intensely to do that. I'd lost intimacy with others. I was alone.

In those settings, I saw the pattern that had developed. I did not know how to treat other people as peers, or equals or as close personal friends. I could be over them, as when I chaired a committee, and I could be under them, as in carrying out my assignments for them, but I could not be with them as a part of the group. I had to dominate or remain quiet and totally withdrawn. It disturbed me deeply.

That revelation, the hunger for intimacy, but not knowing how to be intimate, was the most painful revelation and experience I ever lived through. I was "lonely in a crowd." How could I drop my act and be myself with others? If I let down my guard, would they truly accept me as I am?

Doubtless, some of the people who read these words have experienced something like this—that comes close to being a full-blown social pathology.

I Found the Enemy and It Was Me

During these painful, insightful revelations, I kept wondering why on earth I would consider being a pastor in a church. Perhaps I should start selling cars. Aren't pastors supposed to be kind, caring, loving, gentle, and supremely good listeners? In those moments, it occurred to me that I was lacking all those qualities and that the only thing I could do and do well was to pretend and to put on a front.

If there were any redeeming qualities about this period of intense struggling, it was that I never blamed other people. I seemed to know that there was little or nothing wrong with other people, but something frightfully wrong with me. That I was actually able to identify what was going on and reconstruct my behavior has been nothing short of a miracle. (It was a gift from God.)

The "reconstruction" began when I read and then studied the book *I'm O.K.—You're O.K.* by Dr. Thomas Harris. The author talks about the "OK Corral" and lays out the four fundamental mind-sets of people. They are one, two or all of these positions:

1. I'm not O.K. but you are O.K.
2. I'm not O.K. and you are not O.K.
3. I'm O.K. but you are not O.K.
4. I'm O.K. and you're O.K.

Dr. Harris described the different types of personality disorders that can and often do emerge from the first three types of thinking. Clearly, my behavior was in Category One: "I'm not O.K. but you are O.K." What I came to see and to understand was that my type of thinking and relating was changeable, allowing me a chance to deal with the negative forces that had evolved over those nearly forty years.

What shocked me in the book was to learn about sociopathic behavior, which is Category Three—persons who for whatever reason have this mindset (I'm O.K. but you are not O.K.) often move into a lifestyle of criminal behavior.

In numerous studies of personality types of inmates in our prison system, it was discovered that a large number of them were found to be full-blown sociopaths.

Sociopathic behavior is characterized by a loss or lack of conscience—so that doing bad things, even cruel things, does not make them feel guilty. They are also found to be very compulsive, not unlike the alcoholic who "must" have another drink. Laws, rules, regulations, and standards of behavior were not made for them—but for other people.

In one case, I knew a young boy from a totally dysfunctional family who had been cruelly mistreated—beaten unmercifully and often locked in a closet while his parents went out partying. His comment was that when left alone he was fine—even happy. It was only when other people came, namely his parents, that he suffered and experienced great pain. His modus operandi became "survival" at all costs and keeping his distance from others. By the time he was fifteen he "escaped" from his battering situation, and over the next five years moved into a lifestyle that left him so distant from others that he felt no guilt if he did something to them. He had no principles and that eventually led him to prison.

Despite what you may have been taught about the negative side of guilt, it is, in the final analysis, absolutely essential to good mental health and to acceptable social behavior.

I recall reading that book in the library one day when I began to choke up with tears at the thought that I had not yet sunk so low that I could not still become a healthy, happy person. Yes, I could. Something big, positive, and lasting happened that day in that library with that simple insight from Dr. Harris' book.

It would be foolish to mislead you at this point. You must not conclude that this little miracle was the end of the struggle. It was not. In some respects, it was only the beginning as I began slowly and painfully to turn things around. I recalled the prayer written by Dr. Niebuhr from meetings of the A.A. group. "God, grant me the serenity to accept the things I cannot change, courage to change the things I can, and wisdom to know the difference."

Whatever healing that took place over the next fifteen to twenty years came painfully slowly. I recall "practicing" a style of behavior that forced me to actually listen to what people were saying—to really listen—and when possible to write down on paper what they had said. I also recall making myself "pretend" to like the person to whom I was talking—to value them as though they were sons and daughters of God. The new world which this behavior unfolded for me was at once exciting, rewarding, and frightening.

What I found was that people, all people, had much to give, if only I could slow down, relax, seize the moment, and allow them to tell their story. On several occasions, I was shocked by what I remembered. I went home and shared the interesting insights with Janet. I knew somehow that this new ability to actually listen to what people were saying would prove to be a blessing beyond anything I could ever imagine.

On board our cruise ship recently, I made a point of remembering the names of people that we met. Repeatedly they seemed surprised, even shocked, when I spoke to them by name. However, just when I was feeling good about how well I had learned to listen, my wife asked me if I recalled the names of our professional guides during our on-shore excursions.

She then proceeded to tell me the names of all our tour guides on all fourteen of our stops—and she did it without notes! I realize, even as I write these words, that I still have a long way to go. Help! Help!

I said to her after this splendid demonstration of real listening, "The Bible has it all wrong...It says if you want to know something, you should go home and ask your husband! Wrong," I jokingly added, "because if you want to know something, go home and ask your wife."

I recall Bishop James Armstrong's admonition to his students years ago: "You aren't trying to exhaust the subject in one short sermon or chapter or

even one short book. Don't preach exhaustively," he said, "preach suggestively."

Therefore, my insights are presented to you not in any way as the
answer—or as if to exhaust the topic—but only "suggestively" as you will
want to do your own research and exploration, as painful as it might be.

I have often thought about other people I have known who grew up in
dysfunctional families. A counselor told me that she spends over half her
time with families that are wholly dysfunctional. She then described the
problem areas that included low self-esteem, poverty, sexual perversions,
job problems, and the inability to manage money. She said that in a few
cases these dysfunctional families had suddenly come into large amounts
of money, only to waste it in a matter of months. Without the basics of a
good education, they fell prey to ideas that were designed to strip them of
their newfound wealth.

As she told me some of the types of dysfunctional situations, I could not
help but think of the upside, the humorous side of such stories.

There was the pastor who went to the home of a man whose wife dominated. The pastor asked the children what were their father's last words
before he died. They said, "Pa didn't have no last words. Ma was with him
'til the end."

Perhaps that cannot compare to the well-intentioned husband whose
family and whose marriage was a disaster. He asked his partner at work
why it was that he was always so happy and always saying good things
about his wife.

The partner said, "When I get home and open the door, I shout 'Hi,
honey, I'm home.' I then go to see her, hug her, kiss her, and tell her that I
love her. Then two or three times a week I say, 'Come on, honey, I'm taking you out to dinner.'"

The unhappy husband decided to try it. He went home, yelled out to
his wife that he was home, found her, kissed her, and said, "Come on,
Babe, I'm taking you out for supper."

The wife began to cry. He said, "Honey, what's wrong?"

She said, "The battery in the car went dead, the dishwasher broke down, the kitchen floor was flooded and now my husband comes home drunk." Sometimes you can't win!

However, isn't it an inspiration when we can find people who don't panic, regardless of how bad things might get. They are not unlike the pilot on a four-engine propeller-driven plane. The passengers watched as one engine stopped running and then a second. Finally, the third engine went out. The pilot appeared, holding his microphone and a parachute. He said, "Relax, don't panic. I'm going for help."

The manager of a grocery store nabbed a shoplifter in the act. He was escorting the suspect to the office in the front of the store near the check-out registers. Suddenly, the worst happened. The shoplifter broke from his grip and tried to run but was caught and pinned against the wall.

Relieved to have stopped the perpetrator, he looked up to see a number of surprised customers. The manager said, "Everything's fine, folks," he reassured them. "This guy just tried to go through the express lane with more than five items."

And how do you keep your poise when handling a heckler in an audience who keeps interrupting you, as happened to one speaker. Finally, the speaker stopped and asked the lady heckling him, "How old are you, madam?"

The lady briskly replied, "My age is my business."

"That may be," he replied, "but I can tell you've been in business a long time." She was out-heckled!

Think of the worst that ever happened to you and chances are pretty good that some redeeming factor was present—and very often it was humor. As Bill Cosby said, "You can turn painful situations around through laughter. If you can find humor in anything, even poverty, you can survive it."

And when you can't turn things around with humor, remember what Oprah Winfrey said, "Turn your wounds into wisdom."

11

Seven Steps to Wholeness and Healing

Dealing with the profound issues of life and death is never comforting. It is almost impossible to probe the depths of life's meaning, its ultimate purpose and our own destiny without having a heavy heart. These issues are even more difficult to deal with if you have been traumatized by the sudden and tragic death of a son or daughter.

There are literally millions of people who seem to find great comfort in their faith and their deep religious moorings. The thought that there really is a heaven and a world to come gives them a peace and a sense of comfort about their loss. What they need and need desperately is a sense of calm assurance that there is meaning and purpose in their loss. They need comfort and conversation from people who genuinely care and who will let them respond as they choose to respond, or as they need to respond.

It is well not to be too helpful or to try to relieve their suffering and their pain prematurely or casually. The suffering, tears, grief, anger, questionings, guilt, remorse, bitterness, and feelings of emptiness and despair must not be short-circuited. Sometimes the listeners cannot endure their friend's pain and thereby, for their own sake, try to stifle or end perfectly normal emotional behavior.

What suffering people need from their loved ones and closest friends is a presence—but not necessarily their spoken words. A sign I saw in our travels in Australia recently put it well in describing our work. It said: "Do all you can to reach out to other people who are in need: If necessary, use words."

We should never try to make things too easy for people who are walking through the valley of the shadows of darkness and death. Suffering is often wonderfully healing, cleansing and redemptive. It is often helpful to experience our loss with all its fury and pain, and to allow ourselves to really own the death, and not try to gloss it over by saying or hearing hurtful things like, "Oh, well, life goes on…I've just got to get over this."

How does one go about the almost impossible task of getting through a major loss and finding some meaning in what has happened?

I wish that I could give you a "Six Easy Steps to Total Recovery" leaflet. I wish I could give you the assurance that you will soon get over this death or this loss. I offer no assurance.

The Road to Recovery: First the Tears

I have tried in these pages to show something of the depth of our anguish—that came close to being total despair. The only thing we could do when the news came to us that our son had taken his own life was to cry.

It may seem ironic, paradoxical, or even absurd to say that the road to health, healing and hope comes through tears—but it did for me and for my wife, Janet. If, then, there is a first step to recovery, it has to be giving yourself permission to cry. I don't know how it helped; I don't know why it helped, but it did.

In many ways the tears have never ended, at least they are so close to the surface that today, a full year later, we both choke up when someone wants to know what happened. Life is lived in a forward direction, but it is understood in a backward direction.

As we looked back upon our son's life, we had only glimpses of why he might not want to go on living. Our primary hope was that as we moved forward with our own lives, we might, in the fullness of time, come to understand his act of self-destruction. In the meantime, there will be tears, deep, heavy, strong, and continuous.

You too will find yourself crying to the point you feel there are no tears left. You will scream and yell and be angry and furious. You will say and do things that may seem weird and bizarre. You will talk to him or her, tell them how you feel and ask 1,000 times or more the unanswerable question why, why, why, my God, why?

And then there will be more tears. You will say, "I can't seem to stop crying..." You will cry early in the morning and at noon and at night and when a song is played on the car radio as you try to drive down the street—you will cry.

A thought, a sign on the road, a picture along the way will start the process all over again. You will wake up at night crying. You will think you are losing your mind. You will listen to what others say but never hear them at all. You will probe the depths of despair and wonder about the meaning of life and why God would allow this one you loved to die.

I know that tears really are the price we pay for love—but I did not know that my love was so deep.

Over and over again, I have had other people say to me, "When Bill (or Jane or Lucy) died, I lost the will to live..." One of the great challenges of my life as a pastor was working with people who had lost their will to live. It is well not to argue the point with them. It is better not to debate the topic "to live or not to live." It is best to listen, to draw them out, and to encourage them to talk—always in confidence—which leads me to another step in healing.

Second, Find Someone You Trust To Talk To

As a professional both as a pastor and as a chaplain, I have seen first hand the powerful effect of listening. In perhaps dozens of cases, I have consulted with persons who have walked through their own dark Gethsemane. At least five of them no longer wanted to go on living. I asked them to tell me about what had happened. They always "test the waters" first to determine that you really care about what happened—and that some of their experiences need to be completely confidential. Once people begin to talk, something at once profound, deep, and utterly simple begins to happen.

After they talk through tears (and I always have a box or two of tissues handy), they talk through anger and, all too often, a sense of guilt. They describe in great detail their deepest feelings, their hurt, their loneliness, their grief—and a wish to end their own life. I tried never to interrupt them or to seem shocked or surprised by anything they said. I did ask brief, leading questions that would get them to be free to say whatever they wanted to say—or to explore related areas of their loss.

Almost without exception, the person began to move toward some kind of healing. I often asked myself what it was that I had done or said that made the difference, but was terribly humbled by the realization that the only thing I did was to listen. Anyone can do that.

In the five cases mentioned above, all chose to go on living. One stands out above all the others.

He was a man who appeared to be in his mid-seventies. He was waiting at the back entry of our church as I drove up. I recall that it was Wednesday and I was on my way to play golf—just needed to get my golf hat and then I was on my way.

The man (we'll call him Fred) was gentle, soft, and kind. He seemed to be very intelligent but severely depressed. He said almost casually, "This is going to be my last day and I thought I should tell someone. Are you the pastor?"

Well, I knew right away there would be no golf for me that day, and then in a humorous sort of way, I mentally looked up and said to God, "You owe me one for this."

I asked what he meant, while opening the locked door, turning on the lights, and inviting him into my office.

"Well, this is my last day to live and I wanted you to know."

He was a stranger. I asked for his name later, but knew I had not met him before.

I said, "What happened?"

He said, "Well, do you have time?"

I said, "I've got all day."

There unfolded an almost unbelievable story about a son who had turned to threats to get more money out of his father. The threats had become loud and hostile, with specific actions he would take if his father did not fork over more money.

I recall his saying, "I am tired of dealing with it and with him, and don't want to go on living."

We talked for nearly an hour, and to show you that God really is good, I made it in time for my 9:00 a.m. golf game. I could see as we talked that he was growing stronger, more directed to living and more hopeful about how to deal with the threatening son. I mentioned about three things that I knew could be helpful, and found him ready to hear them.

At the end of a full hour, he stood to leave. His face and eyes came to life. He managed a smile and then said, "Hell, I know how to handle this. I did the same thing ten years ago and I forgot what to do."

Then the thing that intrigued me most. He said, "I don't know why I bothered you with this...It's really no big deal."

When he left, I knew again that the key ingredient was simply listening with an understanding ear. For whatever reason, it really works.

It is important in your own recovery to remember that our friends—and even professionals—may at times say things that are not helpful. Everyone wants desperately to help relieve your suffering, and very often will offer simplistic advice or "aphorisms" which they honestly believe will help. I have said that the very best kind of listening is that which comes from a person's presence. I recall our lead volunteer chaplain, Katie, telling our volunteers, "We are not there to do something but simply to be there."

Why is it that we feel we must rush in with lots of words and words and words—thinking, I suppose, that they want to hear everything we have to say? There is great power in silence—as I have appreciated by observing my chaplain supervisor, Dr. Ron Hamilton.

In addition, there comes a time and a place when the greatest thing we can do for a grieving person is to leave them alone. I hope that experience and sensitivity will tell us when it's time to go.

Not long ago I was called to the surgical waiting room where an older lady had learned that her husband of fifty-four years had died. I told the wife who I was. She asked about the future—the promise of a heaven and the love of God. I told her very briefly what I believed. She asked two more brief and pointed questions and I tried again to tell her what I believed.

There was a long silence—no tears—just silence, and I asked, "Would you like to be alone?"

She smiled and said, "Would you mind terribly? I just want to be alone with him..." Then I left. Outside the door I could hear her crying and talking to him.

I wish there were some way to highlight the importance and power of talking to a trusted friend as an early step on the road to healing. I strongly recommend a program offered by many congregations called "the Stephen Ministry" if you are really earnest about reaching out to people who are grieving. Those who have had training as "Stephen Ministers" have a sensitivity I have not seen among persons who have not had this training. However, with or without the training, all of us can become good listeners and that is what is needed in today's world.

Third, Find Something Worthwhile To Do

Work of any type is a wonderful distraction from our pain and loss. People who are busy doing anything with their hands are less likely to get lost in their deep emotions or grief than those whose only thoughts are centered on their pain. It is among the very best types of therapy known.

This finding has been validated numerous times in special studies. Years ago, I watched as an out-patient in a hospital setting was being wired and monitored by a technician. The patient had very high blood pressure and they wanted some way besides medications to reduce the pressure.

They seated him in a large recliner-type chair and then began having him picture in his mind images of a warm spring day. The technician said, "It was a day of beauty, the sun shining, the flowers in bloom and the birds are singing. You are sitting on the bank and in front of you is a soft blue lake. You are happy, at peace with yourself and the world. Can you see that? Well, you are there just now. Feel it."

Then the incredible happened. I watched as the high blood pressure readings dropped dramatically—returning almost to a normal level.

Find something worthwhile to do. We simply cannot bear to deal with our loss day after day without some type of escape. It seems clear from my work with grieving people that any kind of activity or work that allows people to forget their loss or their suffering, even if for only a few minutes, is therapeutic.

I recall so clearly asking a man in the church whose wife had died very suddenly if he would come to the church to help assemble our weekly newsletters. He declined at first—saying he just needed to grieve alone. I told him I understood, but that we needed someone for only 2 or 3 weeks and then he could resign.

Well, okay, he said. He came on Tuesdays to work with the three or four others around the table. I alerted them that Tom was coming—and they handled his coming like professionals. They greeted him warmly and told him his job. Later I dropped by the assembly room. Tom was smiling and beginning to talk. Later that morning I passed through the area and heard Tom laughing. In less than a year, Tom met a lovely lady who had also come to the church to assemble the mailings. They began going out for lunch and found themselves talking and sharing about their deep but separate losses.

You guessed it—they were married and continued as a team to fold, staple and address the five hundred or so weekly newsletters that went to our church members.

In every case that I recall, none of the grieving people actually wanted to get involved. They all told me "No"—they just needed time to recover and didn't want to do anything. Many of them were afraid of being embarrassed—of crying in public places and feeling humiliated. Great sensitivity is required on the part of leaders when they encourage grieving people to "come and help." In most cases, this involvement process proves to be wonderfully therapeutic.

What can you do? There are dozens of meaningful tasks to be done. My own father-in-law gave five thousand hours to the "Talking Books" program related to the Indiana School for the Blind. He operated the sound system at church, served as a deacon and then as an elder. He made himself available and thereby found deep joy in life, despite the death of his loving wife.

At our two hospitals, care centers and hospice units in the Sun Cities, we have nearly four thousand volunteers—each giving four hours or more a week to help where they are needed. It would, as one volunteer put it, "do your heart good" just to see these people working and themselves coming to life by helping other people.

Some have said to me, "I'll help when I feel better." That may be an honest response. Often, however, people don't start to feel better until they move out in a different direction. There were, for example, two widowed people who joined a weekly bowling group. That little spark proved to be the key to helping them work through their recent loss.

Fourth, Find a "Safe Place"

Following a major personal loss, it is important to find some way to move away to a "safe place" where you can regain your composure. In these safe places, you can focus your attention on other topics or the work at hand. It is helpful to be with people who do not know any of the details about your loss. That exposure gives you a chance to say a few words—finish a whole sentence—without starting to cry.

I found that my "safe place" following our son's death was the hospital where I worked as a chaplain. The wonderful thing about going back to work was that about ninety-nine percent of the people I met knew nothing about our loss. The others who did know respected my privacy so much that they knew how to keep me safe. I recall that both of my supervisors asked me if I needed more time away to recover. They both knew something of the depth of the loss and the anguish and grieving that follows—but they allowed me space to deal with it in my own way. No, I told them, being back at work seems to be the best place for me just now.

The others in the hospital who did know sent cards, waved at me, or, on occasion, lightly patted me on the shoulder and then moved on. I could feel the depth of their caring but they never, even once, intruded.

I was greatly comforted by the responses of our fifteen volunteer chaplains. Not one of them ever asked me for information about our loss. They waited back for me to take the lead; then they responded in ways that made me very proud to be part of their team.

In my ministry as pastor for thirty-five years, I must tell you of the very dangerous "not so safe" places that I saw people take. I recall one man who found an "escape" in alcohol. However, all too often, that leads to total despair and a relinquishment of the will to live. A few others tried "drugs" of one type or another but found them to be far more harmful than helpful.

Still another tried to deal with her loss by running away and traveling all over the world. She would go where her late husband was not, but she soon discovered that she couldn't leave him or his memory behind.

I can think of several others who tried to find their "safe place" through ceaseless activity. One lady agreed to chair three or four major projects for her church and her social organizations. She was on the phone day and night, driving here and there, always running, always in a hurry, until finally nervous exhaustion landed her in the hospital.

There are many safe places and they will vary from person to person. One of our friends has always loved going to shopping centers. Nevertheless, she added that when her husband was living he didn't enjoy shopping, so, for his sake, she stayed home. Now that he was gone, she could go as often as she wished. I chided her about spending all that money and she assured me that the joy was not in the buying but in the looking.

In a similar situation, two ladies lost their husbands. They decided to get together for lunch at the shopping mall, at least weekly. They agreed that they would bring something funny they had heard or read and share it with each other. The combination of tears and laughter had an almost magical effect on their recovery.

One of these ladies told me about the patient who gave up everything that his doctor linked to cancer. The first week he cut out smoked fish and charcoal steaks. The second week he cut out cigarette smoking. The third week he cut out alcohol. The fourth week he cut out all fatty foods and high carbs. The fifth week he cut out paper dolls!

A little common sense goes a long way—even when you are trying to get healthy again.

I think that humor, wherever it appears, can also become for all of us who grieve, a safe place. In my ministry in Arizona over some 17 years, I have worked with nearly a dozen families that had to deal with the devastating disease of Alzheimer's. It is sad, even tragic in its effect on the life of family members. However, right in the middle of this seemingly hopeless situation I have seen humor appear, often from the family members themselves that relieved the hurts a little.

A husband commenting on the "positive" aspects of his wife's Alzheimer's disease said to me, "The good thing about Lucy, with her bad memory, is that everybody she meets, she meets them for the first time—me, her children, everyone."

Our friend, Joyce, who is one of our gifted chaplains, has an infectious sense of humor and told me the following story of "memory."

It seems that an elderly lady called 9-1-1 and reported that her car had been broken into. She was hysterical as she explained her situation to the dispatcher. "They stole my steering wheel, my stereo, the brake pedal, and even the gas pedal," she cried. The dispatcher said, "Stay calm. An officer is on the way."

A few minutes later, the officer radioed back. "Disregard," he said, "the lady got in the back seat by mistake."

Fifth, Make Positive Statements and Simple Affirmations

It may be the hardest thing we ever have to do but for many grieving parents, turning to something positive proves to be among the most healing responses possible.

Find the word or words that feel right for you and either whisper them or, if convenient, say them aloud. For me it was, "Thank you, Eternal Spirit" and "Thank you, Eternal God."

I sang a little tune which I used to sing to both our children when they were small:

> God is so good
> God is so good
> He's so good to me.

I added other phrases or tunes like:

I am loved.
I am not alone.
Life is good.
The Lord is my shepherd.
Thank you for our son.
This is the day which the Lord has made;
Let us rejoice and be glad in it.
My son is alive—thanks be to God.

It sounds childish, perhaps, but saying simple affirmations of your faith, often through tears, seems to help. In addition, even if it didn't help, it is at least worth a try. Positive statements and assertions usually work.

A doctor had bad news for a patient so he wanted to mingle it with something positive and upbeat. He said, "Mr. Jones, I have some good news and some not so good news. The good news is that my son has been accepted at the Harvard Medical School. The bad news is that, over these next four years, you will be paying for it!" Yikes!

Sixth, Enjoy the Comfort of Reading

My wife and I are learning first hand that we were not really able to assimilate or even to appreciate the comfort that may come from intellectual or scientific facts about life and death. Obviously, we knew that "life has a beginning and an ending" and that death is a natural phenomenon.

We were not even comforted by some of the well-intentioned words of others who told us that our son was in a better place, or that his death was a part of God's plan. For us, those responses violated everything that we felt inside, and I kept shouting back in my thoughts, "NO, NO, NO! I don't care about all that. All I want is for our son to come back to us!"

I think that it would have been tragic if people had tried to short-circuit our suffering or our grieving by trying to rescue us before we wanted to be rescued. There is great healing in grieving and both professionals and lay persons alike must allow our grieving friends ample time and space to recover at their own pace.

Do medical facts and data and scientific findings about death help to relieve the anguish of body and mind? Well, probably, but not immediately.

Our friend, Dr. Roy, a retired physician, gave me a remarkable book by Frank Vertasick, M.D. called *When the Air Hits Your Brain*.

He has written about his work as a neurosurgeon. Dr. Vertasick stated something which at first reading shocks our system. He said that death is not a flaw or a failure in biology, but an essential design feature that assures the human race of a constant and continuing existence in an inconstant earth. He goes on to say that our cellular and organic downward spiral from youth to old age is in fact stamped into our genetic code. Our demise assures us that life on earth can and will continue through those who come after us.

In my mind, I know that it would be unthinkable and intolerable if no one died. I can embrace the universal truth that no one in this life lives forever. Even surface thinking causes me to see that if no one died, we would find ways to end life. It is in the very nature of every one of the trillions of cells in the human body to have their "day in the sun" and then to die.

If no one died, there would not be enough food or water or shelter or space for all the people. I know that death is not the enemy, not a mistake when it applies to all of humanity, but I have not resolved in my mind that the premature death of my own son will ever be acceptable.

Help from reading may come from books like *What Happy People Know* by Dr. Dan Baker, psychologist who works in Tucson, Arizona. He says that people with a positive outlook understand that life is a series of events, all of which are potential opportunities for learning. They intuitively grasp that the more profoundly painful the events, the more profound the lessons.

Dr. Barbara Fredrickson, professor at the University of Michigan, says that one's positive good feelings can banish negative emotions. By focusing on something positive like a good book, a movie, or being with people we enjoy, we divert our attention away from the negative experience and it allows us time to recover, recoup, and ultimately cope with life's harsh realities.

Not only reading but writing can help as was demonstrated by a study of breast cancer done at the University of Kansas in 2002. One group of patients was asked to write their deepest feelings about their illness. Another group was asked to write only their positive thoughts. A third group was asked to write only about the fact. At the end of the three month study, the group that wrote about their feelings had more vigor, less stress and fewer appointments for cancer-related problems. By being open and honest about their problems and feelings, the first group of patients became better able to deal with it. (Marsa, 2004)

Readings can offer to us enormous comfort if they address our needs or hurts at the moment. There isn't a person anywhere who hasn't found some vital spark from an old magazine while waiting in a doctor's office. Whether it was how to deal with loss, how to raise children, the certainty of God or a dozen other topics, at that moment it seemed to fit. I think it was Napoleon Hill who said that we are all looking for a magic key to unlock the door of our power source. Yet, all the while, we have the key in our hands.

Besides, if all else fails and nothing written or spoken seems to help, we always have the comfort and consolation of a comic strip like good ole *Charlie Brown.* I love the line, "No problem is so big and complicated that it can't be run away from."

Dr. Samuel Greenberg was for years a professor of psychiatry at the University of Miami School of Medicine. He wrote about the very large number of Americans who cannot seem to enjoy life because of a social-emotional illness called neurosis. Confusing moral values, an overly competitive environment, and too many choices leave us worried, tired, anxious and depressed, leading many to choose not to live any longer.

What may surprise many is Dr. Greenberg's antidote to this disturbing illness. He says you can help yourself if you do some self-analysis and soul searching to find insights on why we behave the way we do. Then he recommended the comfort and wisdom that comes from the Bible and from being with people who are interesting and lively.

Dr. Greenberg's article helps to point all of us in the direction of a less complicated life—one that is guided by standards and principles, by high morals and ethical values. The mad rush of modern American life cannot be good for anyone. The price we pay to gain a few more dollars or more recognition or honor may not, in the end, be worth it.

Fortunately, many people do recover from neurosis without professional help. The body has amazing capacities for recovery. We can tap the forces that lead to good health.

If humor and a positive attitude aren't at the top of the list, they should come in a close second. Some have said, "Laugh and live". That may very well be an oversimplification but it's a worthwhile formula.

Dr. Greenberg's thoughts and analyses are very helpful. In the old days, we did have clear-cut standards. Yes, we had restrictions but we had a sense of stability and of belonging. With all the pain and anguish of my own family life growing up, I recall praying each night that God would make them safe and keep them alive.

How could anyone be cheerful when there is a devastating loss? Is it really possible ever to smile again, to laugh again, or to be positive, upbeat, and "cheerful"? The question and the thought from Max Ehrmann's poem, *Desiderata,* helped me slowly turn in the direction that would make healing possible.

Of all the things I have read, nothing has surfaced that gives us a better picture of the way our life could be lived than the *Desiderata,* which translated from Latin means "things to be desired." I suggest that you take time away from your own mad rush to read this, slowly, reflectively, allowing yourself the permission to act on all the steps that seem to fit. If you read it in haste, it cannot do its work.

Ehrmann was a poet and lawyer, of all things, but included this poem in his Christmas messages in the 1920s. I won't quote it in full but here are a few lines and you can find the entire poem on the Internet and in libraries.

> Take kindly the counsel of the years,
> Gracefully surrendering the things of youth.
> Nurture strength of spirit to shield you in sudden misfortune

But do not distress yourself with dark imaginings.
Many fears are born of fatigue and loneliness.
Beyond a wholesome discipline,
Be gentle with yourself...
With all its sham, drudgery, and broken dreams,
It is still a beautiful world.
Be cheerful.
Strive to be happy.

The other clear memory that comes back was how often we laughed at family reunions and homecomings. When we put together all the ingredients of our total family life, we felt blessed and comforted by all those who seemed to care deeply about our welfare.

My own recovery has been helped by writing this book and reading the Bible, and especially by recalling a line from the poem *Desiderata* that says, "Keep peace in your soul...the universe is unfolding as it should."

The second deep insight came for me in the lines: "Be yourself. Especially do not feign affection. Neither be cynical about love...be cheerful."

Seventh, Fall Back on Your Spiritual Roots

For many adults, the comfort of their religious upbringing fades as the years go by. So many adults that I have talked to over the years have told me how strong their faith in God was when they were small, but how very weak it is now. I would sometimes say, "But you still come to the worship services and you sing the old songs..."

They often add, "Yes, I think I am trying to go back to the faith of my youth. When I sing the old songs I sang as a child, I begin to feel again that all was well with the world."

On numerous occasions, people have told me about needing and wanting scientific proof about the existence of God, about heaven and the world to come and the resurrection. Because there has been no proof, they no longer believe the way they believed as children. Nevertheless, people also tell me that when the lights go out and a disaster hits, there is no comfort—none at all—in not believing. Believing creates a whole new world of hope, peace, comfort, and joy.

One man said to me, "I no longer need to prove anything. I made up my mind not to wait until all the proof has come in. It occurred to me," he said, "that the real power of religious faith is choosing to believe—after all, it is called the 'Christian Faith' and not science or Christian facts."

Those words of wisdom from a number of my parishioners over the years came suddenly back to me at the news of our son's death. I chose to believe. I chose to mix and mingle with the people of faith. I chose to join in the singing of what we used to call the old gospel songs. I chose to believe so I no longer demanded answers. That was comforting beyond my power to describe.

It may not work for you but I believe that it will. For myself, I will not abandon the faith I have embraced all these years and see it shrivel and die. I have decided not to give way to cynicism, hopelessness, existential nothingness, nihilism and ultimately despair. In addition, even if "they" should prove that there really is no God at all, I will keep on singing the old songs and saying my prayers and exalting the majestic God who also watched as our son died. I identify with this same eternal being that suffered just as I have suffered and who now can and does identify with me. In addition, if they are right, at least I had the comfort of thinking and believing in a new world coming.

The skeptics and the doubters may be right. However, I choose to walk the road of faith and I dare say, to use the words of Robert Frost, "that has made all the difference."

Even life's darkest experiences can have about them an element of humor. A Jewish friend who survived the hell of a concentration camp during the war years told me the following story that came out of the Nazi death camp.

They say that Hitler went to a fortune teller to determine how long he had to live and exactly when he would die. The medium said, "You will die on a Jewish holiday."

Hitler said, "Well, which holiday?"

"Sir," said the medium, "any day that you die will be a Jewish holiday."

The Holocaust prisoners who survived their ordeal used to laugh at the starvation diets given to them. Some of them would pretend that the little piece of bread and the small cup of water were really pineapple upside-down cake and red wine. They kidded that they were just so full; they could hardly eat another bite. They found humor in laughing in the face of death.

Humor is clearly a tool of sheer survival, as many prison inmates have found. When a grieving person can find something funny about their own tragic losses, it is a sure sign that hope has not been abandoned.

◆   ◆   ◆

What Is Life's Meaning?

I would never presume to tell anyone the actual meaning of life. I have never met anyone who appeared to me to know the meaning of life. Why are we here? Where are we going? Is there really a Supreme Being whom we call God? If so, where did God come from?

What I have discovered over all these years of searching is that there do not seem to be clear, definitive, verifiable answers to what we are doing here on earth—or even how we can know about God or life after death or heaven and the world to come.

All I have ever been able to come up with is an occasional glimpse into eternity, the world of the Spirit and the meaning of life on earth just for me. On those few and rare occasions, when I have experienced the majesty and glory of this creator God, it seemed to satisfy my intellectual curiosity and my deep emotional hungers as well. I found I no longer had to force the Eternal to supply me with facts and data.

One such glimpse into the meaning of life happened in the simplest and most ordinary way.

It was Sunday afternoon at our suburban church in Pfafftown, North Carolina—and time for the weekly youth meeting. We had a lively group of teenagers who were excellent students and deeply spiritual as well. That afternoon, we welcomed a young teenager named Rick. He was, as I recall, about thirteen or fourteen and had two younger sisters and lived only a few blocks from where we lived.

I asked about his family and if they were interested in church. He said they had an A-frame cabin up in the mountains of Western Carolina, about a 90-minute drive from their home. He said that every Friday the four of them, Mom, Dad and the two sisters would spend the weekend at their mountain cabin.

I asked why he didn't go along. His response stung. He said, "I'm never allowed to go to the cabin—I have to stay here by myself until they come back Sunday night."

"But why," I asked.

"Well," he continued, "they told me that I didn't fit in…that I caused trouble and they didn't want me around…"

"Ouch," I responded. "I bet that really hurts."

"They don't like me," he said, bowing his head as if in embarrassment.

Then the pivotal question from Rick: "Do you play chess?"

"Chess," I exclaimed, "I love chess. Why do you ask?"

"Would you ever be able to play a game of chess with me," he wanted to know.

"Why, yes! How about today after the youth group is over? We'll just sit here at this table and play chess. I have the board out in my car."

For about an hour, we battled each other in the front line trenches of a chess board. Several members of the youth group stayed to watch.

I moved a pawn and he responded. I moved a knight threateningly into his territory and he forced a retreat with a powerful queen. We thought and schemed and planned and tried to look ahead 3, 4, or even 5 moves to find the best vantage point.

I was shocked that a thirteen-year old could have such a grasp of this challenging game. It was obvious that he knew how to play chess—and that he loved it. I could see in his face intensity, determination, and sheer delight at putting up a good fight and at my being there for him and the thought that he really could beat me.

Well, I won—barely edging him out by gaining a new queen. At the end, we were both exhausted. He smiled, repeatedly. He was excited and as I drove him home from the church, I noticed his eyes fill up with tears. I recall his saying, "Can we play again some time?"

"Yes, oh yes," I nodded.

And then Rich said this: "Rev, this is one of the greatest days of my life."

I said goodnight as I let him out of the car and drove toward my home. I recall stopping at the beautiful still lake near our house. It was September and a big bright full moon reflected off the surface of the water as I got out of the car. Standing there, I knew that something deep, perhaps even profound had happened. I knew, somehow, that I had given life to a young teenager who desperately needed to know that someone really cared about him.

I still recall the tears that flooded my eyes as I prayed aloud, "Tonight, dear God, I know why I was born."

No, I still don't know a lot about the meaning of life or heaven and the world to come. But when I give my time, my attention, my love to someone who needs it, I get a glimpse of God's majesty and of the reason I was placed here…and that is enough.

12

How Do You Say "Goodbye"?

I suppose that part of losing a loved one is having to say "goodbye." Saying "goodbye" is one of the hardest things people have to do. I watch people getting ready to go home after being with family or friends for a special occasion. Once we drove to Illinois from Indiana to have Thanksgiving dinner with our relatives. On that particular day, I noted many farewell messages including:

"Well, we'd better start thinking about heading back…"
"I 'spect we ought to get on the road…"
"Well, it's getting late in the day—better get ourselves together…"
"Well, sure wish we could stay longer but Pop has to go to work tomorrow…"

Then with the car packed and everything ready, we began a second round of saying good bye. It went something like this:

"By the way, did you ever get that letter?"
"I really ought to run to the restroom…"

Then there are hugs, more hugs, handshakes for the men and another handshake and finally out at the car where all were gathered, the men shook hands again and the ladies hugged again and then:

"Sure wish you lived closer…"
"I just never get to see you…"

Then began a series of hand wavings. The window of the car went down and the waving continued, then after two or three honks of the horn it was over.

What was happening here? Well, many things but among them is the fact that we really don't know how to say "goodbye."

Perhaps it is just too painful. Perhaps the love is just so deep we cannot bear to leave the ones we love. It's true of dying churches. The members who have been part of a small country church for ten or fifty or one hundred years don't want to see it die. So they hold on and live more on memory than on hope. I recall a church that got down to ten members with only five or six coming to worship on Sunday, but they didn't know how to say "goodbye."

It always looked easy to watch others trying to say goodbye but when I had to do it for a beloved son, it was more than I could bear.

I hold on to the memories, the bright happy moments and find comfort in his warm, winsome personality and his great generosity. What comes to mind is the day in Springfield, Missouri, when he purchased what was for him a very expensive long-sleeved shirt. He threw the old frayed shirt away and put on his new shirt. He felt good, really good. I knew the feeling...

He stopped to pick up a hitchhiker out on an old country road not far from the city limits. The man appeared to be the same size as he. The man was old and poor and his shirt was torn, dirty, and frayed. Our son told the hitchhiker he wanted him to have his new shirt. The man protested but Christopher stopped the car, took off his new shirt, and gave it to the stranger. When he let the stranger off he noticed that the man had tears in his eyes as he turned to walk away.

Our son drove home "topless." He called to tell us and added, "Dad, I felt proud of myself today...I felt really good about myself today..."

We are comforted that he lived by the thought found in Emily Dickinson's poem. It says:

> If I can stop one heart from breaking
> I shall not live in vain
> If I can ease one life the aching
> Or cool one pain,

Or help one fainting robin
Into his nest again,
I shall not live in vain.

Henry Wadsworth Longfellow's words from "Tales of a Wayside Inn" also reflect something of our son's life and his voice and manner, for when he spoke, whether in person or on the phone or in church the few times we heard him give a sermon…

He ended and a kind of spell
Upon the silent listeners fell
His solemn manner and his words
Had touched the deep mysterious chords
That vibrate in each breast alike.

A popular song says, "We've only just begun"…but for our son Christopher, his life, his love, his warm winsome personality and his magical voice can now only live through those of us who knew him and loved him and for some of us, more than life itself.

We will try to say "goodbye" but we will not forget.

◆   ◆   ◆

If you have suffered a similar loss as ours, or if your loss proved to be sudden or traumatic, please drop me a line letting me know how you handled the loss—how you survived.

Perhaps we can publish another book sharing with other grieving persons how we dealt with our loss. It just might help someone. You may send me a letter at E-mail: dnjfarrior@cox.net.

Bibliography

Adams, Scott. *The Joy of Work—Dilbert's Guide to Finding Happiness at the Expense of Your Co-Workers.* New York: Harper-Collins, New York, 1998.

Barry, Dave. *Dave Barry Is Not Taking This Sitting Down!* New York: Crown Publishers, 2000.

Bennett, Howard. "Humor in medicine." *South Med Jo.* 96(12):1257-1261, December 2003.

Bennett, Howard (ed). *The Best of Medical Humor: A Collection of Articles, Essays, Poetry, and Letters Published in the Medical Literature.* Philadelphia, Hanley & Belfus, 1997, ed 2.

Bennett Howard (ed). *The Doctor's Book of Humorous Quotations: A Treasury of Quotes, Jokes, and One-liners about Doctors & Health Care.* Philadelphia, Hanley & Belfus, 2001.

Blair, George *Senior Pursuits.* Miami: Valiant Press Inc., 1993.

Bouvard, Marguerite. "Profiles in Healing—Laughter As Medicine." *Healing Ministry,* 10, (Winter, 2003) 1.

Canfield, J & Hansen, Mark. Chicken Soup for the Soul. Deerfield Beach, FL: Health Communication, Inc. 1993.

Clarke, Caroline V. The healing power of laughter: Liberal doses of humor are a proven prescription for wellness. *Black Enterprise* 5/1/03. Cogan R, Cogan D, Waltz W, et al. Effects of laughter and relations on discomfort thresholds. *J Behav Med* 1987;10:139-144.

Cousins, Norman. *Anatomy of an Illness as Perceived by the Patient: Reflections on Healing and Regeneration.* New York, W.W. Norton, 1979.

Cousins, Norman. Anatomy of an illness (as perceived by the patient). *N Engl J Med* 1976; 295:1458-1463.

Cushner FD, Friedman RJ. Humor and the physician. *South Med J* 1989; 82:51-52.

Edwards Jr, Cooper CL. The impacts of positive psychological states on physical health: A review and theoretical framework. *Soc Sci Med* 1988;27:1447-1459.

Gibson, L. Comedy carts, baskets, and humor rooms, in Buxman K, LeMoine A (eds): *Nursing Perspectives on Humor.* Staten Island, NY, Power Publications, 1995, pp 113-124.

Goode, Erica. "Power of Positive Thinking May Have a Healthy Benefit." *The New York Times.* Sept. 2, 2003.

Goodman JB. Laughing matters: Taking your job seriously and yourself lightly. *JAMA* 1992;267:1858.

Freud, Sigmund. *Jokes and Their Relationship to the Unconscious.* New York, W.W. Norton, 1960, pp 229-230.

Fry WF Jr. The physiologic effects of humor, mirth, and laughter. *JAMA* 1992;267:1857-1858.

Harris, Thomas. *I'm OK—You're OK.* New York: Avon Books, 1973.

Johnson, Barbara. *Pain Is Inevitable But Misery Is Optional So Stick a Geranium in Your Hat and Be Happy.* Dallas: Word Publishing Co., 1990.

Larson, Joan Matthews. *Seven Weeks to Emotional Healing.* New York: Ballentine Publishing Group, 1999, 108-109.

Marsa, Linda. "Natural Health," *The Health and Wellness Resources Center.* Weider Publications, 34, (Jan. 2004) 87.

Martin RA. Humor, laughter, and physical health: Methodological issues and research findings. *Psychol Bull* 2001;127:504-519.

Martin RA, Dobbin JP. Sense of humor, hassles, and immunoglobulin A: Evidence for a stress-moderating effect of humor. *Int J Psychiatry Med* 1988;18:93-105.

Rynk, Peggy. "The Value of a Healthy Attitude," *Vibrant Life,* University of Chicago, 19, (Mar-April 2003) 12.

Schuller, Robert H. *Don't Throw Away Tomorrow: Living God's Dream for Your Life.* San Francisco: Harper, 2005.

Schuller, Robert H. *If It's Going to Be, It's Up to Me: The Eight Proven Principles of Possibility Thinking.* San Francisco: Harper, 1998.

Schuller, Robert H. *Hour of Power: My Daily Book of Motivations and Inspiration.* San Francisco: Harper, 2005.

Schuller, Robert H. *Life's Not Fair But God Is Good.* New York: Bantam, 1993.

Schuller, Robert H. *Power Thoughts.* Thornedike, ME: G. K. Hall, 1995.

Vertasick, Frank. *When the Air Hits Your Brain.* New York: Ballentine Publishing Group, 1996.

Ziegler JB. Use of humor in medical teaching. *Med Teach* 1998;20:341-348.

Ziv, A. "Teaching and learning with humor: Experiment and replication," *J Exp. Educ* 1988; 57: 5-15.

About the Author

Don Farrior is a native of eastern North Carolina. He received his professional degrees in Indiana—A. B. from Earlham and a Masters and Doctor of Ministry at Christian Theological Seminary. He served as Supervisor at two graduate seminaries and as senior pastor of Disciples of Christ congregations in Indiana, North Carolina, Missouri, Florida, and Arizona.

He received the Stubbs award at Earlham College; was inducted in to the Tau Kappa Alpha National Speech Fraternity; served as president of the Seminary Alumni Association; was a host on an in-house television talk show at seminary; was a member of the Mayor's Ethics Committee in Independence, Missouri; a trustee of Lexington Theological Seminary and National Benevolent Association; was president of the Independence Rotary Club; was a founding member of Hope House in Independence, Missouri; and served on the Board of Directors for the Comprehensive Mental Health Center.

Dr. Farrior is currently staff chaplain at the Del E. Webb Memorial Hospital in Sun City West, Arizona. He speaks often in the community on the topics of health, humor, and America's retirees.

He is married to Janet Rubenking and the Farriors have an adult daughter and two granddaughters.

Dr. Farrior's hobbies are golf, chess, and after-dinner speaking.

Dr. Diane Holloway, a Dallas psychologist and author of non-fiction books, happily assisted Dr. Farrior in arranging his book. While on a long cruise, Dr. Farrior wrote out sections of the book and sent them to her from each port. He came home to a complete book compiled by this unusual and interesting method of collaborative writing.

978-0-595-37359-8
0-595-37359-3

Printed in the United States
54906LVS00004BA/244-267

9 780595 373598